New Edition

first certificate
expert

STUDENT'S RESOURCE BOOK
with key and audio CD

Richard Mann • Nick Kenny • Jan Bell • Roger Gower

PEARSON
Longman

Contents

Unit	Vocabulary	Language Development 2	Reading
1B **Customs and traditions**	**Topic:** special occasions Comparing two photos of special occasions. **Exam strategy:** coping with words you don't know in the speaking exam. (p.10)	Comparatives and superlatives. Modifying adjectives and adverbs. (p.11)	**Paper 1 Part 3** Multiple matching. Magazine article: *The Art of Giving*. (pp.12-13)
2B **A learning experience**	**Topic:** educational systems. Commonly confused words. Agreeing and disagreeing. (p.18)	Articles and determiners. *some/any, something/anything*. Key word transformations. (p.19)	**Paper 1 Part 1** Multiple-choice questions. Magazine article: *Carry on Learning*. (pp.20-21)
3B **Our natural heritage**	**Topic:** the environment. **Exam practice: multiple-choice cloze.** (pp.27-28)	*-ing* forms and infinitives. Prepositions + *-ing* forms. Verbs with a change of meaning. Key word transformations. Extra word. (pp.28-29)	**Paper 1 Part 3** Multiple matching. Newspaper article: *Clever Claws*. (pp.30-31)
4B **Sport**	**Topic:** describing sports. Informal expressions. Sports quiz. (pp.37-38)	Quantity. Countable and uncountable nouns with *a, some, any*. Determiners: *much, many, plenty/a great deal of; few/a few; little/a little*. Key word transformations. **Exam practice: open cloze.** (pp.38-39)	**Paper 1 Part 2** Gapped text. Newspaper article: *Business calls the shots*. (pp.40-41)
5B **Technology**	**Topic:** modern inventions. Agreeing and disagreeing. Commonly confused words. **Exam practice: word formation.** (pp.47-48)	Reflexives. Structures with question words. Key word transformations. (pp.48-49)	**Paper 1 Part 2** Gapped text. Newspaper article: *In search of simplicity*. (pp.50-51)
6B **Art and entertainment**	**Topic:** talking about the arts. Definitions. Adjective + noun collocations. **Exam practice: multiple-choice cloze.** (pp.57-58)	Adjectives and nouns + prepositions. *be used to/get used to* + *-ing*. **Exam practice: open cloze.** (pp.58-59)	**Paper 1 Part 1** Multiple-choice questions. Magazine article: *For the art, turn left at the dance floor*. (pp.60-61)

Contents

1A | Family life

Vocabulary ▶ GR pages 10–11

Exam strategy

You will often need to use a dictionary during your English course in order to expand your vocabulary. You should use a good **English–English dictionary** (such as the *Longman Exams Dictionary*) when you check your answers to exercises in Paper 3 (Use of English). You will also need to use a dictionary when you write compositions, reports, etc. for Paper 2 (Writing).

When doing reading tests, however, it is better to try to guess the meanings of words as much as you can. Afterwards you can go through the texts again and add any new words to your vocabulary notebook.

1 Understanding your dictionary

Look at the extract from the *Longman Exams Dictionary*. Match each of the numbered boxes (1–8) to one of the explanations (a–h) below. Write the correct letter in the box.

| 1 | b | | 2 | |

| 3 | |

gen·e·ra·tion AC S2 W2 /ˌdʒenəˈreɪʃən/ *n*

| 4 | |

1 [C also + plural verb] *BrE* all people of about the same age: *Like most of my generation, I had never known a war.* | *In my generation the divorce rate is very high.* | *the need to preserve the planet for future generations* | **[+of]** *the post-war generation of writers* | **the younger/older generation** (=the younger or older people in society) *The younger generation don't know what hard work is.* | *The story has been handed down from generation to generation.* | *If the gene is passed from father to son through the generations, the disease becomes increasingly severe.*

| 5 | |

| 6 | |

| 7 | |

| 8 | |

2 [C] all the members of a family of about the same age: *Friction is common when three generations live together* | *In some families there is little verbal interchange between the generations.* | **first-generation/second-generation etc** (=being a member of the first, second etc generation to live or be born in a country) *a third-generation American* | *As many as 40% of the fathers were first-generation immigrants.*

a the meaning or definition of the word
b the pronunciation of the word, using the International Phonetic Alphabet
c the word class – verb, noun, adjective, etc.
d a second meaning of the word – indicated by a number
e a common expression or set phrase
f British English (not American English) usage
g an example sentence showing how the word is used
h grammatical information (e.g. countable noun)

2 Using your dictionary

Look at these extracs from the *Longman Exams Dictionary* and answer the questions.

in·her·it /ɪnˈherɪt/ *v*
1 [I,T] to receive money, property etc from someone after they have died: **inherit sth from sb** *He inherited a fortune from his grandmother* | *inherited wealth* **2** [T] if you inherit a situation, especially one in which problems have been caused by other people, you have to deal with it: *The present government inherited a closed, state-dominated economy.* **3** [T] to have the same character or appearance as your parents: **inherit sth from sb** *Mr. Grass inherited his work ethic from his father.* | *I inherited my mother's curly hair.*

1 When we say the word *inherit* do we stress the first, middle or last syllable?
2 Do we pronounce the middle part of *inherit* as *hear*?
3 As a verb, does *inherit* take a direct object?

house·hold¹ /ˈhaʊshəʊld $ -hoʊld/ *n* [C]
all the people who live together in one house **SYN house**: *A growing number of households have at least one computer.* | *Families are classified by the occupation of* **the head of the household** (=the person who earns the most money and is most respected in a house). | *There are 7 million single-person households in this country.*
household² *adj* [only before noun]
1 relating to looking after a house and the people in it **SYN domestic: household goods/products/ items etc** *washing powder and other household products* | *household chores* | *The government had set a target of recycling 25% of household waste by the end of the 20th century.* **2 be a household name/word** to be very well known: *Coca Cola is a household name around the world.*

4 When we say the word *household*, do we stress the first or second syllable?
5 Is the word *household* an adjective as well as a noun?
6 As a noun, is *household* countable or uncountable?
7 Is it correct to say: '*I bought some items which are household*'?
8 Could we say that Madonna is a *household name*?

Language development 1
Present and past habits ▶ GR pages 12–13

1 Position of frequency adverbs ▶ GR page 194

a Read the examples in the box and complete the rules with *before* or *after*.

---

*I **usually** go out every Saturday night.*
*The cat will **occasionally** disappear for days.*
*My mother's stories are **sometimes** very funny.*
*I **often** used to play chess with my father and he would **always** win.*

Rules
We put frequency adverbs such as *always, sometimes, often*:

- .... simple tenses of the verb *be*
- .... simple tenses of other verbs
- .... the auxiliary verb in complex tenses
- .... *used to* but .... *would*.

Adverbial phrases such as *every day, three times a week,* etc. can go at the beginning or the end of a clause. Initial position is more emphatic.

---

b Rewrite the sentences, putting the words in brackets in the correct place.

1 Adam leaves for school at seven o'clock in the morning. (*always*)
....

2 He goes to school by bus. (*every day*)
....

3 In the past, he used to wait very long for the bus. (*never*)
.... he never used to wait very long ......

4 The bus would be two or three minutes late. (*sometimes*)
....

5 Nowadays, the bus is late. (*often*)
....

6 As a result, Adam arrives late for school. (*frequently*)
....

7 Fortunately, his teacher doesn't complain. (*usually*)
....

8 Adam does his homework on the bus. (*regularly*)
....

9 He doesn't get home until after six o'clock. (*on some days*)
....

2 Present simple or continuous? ▶ GR page 197

Complete the sentences with the correct form of the verb given.

1 **have**
  a Sandra ....*has got*.... a large collection of DVDs.
  b Mum, answer the phone, please! I can't answer it because I ..*'m having*.. a shower.

2 **see**
  a I ....*see*.... why your sister gets so annoyed with you. You're always borrowing her things!
  b My brother isn't going out with Stella anymore. These days he ..*is seeing*.. Tina instead.

3 **feel**
  a I ...*feel*... much better today. The antibiotics are obviously working.
  b My dad ..*feels*.. that I should stay at school but I want to get a job now.

4 **think**
  a You haven't said anything all evening. What ....*are*.... you .... about?
  b What .... you .... about the new History lecturer?

5 **appear**
  a Although my dad .... to be very strict, he's not really.
  b Alex Cameron .... as Hamlet at the Theatre Royal all week.

6 **smell**
  a Why .... you .... those roses? Don't you know they're made of plastic?
  b The biscuits my sister made this afternoon ..*smell*.. delicious.

7 **look**
  a Today our family's going on a picnic, but it ..*looks*.. as if it might rain.
  b Why .... you .... at me like that? Have I done something wrong?

8 **expect**
  a I .... you are tired after playing football all afternoon.
  b I can't go out tonight because I .... a phone call from my aunt in America..

3 Past habit: form ▶ GR pages 198–199

Some of these sentences contain mistakes. Tick (✓) the correct sentences. Correct the ones with mistakes.

EXAMPLES: When I lived at home, I used to ~~going~~ fishing with my father every Saturday. ....*go*....

My mother would make us sandwiches for the day. ✓

1 I remember how we would have spent hours waiting for a fish to bite. ......✓......

2 Sometimes we didn't used to come home until after dark. ....

3 I remember how my mother used to look at us when we were late. ....

4 My father used to taking me with him on long walks in the mountains. ....*take*....

5 I used love listening to him talk about nature. ....*to love*....

6 Did I ever used to get bored? Never! There were so many things to do. ....

4 Past habit: use ▶ GR pages 188–189

Exam strategy

For Paper 2, Writing, it's important to vary the grammatical structures and verb forms you use. This makes your writing more interesting for the reader. But you have to be careful. Sometimes, a particular form may not be possible.

Read the text below and mark the best verb form in each pair. Make sure the form you use is grammatically possible. Both forms may be possible, but don't repeat the same form in one sentence.

We (1) *used to / would* live in London when I was a child. My bedroom (2) *was / would be* at the top of the house, in the attic, and I (3) *used to / would* love spending time there. It (4) *used to / would* be my private space and I (5) *didn't use to / wouldn't* let my parents change anything. My mother always (6) *used to / would* wake me up at 7:30 in the morning. She usually (7) *brought / would bring* me a cup of tea in bed, and she (8) *turned / would turn* on the radio very loud. About ten minutes later, she (9) *left / would leave* for work, and her last words to me always (10) *were / used to be* 'Time to come down and face the world again, darling!'

Listening Extracts: multiple choice
(Paper 4 Part 1)

1 Before you listen

a Read the instructions for the listening task. How many extracts will you hear? The extracts are not related.
(Note that in the exam you will hear eight extracts.)

b For questions 1–6, read the sentence that gives the context of the extract, the question and the three options A–C. Think about the situation, who will be talking and what they will be talking about. Mark key words in each question. (The first two have been done for you.)

2 🎧 Listening for gist

a You will hear each extract twice. As you listen, focus on the speaker's main idea – don't worry if you don't understand every word.

b Choose one of the options after listening the first time. If you don't know an answer, have a guess and go on to the next question.

c Listen again to check your answers.

You will hear people talking in six different situations. For questions **1–6**, choose the best answer **A**, **B**, or **C**.

1 You hear a woman talking about her car. What is she describing?

  A what she dislikes about her car

  B how she depends on her car

  C why she needs a new car ☐ 1

2 You hear a sound recording engineer talking about his training.

  How does he feel about the course he followed?

  A unsure how useful it was

  B sorry that it was only part-time

  C grateful for the basic skills it gave him ☐ 2

3 You hear a woman talking about shopping. What is she doing when she speaks?

  A disagreeing with some recent research

  B justifying a decision she has made

  C defending an activity she enjoys ☐ 3

4 You hear the beginning of a radio programme. What is the programme going to be about?

  A ways of learning new skills

  B helping people who have no skills

  C keeping your own skills up-to-date ☐ 4

5 You hear a student talking about living and studying in London.

  What did she find most difficult?

  A managing on a restricted budget

  B keeping a record of her spending

  C being criticised by her parents ☐ 5

6 You hear a man talking about how he lives. What point is he making about the furnishings in his home?

  A They needed to reflect his lifestyle at work.

  B The things he chose were modern in design.

  C He didn't want them to remind him of work. ☐ 6

Writing Informal email (Paper 2 Part 2)

▶ CB pages 14–15, WR page 199

1 Understand the task

Read the task below and answer the questions.

1 Who are you writing to?
   (a) someone you know well
   b someone you know a little

2 What is the main purpose of the email?
   a to entertain the reader
   (b) to provide important information

3 What information MUST you include? Mark the parts of the task that tell you.

> You and your brother or sister have been invited to stay for two weeks with an English pen friend over the summer. Write an email to your pen friend, accepting the invitation and saying a little about your brother or sister, whom your pen friend does not know.
>
> Write your **email** in **120–180** words in an appropriate style.

2 Check and improve a sample answer

a Read the email that a student wrote, then look at the parts of the task you marked in Exercise 1. Does the email include the required information?

Exam strategy

Always check your work for basic errors when you finish writing. You will lose marks if basic errors make your work unclear or difficult to understand. Double-space your writing so that you have room to make corrections if you need to. Make sure that your handwriting is neat and easy to read.

b The student's teacher has underlined all the mistakes in the email and used symbols to identify the types of mistakes. Look at the key below to see what the symbols mean.

c Rewrite the email in your notebook, correcting the mistakes.

New Message

Hi Elizabeth!

Thank you,ᴾ for inviting me and my sister to stay with your family this summer. We would both love to come. We can come ᵂᵒ for two weeks in August?

I know that you never have ᵂᵒ met my sister, Angela, but I am sure you'll like her very much. She is a very easy-going person. She is two years smaller ᵂʷ than me and studies ᵀ to be ᴳʳ doctor.

Like me ᴾ Angela likes walking and horse riding. She is also very good in ᴳʳ tennis. There is one only ᵂᵒ thing that Angela is not very keen on. Swiming. ˢᵖ Its ᴾ rather strange because we were used to ᴳʳ go with our family to Lake Balaton every year when we were children. Our family even have a house their ˢᵖ now.

I won't write any more, Elizabeth, because I take ᵀ exams at the moment and I am very occupied ᵂʷ. Thank you again for your invitation. I am looking forward to see you ᴳʳ and your family this summer. I've told Angela all about you! Please let me know if we can come in August, won't you. ᴾ

Yours faithfully ˢᵗ

Suzanna

> **Key to correction symbols**
> P = punctuation
> Sp = spelling
> Gr = grammar
> T = verb tense
> Ww = wrong word
> Wo = word order
> St = style

Vocabulary ▶ CB pages 16–17

1 **Topic: special occasions**
Match words and phrases from the list below to the correct photo, A or B.

university B   olive leaves A   medals A   degree B   athletes A
sports event A   shake someone's hand B   graduate B

Photo A	Photo B

A

B

2 **Comparing photos**

Exam strategy

When you talk about photos, you may not know what something is called in English. Try to describe it using words you **do** know. Useful phrases for doing this include:

It's like … .
It's a kind/sort of … .

a **Read how one student compared the two photos and complete the text. Use only one word in each space.**

b **Mark the expressions the student uses to do the following.**
 1 talk about similarities
 2 talk about differences
 3 express an opinion
 4 paraphrase an unknown word

Both these photos (1) *have been* ~~folden on~~ special occasions or ceremonies.

The first picture was obviously (2) *taken* at the Olympic Games. I can see three (3) *women*, who are holding their (4) *hands* and looking very happy. In the second photograph, a university student is holding some kind of document – I think it's called a (5) *diploma* in English – and shaking an older woman's hand. (6) .... the people in the first photo, she also looks very happy. Both the ceremony in the first picture (7) *and* the ceremony in the second picture are very formal occasions. People have been given a prize or award for what they have achieved.

The main difference (8) *between* the two photographs is that these athletes have done well in a sports (9) *competition* at the Olympics, (10) *whearean* the student here has just – what's the word? – graduated? – from a university. She is now called a (11) *graduate*, I think. It's interesting that the athletes are wearing (12) *olive leaves* on their heads; the student here is also wearing a sort of hat on her head.

I really love sport, so I think I'd prefer to attend the ceremony in this photograph, at the Olympic Games. I think it must be a very happy time for everyone there, and incredibly exciting.

Language development 2

Comparatives and superlatives ▶ CB page 19, GR page 185

1 Modifying adjectives and adverbs

a Look at the table comparing the Olympic Games which were held in Athens, Sydney and Atlanta. Decide if the statements below are *True* or *False*.

Number of:	Athens 2004	Sydney 2000	Atlanta 1996
athletes (total)	11,099	10,651	10,320
athletes (women)	4306	4,069	3,523
athletes (men)	6793	6,582	6,797
events	301	300	271
American gold medallists	36	40	44
Australian gold medallists	17	16	9
Greek gold medallists	6	4	4
seats in Olympic Stadium	72,000	110,000	85,000

1 Slightly more athletes took part in the Olympic Games in Sydney than in Atlanta. T

2 A far larger number of women than men took part in the Sydney Olympics. F

3 In Athens, Sydney and Atlanta, the USA won by far the most gold medals. T

4 There were nowhere near as many events in Sydney as there were in Atlanta. F

5 The USA won a lot more gold medals in Athens than in Sydney. F

6 There were nearly as many Australian gold medallists in Sydney as in Athens. T

7 At the Athens Olympics there were almost five times as many men athletes as women athletes. F

b Mark the expressions in sentences 1–7 which express:
1 a big difference.   2 a small difference.

c Use the information in the table and the prompts below to write more correct sentences comparing the three Olympic Games. Choose one expression only from the words in brackets.

EXAMPLE: large / number of athletes / take part / Athens Olympics / Sydney Olympics. (*slightly / much*)

A much larger number of athletes took part in the Athens Olympics than in the Sydney Olympics.

1 the number of women / take part / Atlanta Olympics / small / Athens Olympics (*a bit / a lot*)

2 Athens / organise / more / events / Sydney (*slightly / a lot*)

3 Atlanta / not organise / many / events / Athens (*quite / nearly*)

4 Australian athletes / successful / Sydney Olympics / Atlanta Olympics (*not nearly / far*)

5 American athletes / do / worse / Athens Olympics / Atlanta Olympics (*slightly / far*)

6 Greek athletes / win / many / gold medals / Sydney / Atlanta (*nearly / exactly*)

7 Olympic Stadium / Atlanta / big / Olympic Stadium / Sydney (*nowhere near / a lot*)

8 Olympic Stadium / Athens / small / Olympic Stadium / Sydney (*slightly / a lot*)

2 Comparatives and superlatives

Put a tick next to the sentences which are correct. Rewrite sentences which are incorrect.

✓ 1 The food I ate at that restaurant in Sydney was the most spiciest I have ever eaten.

✗ 2 The first event we saw was far better one than the others. *much*

3 The opening ceremony in Athens was much more exciting that the ceremonies in Sydney or Atlanta. *n*

✓ 4 The fireworks for the Sydney Olympics were by far the best I have ever seen.

5 He is a more faster sprinter than all the other athletes.

6 The people in the town were not nearly as much friendly as the villagers.

7 The stadium they are building must be just about the biggest stadium ever built.

8 Unfortunately, we didn't have nowhere near as much time to spend shopping in Athens as in Sydney.

Reading Multiple matching

(Paper 1 Part 3)

1 Before you read
Look at the title of the article opposite and the photo. What information will the article contain?
a) what gifts you can give in different countries
b how to behave towards foreign visitors

2 Scanning and skimming
a The text mentions four different countries. The names of the countries are in bold. Scan the text to find them. How many paragraphs deal with:
1 the first country?
2 the second country?

b Skim the text to answer these questions.
1 Which country seems to have the strictest rules about gifts?
2 In which country are gifts least important?

3 Multiple matching
a Look at the example (0) in the exam task opposite. Key words in the question are highlighted. Mark the part of paragraph 1 in the text that tells you the answer is A, *Egypt*.

b Look at question 1.
• Mark key words in the question.
• Scan the text and mark the part which expresses the same idea.
• Read this section carefully and mark the place where you find the answer.
• Check that the text you have found exactly matches the question.

c Now continue with questions 2–11. (In the exam you will have 15 questions.)

You are going to read an extract from a book which gives businesspeople advice about social customs in different parts of the world. For questions **1–11**, choose from the countries **(A–D)**. Some of the countries may be chosen more than once. There is an example at the beginning **(0)**.

A	EGYPT
B	JAPAN
C	THAILAND
D	AUSTRALIA

According to the writer, in which country

did a politician receive an unexpected gift?	**0** **A**
is the price of the gift unimportant?	**1**
are you expected to give a gift as large as the one you've received?	**2**
are most gifts specially made to celebrate a particular event?	**3**
have the rules of gift-giving been established for generations?	**4**
is it common not to open gifts in front of the giver?	**5**
is it unwise to say you like someone else's possessions?	**6**
are there rules about how different types of gifts must be presented?	**7**
might people be unimpressed by a large gift?	**8**
is it important not to damage the packaging of a gift?	**9**
will you be forgiven if you get the details of gift-giving wrong?	**10**
have the rules of gift-giving become less important in recent years?	**11**

The Art of Giving

In many countries it is customary to give gifts to your guests and hosts, but different cultures have different customs. How does the foreign visitor know what to do where?

When the US President Jimmy Carter visited **Egypt** in 1978, a camel trader was asked to show him round a camel market. The trader was so honoured that he not only gave the tour,
5 but also presented the president with a six-year-old camel, a pink ribbon tied around its neck. The camel trader's action was typical of the hospitality and generosity shown in many parts of the Arab world, where good manners are an
10 essential ingredient in a person's character, and generosity to guests is essential to a good reputation.

Because there are accepted rules of behaviour in gift-giving, the foreign businessperson must
15 be careful. For example, admiring a painting or ornament in a client's home or office might oblige them to present you with it as a gift. What's more, your Egyptian colleague will probably begin a round of gift-giving and will
20 expect you to reciprocate, if not immediately, then on the next possible occasion, and the gift should match theirs in size and cost, if possible.

And the Arab world is not the only place where gift-giving follows set rules. In **Japan** they are
25 even stricter. As an American who volunteered to teach English to a Japanese woman reported: 'Before each lesson, and on each and every visit, the Japanese lady brought me a gift – a book, some paper sculpture or flowers.' Unknowingly,
30 this American was experiencing a ritual rooted centuries deep in Japanese culture. According to *Business Tokyo* magazine, among the Japanese 'gift-giving is a necessity, not merely a nicety as it is in the West.'

35 In Japan the proper gift is thought to express the giver's true friendship, gratitude, and respect far better than words can. And specific gift-giving rules have prevailed in Japanese society for centuries. They spell out the type of
40 gift to give and how the various types of gifts should be wrapped. So if you plan to visit Japan, be prepared. But don't worry about getting the protocol wrong – foreigners are not expected to know all the rules!

45 Another country which takes gifts seriously is **Thailand**. When visiting a home in this country, take flowers or a box of chocolates from the local market. The value is not important; it is the thought and the act that
50 count. It is the tradition in Thailand to wrap gifts beautifully with colourful ribbons, and the custom has long been to put the gift aside to be opened later, so don't be offended if the gift seems to go unappreciated. But this custom is
55 not as rigid today as it was and you may be invited to open a gift in front of the giver. But in this case do avoid ripping open the beautiful wrapping, as this is considered rude.

And of course, there are countries where
60 businesspeople rarely exchange gifts, and **Australia** is an example of this. Modest gifts, such as a business diary, a paperweight or a coffee mug might be presented as a memento of a visit or business meeting, and sales
65 conferences and trade shows often give out T-shirts, ties or baseball caps as mementos. However, anything more than these types of gifts could cause embarrassment in a society known for its friendly informality, as people
70 might regard them as pretentious.

2A Work

Vocabulary ▶ CB pages 24–25

Exam strategy

For Paper 5 Part 1, be prepared to talk about the job you do or hope to do in the future. You may be asked to describe what you enjoy most about your job, or to say what kind of job you would most like to do.

1 Topic: job factors

Look at the list of factors which people consider important in a job. Tick (✓) the three factors which are the most important for you.

- [ ] the salary
- [ ] the location (e.g. town, region) of the job
- [ ] opportunities for promotion
- [ ] a friendly working environment
- [ ] good facilities (e.g. car park, canteen, gym)
- [ ] long holidays
- [ ] opportunities to work independently
- [ ] a company car
- [ ] opportunities for creativity
- [ ] a company pension
- [ ] flexible working hours
- [ ] opportunities for travel

2 Describing jobs

a Read what six people say about their work opposite. What job does each person do? Write the name of the correct job from the list next to each person. There are four jobs you do not need to use.

actor   journalist   lecturer   lawyer   scientist
architect   accountant   engineer   musician
bank clerk

> I'm very good at maths and statistics. I like my job because I can work on my own a lot. It's also creative. I love testing my theories in the laboratory to see if they are right.

1 ....

> I enjoy working with figures. Some people might think that my job is boring, but they're quite wrong. Looking after so much money is actually really interesting.

2 ....

> I've always been good at persuading people to do or believe things. Now I do it every day in court. My salary is excellent, of course, and there are good career opportunities.

3 ....

> My job is very creative. I have to practise a lot, of course, and being on tour with an orchestra can be rather tiring. However, I can take long holidays if I want to.

4 ....

> I've always been keen on designing and building things. Now I am well-paid for doing what I enjoy. It's a creative job because you combine theory and practice. You also need to know a lot about different materials.

5 ....

> For my job you need to have a good command of English. You work on your own a lot, particularly when you're following up a big story. The salary's not great, but it's an interesting, rewarding job.

6 ....

b Read the comments again. What are the advantages of each job, according to the six people? Underline them.

c In your notebook, write a short paragraph describing your own job, or the job you would like to do. Use some of the ideas and language above.

3 Verb + noun collocations

Read the text below and decide which answer A, B or C best fits each space.

MY CAREER

My name is Helena. Although I did well at school and managed to (1)............... all my exams when I was 18, I decided not to go to university. I wanted to make lots of money instead. I (2).............. for three jobs with large international companies and (3).............. an interview with one of them the following week. They offered me the job. I was now Helena Roberts – Assistant Marketing Manager!

For the first two years I (4).............. very little money, but I worked conscientiously. As a result, I soon (5).............. promoted. My dream was to become Managing Director. That was my first big mistake. The company closed down a month later and I was (6).............. redundant!

In my next job, the working conditions were awful. I wanted to (7).............. and look for something else. My colleagues, however, persuaded me to (8).............. on strike with them for better pay. That, of course, was my second big mistake. The boss immediately (9).............. us the sack! It was six months before I found another job.

I've been with my present company for five years now. I am extremely happy and intend to stay here until I (10).............. at 65. I no longer dream of being Managing Director. Having a job is enough for me.

1 **A** pass	**B** take	**C** succeed
2 **A** looked	**B** applied	**C** offered
3 **A** went	**B** attended	**C** made
4 **A** gained	**B** won	**C** earned
5 **A** became	**B** got	**C** took
6 **A** made	**B** become	**C** told
7 **A** resign	**B** dismiss	**C** release
8 **A** make	**B** go	**C** put
9 **A** put	**B** showed	**C** gave
10 **A** retire	**B** graduate	**C** withdraw

4 ⌒ Pronunciation

a Say the following words aloud. Is the *-ed* ending pronounced *-t, -d* or *-id*?

wanted   passed   applied   worked   attended   earned   persuaded   closed   offered   promoted

b Listen to the recording and write the verbs in the correct column in the table.

-t	-d	-id

Language development 1

Past simple and present perfect

▶ CB pages 26–27, GR 188–189

1 Past simple or present perfect?
Complete the email with the past simple or present perfect form of the verb in brackets. Mark the time expressions which help you to decide.

Hi Maria!
I've just read your message. Yes, I'd love to come and help you at your office. I (1)....................... (*take*) my final exams last week and I (2)....................... (*not/have*) anything to do since then. Some work would be great! I still (3)....................... (*not/learn*) to type, I'm afraid, but I could put your files in order. In January, I (4)....................... (*organise*) all the files for the Students' Union. Up to now, nobody (5)....................... (*complain*), I'm proud to say. I know you (6)....................... (*not/find*) a receptionist yet, so I could do that job as well. The other day, I (7)....................... (*answer*) some phone calls from college applicants, and I really (8)....................... (*enjoy*) it. So you see, Maria, I have already had lots of experience!

Love, Alexia

2 *yet, still, already, just*

a Complete the sentences with *yet, still, already* or *just*. Use the explanations in brackets to help you.
1 I have .... received a fax from Texas Computers. Do you want to see it? (= *a short time ago*)
2 We've written to him three times and he .... hasn't replied. (= *up to now but we expected it to happen by now*)
3 Mr Smith is looking for you. Has he spoken to you ....? (= *up to now but we expect it to happen*)
4 There's no need for you to phone the bank – I've .... done it. (= *before now/earlier than expected*)

b Now complete these sentences in the same way.
1 I can't give Mrs Hudson my report, because I haven't finished it ....
2 You don't need to write to Mr Jones – I've .... written to him.
3 My car broke down last week, and the garage .... hasn't fixed it.
4 We've .... heard that Sally's been promoted. It's great news, isn't it?

3 Present perfect simple or continuous?

a Mark the correct verb form in each pair.

1 Have you *lived / been living* in Vienna all your life?
2 I'm exhausted! I've *studied / been studying* for my accounting exams all day.
3 Oh dear! We've *missed / been missing* the bus!
4 My boss is away at the moment, so I've *worked / been working* overtime.
5 Can you phone Maria urgently? She's *phoned / been phoning* for you four times this afternoon.
6 Stephen's *tried / been trying* to contact you all day. Where have you been?

b Use the prompts to make sentences with the present perfect simple or continuous.

1 I / just / write / two letters of application / Can you post them?

....

2 George / work on / his CV / all day / but / he still / not / finish it.

....

3 Joanna / still / not / arrive. / Do you think she / get lost?

....

4 Although I / learn / English / for over five years / I / never / go / to England.

....

5 Call the police! / Someone / steal / the money from the safe.

....

6 I / try / to phone Sue / all afternoon / but I / not / be able / get through yet.

....

4 Key word transformations

Complete the second sentence so that it has a similar meaning to the first sentence, using the word given. Do not change the word given. You must use between two and five words, including the word given.

1 I have never been to the National Museum. **still**
I .... the National Museum.
2 The last time I saw Jenny was ten years ago. **for**
I .... ten years.
3 John can still remember how nervous he felt on his first day at work. **never**
John .... how nervous he felt on his first day at work.
4 She began working for this company when she was 18. **been**
She .... for this company since she was 18.
5 Mr Thomas phoned a moment ago to say he will be late. **just**
Mr Thomas .... to say he will be late.
6 It's been a long time since our last meeting. **met**
We .... a long time.

Listening Multiple matching
(Paper 4 Part 3)

1 Before you listen

a Read the instructions for the listening task below. Answer these questions.
1 How many speakers will you hear?
2 What do they all have in common?
(Note that in the exam there will be an extra option that you do not need to use.)

b Read the statements A–E and mark key words. (The first two have been done for you.)

c Think of other ways of expressing this information.

2 🎧 Listening for gist
Listen to the recording once, and decide which of the speakers mentions the ideas you've marked.

3 🎧 Listening for specific information
Listen again to check that the ideas expressed exactly match the wording of the options.

You will hear five people who have given up stressful jobs in the city talking about their decisions. For questions **1–5**, choose from the list **A–E** the statement which best matches what each person says.

A I'm not absolutely sure I've done the right thing.

B I find I can manage on a much lower income.

C A sudden change led me to make my decision.

D I had some money to invest in a new career.

E I realised that my way of life was making me miserable.

Speaker 1 [1]

Speaker 2 [2]

Speaker 3 [3]

Speaker 4 [4]

Speaker 5 [5]

Writing Formal letter (Paper 2 Part 2)

▶ CB pages 28–29, WR page 200

Exam strategy

In Paper 2, it's important to organise your ideas clearly and divide them into paragraphs. You will lose marks in the exam otherwise. Making a paragraph plan before you write will help you to do this.

1 Understand the task

Read the task below and answer the questions.
1 Who are you writing to?
2 What is the purpose of your letter?
3 What style should you use?
4 What information MUST your letter supply? Mark the parts of the task that tell you.

You have seen this advertisement in a student magazine. You are interested in applying for the job.

Tour Guide
needed!

Would you like to work as a tour guide this summer, taking groups of English-speaking tourists to see the attractions of your town? Full training provided!

Write to Peter Harlow, giving details of previous work experience and explaining why you are the person we need.

Write your **letter** in **120–180** applying for the job. Do not give any postal addresses.

2 Plan your letter

a **Which of the following points will you include in your letter? Tick (✓) the ones that are relevant to the task.**
1 details about your present job
2 what you hate about your present job
3 details about any relevant knowledge/skills
4 what kind of person you are
5 your reason for writing/where you heard about the job
6 names and addresses of people who can recommend you
7 details about yourself/qualifications/ previous experience
8 details about your home and family
9 availability for interview/concluding remarks
10 the kind of clothes you usually wear
11 why you want the job/why you are suitable for the job

b How will you organise the points? Make a paragraph plan for the points you ticked above.

Paragraph 1: ....
Paragraph 2: ....
Paragraph 3: ....
Paragraph 4: ....

3 Check and complete a sample answer

a Complete this student's letter with a suitable word or phrase for each space.

b Does the letter include all the relevant information? Compare it to your list in Exercise 2.

c The letter has no paragraphs. Mark where each new paragraph should begin.

---

(1)................................

I would like **(2)**........................ tour guide, which I saw advertised in our student magazine. I am 23 years old and have just completed a first degree in History at Szeged University. **(3)**........................ I am thinking of continuing my studies at postgraduate level next year. Although I am not actually from Szeged, I have lived here for many years and know the town and surrounding area very well. I have **(4)**........................ English and German, and have been learning Spanish for the past two years. Last summer, I worked for three months as a receptionist in a hotel in Budapest. This job involved giving foreign tourists information about the city. I feel **(5)**........................ for the job you describe in the advertisement because I know a lot about Szeged and its history. I think it is a beautiful town and I would enjoy showing tourists its attractions. It would also be a wonderful **(6)**........................ for me to meet people from other countries. I hope you will **(7)**........................ seriously. I am **(8)**........................ whenever it is convenient.

(9)................................

János Kelemen

Vocabulary ▶ CB pages 30–31

Exam strategy
For Paper 5 Part 1, you may be asked about your studies and what you enjoy/enjoyed most about them. For Paper 2, you may have to write a letter or report on the topic of education in your country, for example. Make sure you are familiar with the vocabulary you need.

1 Topic: educational systems

a **Look at the statements about the educational system in the UK. Tick (✓) the statements which are also true for your country.**

1 Education is compulsory until the age of 16.
2 Education in state schools is free until the age of 18.
3 Children start primary school at around the age of five.
4 Children in primary and secondary schools take national tests to monitor their progress.
5 At the age of 16, students usually take important exams in several different subjects.
6 Students who want to continue their studies take advanced level exams in two to four subjects at the age of 18.
7 About 40 per cent of young people go to college or university after school.
8 For most subjects, an undergraduate university course (leading to a bachelor's degree) lasts three or four years.
9 Some 'sandwich' courses at college or university include a certain amount of work experience.
10 Nowadays many colleges and universities have a system of 'continuous assessment' rather than formal exams.
11 If a student does very well at university, he or she will be awarded a 'first-class' degree. Weaker students will receive a second-class, third-class or pass degree.
12 A postgraduate course leading to a master's degree usually lasts one year. It may take longer if students have to carry out some research.

b **Rewrite any statements you did not tick and make them true for your own country.**

2 Commonly confused words
Complete the sentences with the correct word. Use each word once only.

1 **professor / teacher**
   a When I was 12, my English .... encouraged me to write stories.
   b Our .... at university was more interested in his research than in teaching.

2 **check / control**
   a Before you hand in written work, you should .... it carefully for mistakes.
   b The children in Mr Adam's class are so naughty that he cannot .... them.

3 **career / course**
   a Dr Jenkins ruined his .... when he gave several patients the wrong drug.
   b They sent him on a two-week .... to learn how to use the new computer.

4 **subject / lesson**
   a Monday's French .... was so boring I thought it would never end.
   b I think physics is a difficult .... to study at university level.

5 **educate / train**
   a I'm sure your company will .... you to use the new equipment.
   b Many people feel that schools do not .... children very well these days.

6 **degree / grade**
   a I think this composition deserves a better .... than C, don't you?
   b Although my .... was in chemistry, the headmaster still let me teach biology.

3 Agreeing and disagreeing
Two students are discussing this question:
'Do schools prepare children for the "real world"?'

Complete their discussion with phrases from the list.

- up to a point   • couldn't agree   • you think so
- you're right   • don't you think   • quite true
- what about   • suppose so

Alan: I'm sure that what you study at school is very useful when you start work.
Jane: Do (1)..........................? Some subjects you study don't prepare you for work at all, I'd say. (2).......................... Latin?
Alan: Well, perhaps (3).......................... about Latin. But other subjects help you when you leave school. (4).......................... that mathematics is useful?
Jane: I (5).......................... . But they could have made it more relevant to everyday life.
Alan: I (6).......................... more. Perhaps the problem is not the subjects we learn, but the way they are taught? Take geography – they could make it really interesting.
Jane: I agree (7).......................... . But not entirely. You probably learn more about geography when you start to travel. I don't see why it's useful to study it at school.
Alan: That's (8).......................... . But some people may not have the opportunity to travel when they leave school.

Language development 2

Articles, *some/any, something/anything*

▶ CB page 34, GR pages 182–183

1 Articles

Mark the correct alternative in each pair. (Ø = no article.)

1 My brother wants to join Ø / *the* army when he leaves Ø / *the* school.

2 I have Ø / *a* degree in Ø / *the* chemistry from Ø / *the* University of York.

3 Twice *a* / *the* week, we have Ø / *a* lecture by Ø / *the* Professor Hawking.

4 Do you want to go to Ø / *the* cinema tonight, or would you rather go to Ø / *the* theatre?

5 When did Ø / *the* Poland join Ø / *the* European Union?

6 I'd like to come out for Ø / *a* drink this evening, but I have to revise for Ø / *the* end-of-semester German exam.

7 Although my brother had Ø / *a* good school education, he didn't know that Ø / *the* River Danube flows through Budapest.

8 *A* / *The* computer has changed Ø / *the* way many people live and work.

9 My little sister is making Ø / *the* excellent progress at Ø / *the* school she goes to.

10 Although people say that Ø / *the* English are very reserved, I have Ø / *an* English girlfriend who is just the opposite!

2 Some / any, something / anything

Put a tick next to the sentences which are correct. Rewrite sentences which are incorrect.

1 My flatmate, Mark, wanted to do anything special last night.

2 He had just heard some good news and wanted to go out to celebrate.

3 He phoned any friends of his to ask them if they'd like to come as well.

4 It took Mark's friend some time to arrive, so we didn't leave the flat until after 10 o'clock.

5 We went to three or four different restaurants, but didn't like any of them. In the end, we decided to go for a pizza.

6 Mark was in a good mood In the local pizza restaurant he said, 'You can have anything you like – I'll pay!'

7 Unfortunately, it was late and the owner said that he had hardly some pizzas left.

8 'Give us something you have then. It doesn't matter what it is!' Mark told the owner in desperation.

9 The owner returned with two sad-looking pizzas and half a dozen sandwiches. Some them looked distinctly stale.

10 'Next time we'll stay at home and make the food ourselves. Something's better than this!' Mark groaned.

3 Extra word

Look at the sentences below. Some are correct and some have a word which should not be there. If a sentence is correct, put a tick (✓) by it. If a sentence has a word which should not be there, cross the word out.

EXAMPLE: In the UK, some ~~of~~ teenagers leave school at the age of 16.

1 Undergraduate courses in the USA usually last longer than in the UK.

2 My brother doesn't have hardly any homework to do during the summer holidays.

3 I went to the school my father went to when he was a boy.

4 Almost all the countries in the world regard the education as extremely important.

5 My brother got the high grades in every subject when he was at school.

6 I had a bad cough, so I had to spend a couple of days at the home.

7 My friend wanted to study medicine at the University of Birmingham, but there weren't any of places available.

8 I couldn't answer some of the questions in the history exam I took yesterday.

9 Even with a good degree, it is sometimes difficult to find a work these days.

4 Key word transformations

Complete the second sentence so that it has a similar meaning to the first sentence, using the word given. Do not change the word given. You must use between two and five words, including the word given.

1 Do you have a computer in your house? **got**
   Have .... home?

2 We went to Paris by train. **on**
   We went .... Paris.

3 My little cousin wants to drive a bus when he leaves school. **driver**
   My little cousin wants .... when he leaves school.

4 Is he a good pianist? **play**
   Does .... well?

5 We watched a television documentary about Scotland last night. **on**
   We watched a documentary .... last night.

6 How about going to see a film this evening? **cinema**
   Why don't .... this evening?

7 I think she is lying about what happened. **truth**
   I don't think she .... about what happened.

8 Germany is well-known for making very good cars. **reputation**
   The Germans .... for making very good cars.

Reading Multiple-choice questions
(Paper 1 Part 1)

1 Before you read

a Read the instructions for the reading task. What do they tell you about the text? Think about these questions.

1 Where would you read a text like this?
2 Who is the writer?
3 What style do you expect it to be in?
4 What sort of things do you think the text will talk about?

b Now look at the title and subheading of the article. What more do you find out? Mark the words which tell you about the writer's attitude.

2 Skimming

Read the text quickly once.

1 Were your predictions about the content and the writer's attitude correct?
2 Which of the three photos A–C below do you think shows the writer?

3 Reading for detail

a Read the questions 1–8. Don't look at the options A–D yet. Find the place in the text where the information is contained. (The questions are in the same order as the text.) Try to answer the question yourself and mark the relevant part of the text.

b Now read the options A–D and choose the one closest to your answer. Read the part of the text again carefully to check that your answer is right and that the other options are definitely wrong. Look for parallel words and phrases in the text and the option you have chosen. The first one has been done for you.

You are going to read a magazine article written by a woman who has returned to studying in retirement. For questions **1–8**, choose the answer **A**, **B**, **C** or **D** which you think fits best according to the text.

1 What did June discover when she first retired?

A She had more free time than she expected.
B She had not really been very happy in her job.
C She needed activities she could do on her own.
D She no longer found her old hobbies satisfying.

2 What first attracted June to the 'access course'?

A Some of her friends were doing it.
B She knew somebody who taught on it.
C She'd decided she wanted to study full-time.
D Pensioners who did it were offered a discount.

3 The word 'clinched' in line 30 means

A made up my mind for me.
B put me under pressure to decide.
C made me reconsider my decision.
D left me unsure what to do next.

4 What does June say about the teachers on the access course?

A They are very patient with the more mature students.
B They need to know a lot about a wide range of subjects.
C They appear to be genuinely interested in what they teach.
D They have problems dealing with such a variety of students.

5 What does 'one' in line 46 refer to?

A a subject June has to study
B a student on the course June is doing
C a new way of approaching art history
D an experience June can share with others

6 When June had to write an essay,

A she wrote about a college she had once attended.
B she rewrote one she had written years ago.
C she wasn't allowed to choose the subject.
D she found it easier than she had expected.

7 What disadvantage of the access course does June mention?

A It tends to limit her freedom in some ways.
B It attracts students who are not really committed.
C It involves keeping a journal which is rather boring.
D It doesn't give her the opportunity to take exams.

8 From the last paragraph, we understand that June is

A anxious about her garden.
B determined to take a degree.
C enjoying what she's currently doing.
D unsure whether studying is really for her.

Carry on Learning

Everyone, whatever their age, can share in the joy and fulfilment of learning, as June Weatherall found out

When I first retired, I thought I'd love spending more time on the gardening, needlework, and other creative activities I'd found so relaxing after my demanding job. But it didn't turn out that way. I
5 found that I didn't want, or need, that kind of relaxation anymore, I wanted to stimulate my mind instead. Also, they're all solitary activities and I missed the company and interests of my old work companions.
10 So, with a couple of friends, I went along to an art appreciation evening class at our local regional college. It was wonderful, but only lasted a year. At the end, I asked my tutor, 'What next?' He suggested I attend his history of art access course.
15 'Whatever's that?' I asked. The college had an open evening coming up, so I went along to find out.

A full-time access course takes one year and gives you access to university if, like me, you left school without any qualifications, and it's free if
20 you do it full-time. I only wanted to do the art history bit, but even so, with my pensioner's discount, it would cost a mere £30 per term.

Lyn, who organises the courses for the college, was enthusiastic. 'Why don't you do the whole
25 course? You could start in the spring term with art history, do another module in the summer, then go full-time in the autumn and do all the subjects.' It sounded wonderful, but wasn't I a bit old, at 63, to start being a student? A definite 'no'. One of the
30 students that year was 82. That **clinched** it. It must be worth having a go.

The art history part of the course, which I've just completed, was stimulating and involved a trip to the Louvre museum in Paris – which was wonderful.
35 The tutors are enthusiasts and infect us all with their enjoyment of the subjects they teach. 'Lively' would be the word to describe the classes. My fellow students, who are also doing subjects like psychology, maths, biology, etc., are good company.
40 They're mainly people in their thirties with children, taking a second bite at the educational cherry. There's a crèche to help those with toddlers and an excellent library. They're kind enough to say they find the older students offer a lot in experience
45 – they certainly give a lot to us in newer ways of looking at things. **One**, a nurse, is changing direction and has a place at Anglia University to do a degree course in art history. Another has been accepted to do English.
50 We have homework and have to do an essay each term for each subject, and sit exams. For art history, I opted to write about the Bauhaus – a college for all the arts set up in Germany in the early twentieth century. The last essay I'd written had been a
55 lifetime ago – in 1955 – so I was a bit apprehensive, but I managed fine. We also had to produce a journal about all the painters we'd learnt about – which was fun, but rather time-consuming. Occasionally, I envy the more typical mature students, who just do
60 courses for pleasure and don't have to do exams or essays as I do, but really I'm a very happy lady. There are drawbacks, however. The main one is you have to make a commitment. During term time, you can't just drop everything and go out for the day if the sun
65 shines – one of the supposed joys of retirement.

Will I go on to university if I'm successful? I'll see how next year goes. Meanwhile, exercising my brain cells is working well for me. I feel alive. The garden's getting a bit out of control, but that's the least of my
70 worries!

3A Our cultural heritage

Vocabulary ▶ CB pages 38–39

1 Topic: cities and culture

a In the diagram below, only one adjective collocates with each noun or noun phrase. <u>Underline</u> the adjective which collocates.

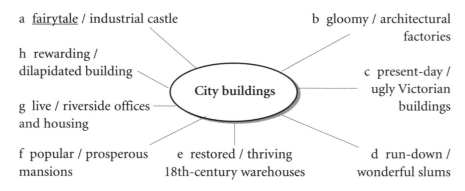

a <u>fairytale</u> / industrial castle

b gloomy / architectural factories

h rewarding / dilapidated building

City buildings

c present-day / ugly Victorian buildings

g live / riverside offices and housing

f popular / prosperous mansions

e restored / thriving 18th-century warehouses

d run-down / wonderful slums

b Check your answers by reading the magazine advertisement below. Do not worry about the numbered gaps.

c Put the adjectives from Exercise 1a which you did <u>not</u> underline in the numbered gaps in the advertisement. Use each adjective once.

Forget Edinburgh ... Come to Glasgow instead!

It may not have Edinburgh's fairytale castle, but Glasgow is a far more (1) .... place to visit. You'll find the people are friendlier too!

Forget those images of gloomy factories, ugly Victorian buildings and abandoned shipyards ... Haven't you heard that Glasgow has changed?

Some people say that Glasgow still seems a little grey and depressing when you first arrive. To some extent they are right. You'll still find the occasional dilapidated building in the city centre; there are still run-down slums on the outskirts. But Glasgow is now a proud city – proud of its (2) .... and shipbuilding past, proud of its architectural heritage and proud of its (3) .... role as a leading UK tourist destination.

Four million people visit Glasgow every year. They come as much for the shopping as for the museums and art galleries. There's also a (4) .... theatre scene, and (5) .... music events take place almost every night of the week. Then there is the (6) .... architecture. From the restored 18th-century warehouses of the Merchant City to the prosperous mansions around George Square, the (7) .... legacy of Glasgow is among the most striking in the UK.

It's not by accident that £500 million has recently been invested in new riverside offices and housing. Or that the city is one of the most (8) .... conference destinations in Europe. Glasgow has something to offer everyone.

Come to Glasgow and see what Glasgow can offer you!

2 Word formation.

Complete the table.

Adjective	Verb	Noun	Adjective	Verb	Noun
strong	strengthen	1	▬▬▬	8	achievement
prosperous	2	3	9	▬▬▬	culture
optimistic	▬▬▬	4	10	▬▬▬	architecture
threatening	5	6	declining	decline	11 ....
7	▬▬▬	economy	▬▬▬	solve	12 ....

3 Exam practice: word formation

(Paper 3 Part 3)

> Read the text below. Use the word given in capitals below the text to form a word that fits in the space in the text. There is an example at the beginning (0).

KRAKOV

In the past, Krakov was a city of great political (0)...importance... . It was the ancient capital of Poland and the official (1)............................. of the country's kings. The city still has (2)........................... medieval architecture, and is listed by UNESCO as a world heritage site because of its great (3)........................... and artistic (4)........................... . Krakov had the largest square in medieval Europe and this is still the (5)........................... centre of the city, and the best place to begin your (6)........................... of the winding streets of the old quarter. These streets were home to Poland's (7)........................... artists, writers and thinkers, many of whom studied at the city's (8)........................... university. The area still has a (9)........................... atmosphere and it's a pleasure just to wander round. But there is also plenty to do and see as a thriving (10)...culture... life continues today.

(0) IMPORTANT	(6) EXPLORE
(1) RESIDENT	(7) GREAT
(2) IMPRESS	(8) FAME
(3) HISTORY	(9) ROMANCE
(4) SIGNIFICANT	(10) CULTURE
(5) COMMERCE	

Language development 1

Adjectives and adverbs

▶ CB pages 40–41 ▶ GR pages 183–184

1 Which word?

Complete the sentences with the correct word.

1 **good / well**
   a You don't look very .... Are you feeling OK?
   b Ask Sue what this word means – her Italian is really ....

2 **steady / steadily**
   a Since 1990, there's been a .... increase in tourism to this town.
   b Over the past 20 years, the quality of hotels has .... improved.

3 **late / lately**
   a There have been a lot of strikes at the airport ....
   b The announcement said that the plane would take off ....

4 **hard / hardly**
   a Sarah was so suntanned I could .... recognise her.
   b I worked extremely .... to pay for this holiday.

5 **wide / widely**
   a Can you close the window? It's .... open at the moment.
   b Mark travelled .... in Europe when he was a student.

6 **direct / directly**
   a We can fly .... to Rome from this airport.
   b If you lose your passport, you should go .... to the police.

2 Adverbs of degree

a **Write these adjectives in the correct column.**
~~marvellous~~ ~~powerful~~ decisive tremendous lively fantastic well-known bleak furious fragile romantic awful impressive fast unique

Gradable	Ungradable
powerful	marvellous

b **Complete the sentences with *very/extremely* or *absolutely*.**

1 When we arrived in Rome, the weather was
.... awful.

2 Many of the monuments of Rome are
.... well-known.

3 That porcelain vase you bought looks
.... fragile.

4 Verdi played a(n) .... decisive role in
the development of opera.

5 When my father heard the bad news he was
.... furious.

6 The service at our hotel was .... impressive.

7 I found the Colosseum in Rome ....
unique.

8 Anna's two-year-old daughter is .... lively.

9 With no money and no job, my prospects
seemed .... bleak.

10 Volunteers are making .... tremendous
efforts to rescue artworks threatened by the floods.

3 **Key word transformations**

Complete the second sentence so that it has a similar
meaning to the first sentence, using the word given.
Do not change the word given. You must use between
two and five words, including the word given.

1 A lot of snow fell yesterday in Vienna.
hard
It .... in Vienna yesterday.

2 There has been a steady increase in prices over
the last year.
steadily
Prices .... over the past year.

3 My hometown is a fairly big industrial city.
quite
My hometown is ....
industrial city.

4 Prague is rather expensive.
bit
Prague is .... expensive city.

5 I have almost no money left after my holiday.
hardly
I have .... money left after
my holiday.

6 The number of tourists I saw was really amazing.
absolutely
I .... the number of tourists I saw.

7 Can I fly to Bratislava without having to change
planes?
direct
Is there .... to Bratislava?

8 Keith really lost his temper when they told him to
show his passport again.
extremely
Keith .... when they told
him to show his passport again.

4 **Exam practice: open cloze** (Paper 3 Part 2)

Read the text below and think of the word which
best fits each space. Use only **one** word in each
space. There is an example at the beginning (**0**).

EVERY PICTURE TELLS A STORY

More (**0**)........than........ 230 years after his death,
the Venetian painter Canaletto is helping to save
his beloved city. Scientists (**1**)..............................
discovered that his highly accurate paintings of
eighteenth-century Venice provide
(**2**).............................. with a record of sea levels a
century and (**3**).............................. half before modern
measurements began. They hope that this
information will help them to save Venice and its
rich cultural heritage from being lost beneath the
waves.
(**4**).............................. Venice is built on a lagoon, it is
highly vulnerable to the changing sea levels
brought on (**5**).............................. global warming. High
tides often flood the city. As well as causing
problems for residents, this means that sea water
gets into the buildings and it has begun
(**6**).............................. rot them away.
Instruments were first used to measure sea levels
in 1872, and scientists have (**7**)..............................
looking for ways to find (**8**).............................. what
happened before then, as this could help them
predict what might happen in future. Then
somebody realised that Canaletto, unlike most
modern painters, painted exactly (**9**)..............................
he saw, so his pictures are almost
(**10**).............................. accurate as photographs. If you
look at them closely, you can see a brown-green
line on the buildings (**11**).............................. marks the
average high-tide level at the time. The scientists
can therefore see that the sea level in Venice has
risen by about 2.7 millimetres per year
(**12**).............................. Canaletto's day.

Writing Email

(Paper 2 Part 1) ▶ CB pages 42–43, WR pages 197–198

Exam strategy

In Part 1 of Paper 2, you have to use the given information to write an email. (The email may be formal or informal.) Read the input material very carefully, and mark key words and phrases. Make sure you include all the points in the task, or you will lose marks. When you've finished, check by ticking the parts of the task you marked.

1 Understand the task

Read the task below and answer the questions.

1 Who are you writing to?
   a someone you know   b someone you don't know
2 What style should you use?
   a formal   b informal
3 What information MUST you include in the email? Mark the parts of the task that tell you.

You are studying in the UK, and have recently received an email from an English friend, Peter, who is thinking of going on a two-day organised tour of a historic town near you. Read Peter's email and the notes you have made. Then write an email to Peter, using all your note

---

New Message

I'm thinking of going on that two-day tour of Loxford that you went on last year. Would you recommend it? Was it well organised?   *Yes, say why*

The advertisement says that Loxford was originally a Roman town and that the town's museum is well worth visiting. Do you agree or do you think I might find it a bit boring?   *Yes, give details*

What about the hotel where you stayed? Did you like it? It's a modern 3-star hotel, so it should be okay.   *modern, but ...*

The evening lecture about Loxford's history sounds interesting. Was there a lecture at the hotel when you went on the tour last year?   *Yes, give details*

Reply soon.
Peter

Write your **email** of between **120–150** words. You must use grammatically correct sentences with accurate spelling and punctuation in a style appropriate for the situation.

2 Check and improve a sample answer

a Read the email below. Tick (✓) the points which are included. Check back to the task. Which two pieces of information are missing?
1 Information about the ....
2 Information about the ....

New Message

Hi Peter
Thanks for your email. I'm glad you are thinking of visiting Loxford. Its a really beautiful town.
The tour I went on last year, was very well-organised. A coach took us to all the main sights. I particularly remember Loxford Museum.
The Hotel, where we stayed was quite nice. We ate all our meals there.
After dinner, there was a lecture at the hotel by a local historian. His name was dr Rawlings. It wasn't really a lecture at all, it was so relaxed and informal.
I think you should go on the tour, Peter. I enjoyed it and I'm sure you would as well. Tell me how you get on!

Lot's of love
Maria

---

b Write sentences to include the missing information and mark where they should go in the letter.

c Find and correct these punctuation mistakes.
- Two mistakes with apostrophes
- Two mistakes with capital letters
- Two mistakes with commas

d Rewrite the letter in your notebook.

Listening Sentence completion
(Paper 4 Part 2)

1 Before you listen
Read the instructions for the exam task below and look at the photos. When do you think they were taken? What can you see?

2 ∩ Listening for gist
Listen to the recording once and number the photos in order.

3 ∩ Listening for specific information
a Read sentences 1–10 and try to predict what kind of information is missing.
  1 Which answers do you think will be numbers? What type of numbers will they be?
  2 Which answers do you think will be proper names?
  3 Which answer do you think will be a form of transport?

b Now listen and complete the sentences, using no more than three words. The words you need are on the recording.

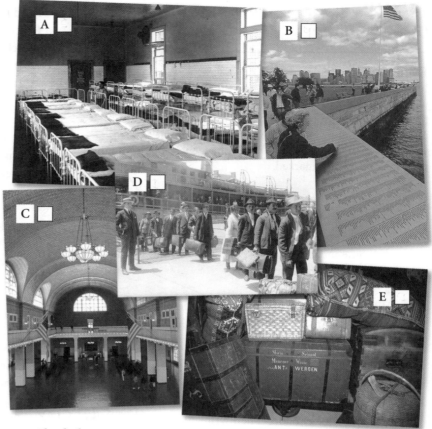

c Check that:
  • your answer fits the gap to make a good sentence
  • your answers are single words, numbers or short phrases
  • you have written numbers as figures, not words
  • your spelling is correct.

You will hear a tour guide talking to a group of tourists in New York about a visit they will make to the Museum of Immigration on Ellis Island. For questions **1–10** complete the sentences.

Ellis island was busiest between the years [and | **1**].

The group of tourists will arrive at the museum by [| **2**].

The first part of the museum you go through used to be the [| **3**] room.

In the Registry Room, immigrants had both [| **4**] and medical check-ups.

What's called a [| **5**] records the names of immigrants who passed through Ellis Island.

Immigrants staying overnight on the island slept in the [| **6**] Room.

The movie you can see at the museum is called [| **7**].

The play in Theatre 2 begins at [| **8**].

Instead of the play, the tourists can visit the [| **9**].

The *Peopling of America* exhibition can be found in what used to be a [| **10**].

3B Our natural heritage

Vocabulary ▶ CB pages 44–45

▶ CB pages 44–45

Exam strategy

For Paper 2, Writing or Paper 5, Speaking, you may be asked to give your opinions about problems related to the environment and what we can do about them. Make sure you are familiar with the necessary vocabulary.

1 **Topic:** the environment

a Skim the text extracts 1–5 and match them to the pictures. There may be more than one possibility. (Ignore the numbered words at this stage.)

b Read the texts again and mark the correct word in each pair.

c In your notebook, list two or three of the most important environmental problems in your country or region. Note down possible solutions.

1 The world's rainforests are quickly disappearing. People **(1)** cut *down / up* thousands of trees every day, which is a **(2)** *shame / catastrophe* for the animals and plants that live there. Rainforests are the natural **(3)** *locations / habitats* for thousands of **(4)** *forms / species* of animals, birds and plants. If you **(5)** *destroy / demolish* the rainforests, these creatures will become **(6)** *extinct / vanished*. Governments must **(7)** *take / put* urgent action to save the rainforests.

2 Burning coal and oil releases carbon dioxide (CO_2) into the atmosphere. In large amounts, this gas traps the heat of the sun and causes the **(8)** *hothouse / greenhouse* effect. The problem of global **(9)** *heating / warming* is already affecting the climate of the world. We should start now to look for other forms of energy. Hot countries, for example, could use **(10)** *solar / sun* energy on a larger scale.

3 **(11)** *Poisoned / Poisonous* gases from cars and factories cause atmospheric pollution and make the air dangerous to breathe. Factories **(12)** *emit / dump* dangerous chemical waste into rivers and seas, causing the death of thousands of fish and sea animals. **(13)** *Atomic / Radioactive* waste is particularly dangerous, and has a terrible **(14)** *effect / influence* on the environment. We should **(15)** *abolish / ban* cars from city centres and force factories to be cleaner.

4 Many of the world's natural resources are going to run **(16)** *off / out* in the near future. We should do something about this before it's too late. For example, we could **(17)** *exploit / recycle* paper, metal and glass rather than just throwing them away.

5 Most farmers these days spray their crops with chemical **(18)** *soils / fertilisers* and pesticides. What's more, increasing numbers of farmers are planting genetically **(19)** *modified / changed* crops, even though many people believe that they might be dangerous to our health. Governments should encourage farmers to **(20)** *grow / manufacture* organic crops. Organic fruit and vegetables are much tastier and better for you.

2 Exam practice: multiple-choice cloze (Paper 3 Part 1)

Read the text below and decide which answer **A**, **B**, **C** or **D** best fits each space. There is an example at the beginning **(0)**.

0 A nearby **B** closely **C** vicinity **D** neighbourly

LIGHT POLLUTION

Some years ago, when I was working as an astronomer at the Greenwich Observatory in London, I received a letter from an elderly lady living **(0)**.....A..... who said: 'When I was a girl, we could see so many stars, but they're not there any more. Have they faded?' Walking down the hill on which the observatory stands, I **(1)**............. the truth of what she said. **(2)**............. me were all the lights of London and above me was the orange glow they **(3)**............. up into the night sky. But I could **(4)**............. see any stars.

If light pollution – as this effect is known – continues to increase at its present **(5)**............. , our grandchildren will only **(6)**............. the chance to see the stars if they visit an observatory **(7)**............. the one in Greenwich. Light pollution is almost **(8)**............. for granted in most cities, and it is fast spreading into rural areas too. **(9)**............. recent research, almost half of all Europeans and two-thirds of North Americans can no longer see the Milky Way. And this type of pollution doesn't only **(10)**............. our view of the night sky, it also wastes money and causes environmental pollution. For example, a single light bulb, **(11)**............. all year, releases around a quarter of a tonne of carbon dioxide into the atmosphere, **(12)**............. global warming even worse.

1	**A** regarded	**B** realised	**C** remarked	**D** reacted
2	**A** Across	**B** Between	**C** Aside	**D** Beneath
3	**A** give	**B** send	**C** keep	**D** fill
4	**A** clearly	**B** surely	**C** hardly	**D** faintly
5	**A** case	**B** rank	**C** grade	**D** rate
6	**A** carry	**B** draw	**C** get	**D** catch
7	**A** like	**B** similar	**C** same	**D** as
8	**A** brought	**B** taken	**C** felt	**D** passed
9	**A** According to	**B** Apart from	**C** Instead of	**D** In addition to
10	**A** destroy	**B** deny	**C** defeat	**D** delay
11	**A** set off	**B** put in	**C** left on	**D** joined up
12	**A** letting	**B** resulting	**C** causing	**D** making

Language development 2

-ing forms and infinitives

▶ CB page 48, GR pages 194–195

1 *-ing* form or infinitive?

Six of the sentences contain mistakes with *-ing* forms and infinitives. If a sentence is correct, put a tick (✓) by it. Find and correct the mistakes.

EXAMPLE: In late January 2006, thousands of people in London were astonished when they saw an enormous whale <u>to swim</u> in the River Thames. ....swimming.........

1 Millions of TV viewers from around the world found it hard to believe their eyes. ....

2 Onlookers enjoyed to watch the northern bottle-nosed whale as it made its way past Waterloo Bridge. ....

3 The magnificent creature appeared being lost and very weak. ....

4 Everyone wanted to believe that the whale would find its way back to the sea. ....

5 The two-ton whale was obviously exhausted and injured, but people refused giving up hope. ....

6 During the night, rescuers at Battersea Bridge managed lifting Willy (as he was now affectionately called) onto a special boat. ....

7 They hoped to transfer Willy to a bigger ship, which would take him to the Atlantic Ocean. ....

8 Willy was having problems to breathe and suffering from dehydration. ....

9 Willy's condition suddenly got worse, so vets decided to put the animal to sleep with an injection. He died before they could do so. ....

10 Willy – who turned out to be a female whale – made millions of people to feel a sense of wonder for the natural world. ....

2 Prepositions + -ing forms

Complete the sentences with the correct preposition from the list.

about (x 3)   for (x 3)   on (x 2)   to   at   in (x 2)

1 Rick insisted .... coming with us to the zoo.
2 I succeeded .... persuading my father to lend me his new camera.
3 We were really excited .... seeing the polar bears.
4 I've always been interested .... learning about animals.
5 We talked .... going on a safari one day.
6 Rick objected .... having to pay to visit the aquarium.
7 My sister is good .... imitating animal sounds.
8 We talked to the man who was responsible .... feeding the lions.
9 I'm very keen .... taking photographs of wildlife.
10 I apologised .... being half an hour late.
11 You don't seem very enthusiastic .... having a picnic.
12 Dr Tibbet is famous .... carrying out research on the way dolphins communicate.

3 Verbs with a change of meaning

Mark the correct form of the verb in each pair.

1 **stop**
   a They claim that hunters have stopped *killing / to kill* protected animals in the area.
   b On the way to the village, we stopped *taking / to take* photographs.
2 **remember**
   a I hope you remembered *bringing / to bring* the video camera.
   b I clearly remember *putting / to put* our passports in my travel bag.
3 **try**
   a Why don't you try *taking / to take* sleeping pills, if you can't sleep?
   b I tried *persuading / to persuade* him to come with us, but without success.
4 **regret**
   a I regret *telling / to tell* you that the trip tomorrow has been cancelled.
   b I regret *paying / to pay* so much for this tent – it's not even waterproof!
5 **forget**
   a Our guide forgot *mentioning / to mention* that the road was full of holes.
   b I have not forgotten *seeing / to see* what hunters had done to those elephants.

6 **mean**
   a The government means *taking / to take* action to protect wildlife.
   b Protecting wildlife means *changing / to change* the law.

4 Key word transformations

Complete the second sentence so that it has a similar meaning to the first sentence, using the word given. Do not change the word given. You must use between two and five words, including the word given.

1 I really don't like travelling by bus in the morning. **stand**
   I .... by bus in the morning.
2 I decided to go to Africa on my own. **decision**
   It .... to go to Africa on my own.
3 I didn't have enough money to go to Rwanda by plane. **afford**
   I .... to Rwanda by plane.
4 It took me ages to get all the documents I needed. **spent**
   I .... all the documents I needed.
5 It was difficult for me not to smile when they told me the news. **help**
   I couldn't .... heard the news.
6 I can hear laughter coming from the neighbours' flat. **people**
   I .... in the neighbour's flat.
7 They said they would go to the police if we didn't help them. **threatened**
   They .... the police if we didn't help them.
8 I can't wait to visit the new safari park. **forward**
   I'm .... the new safari park.
9 I'm glad I went to Africa to see animals in their natural environment. **worth**
   It .... Africa to see animals in their natural environment.
10 The idea of waiting for five hours at the airport does not appeal to me. **keen**
   I'm not .... waiting for five hours at the airport.

5 Extra word

Look at the sentences below. Each one has a word which should not be there. Cross this word out.

BIRDWATCHING

EXAMPLE: I am thinking of going ~~to~~ birdwatching this weekend.

1 I am taking my daughter with me as she is keen for to learn about the countryside.
2 She is looking forward to be seeing the wild birds she has learnt to recognise.
3 I've told Lorna that it's important to remember taking her binoculars.
4 But of course, it's also worth to taking a camera so she can keep a record of what she sees.

Reading Multiple matching (Paper 1 Part 3)

kea parrot

orang-utan

octopus

1 Before you read
Which of the animals in the list do you expect to be the most intelligent? Tick (✓) them.

seal   rat   pigeon   fox   elephant   parrot   octopus   leopard   orang-utan

2 Scanning
Scan the article opposite and find where each animal in Exercise 1 is mentioned. Then look at the text about each animal more carefully. Were your predictions right or wrong?

3 Multiple matching
a Look at the example (0) in the exam task opposite. Mark the part of text B that tells you the answer.

b Look at question 1.
   • Mark key words in the question.
   • Scan the text to find the section(s) which may contain the answer.
   • Read this section carefully and mark the place where you find the answer.
   • Check that the text you have found exactly matches the question.

c Now continue with questions 2–15.

You are going to read an article about animal intelligence. For questions **1–15**, choose from the paragraphs **(A–G)**. Some of the paragraphs may be chosen more than once. When more than one answer is required, these may be given in any order. There is an example at the beginning **(0)**.

Which paragraph mentions

a type of animal that is now extinct?	**0** B
an animal which has prevented humans controlling its behaviour?	**1**
an example of intelligence that may not have a positive outcome?	**2**
the way the majority of animals react to things?	**3**
an animal that managed to solve a problem quickly?	**4**
an animal that was able to remember things?	**5**
animals that will not appear in the programme?	**6**
an animal which performs well in experiments?	**7** **8**
an animal which has followed a human example?	**9**
animals overcoming man-made obstacles to get food?	**10** **11**
an animal that exploits aspects of the man-made environment?	**12**
environmental problems which are affecting animals?	**13**
when you'll be able to see the programme?	**14** **15**

Clever Claws

A new wildlife series begins on TV next week

A

What is the world's most intelligent animal? Television producer Mike Beynon and his team of animal experts have searched the world for the new TV series *Clever Claws*, which will be
5 broadcast this autumn. You won't find any performing seals among the contenders, however, because all the animals featured use their brains to solve problems encountered in their natural environments. Mike points out that the brainiest
10 creatures are often those that we think of as pests. 'Rats, foxes and pigeons are pretty intelligent,' he says. 'We only call them pests because they have learnt to exploit us, instead of being frightened.'

B

In the last century, animals have had to cope with
15 enormous changes, from pollution to climate shifts. The clever creatures are those that learn to survive by adapting; those that don't, like the dinosaurs, tend to die out as the world around them changes. '99 per cent of animal behaviour is
20 controlled by instinct,' says Mike. 'Give most creatures something new and they don't know what to do – it's only the clever ones which accept the challenge.' And the first programme in the series, which you can see next Monday
25 evening, includes a few examples of just that.

C

Can an elephant be as quiet as a mouse? It seems it can! When farmers in Thailand suspected elephants of stealing their banana crops, they hung a bell around each animal's
30 neck so that they'd get warning of an attack. But one elephant has worked out how to stop his bell ringing, so he can get to the bananas undetected. The elephant fills the bell with mud which stops the sound. But that's not all. By
35 morning, the mud has dried and fallen out and so the locals still can't identify the mystery banana burglar!

D

And it's not only land animals that prove to be quite bright. Octopuses have fantastic eyesight and
40 big brains for their size, so Mike and his team put one in a specially designed tank, designed like a maze with lots of tunnels that led nowhere and choices to make about whether to go left or right at junctions. 'The octopus had a good memory
45 and solved our puzzle by trial and error. After two weeks, it could get out of that maze in under a minute,' says Mike.

E

Just like humans, animals use their intelligence to their own advantage. Sometimes they even use
50 man's inventions to get ahead of the competition. Big cats such as cheetahs and leopards have been spotted standing on safari vehicles, ready and waiting to leap out at their prey. Clever, but worrying, says Mike. 'If a cheetah uses a man-
55 made object to gain an advantage over an antelope in an attack, then that is very dangerous, because it puts nature out of balance.'

F

And hunger is one of the great motivators of intelligence in animals. New Zealand kea parrots
60 are some of the cleverest. On the programme we see that parrots can actually be very accomplished locksmiths. In order to get at the tasty snack inside a locked box, one such bird had to undo one lock, pull a pin out of a second and then
65 turned a key ten times to open a third. No problem! After only 45 seconds the kea reached its meal!

G

For a programme about brainy animals, apes and monkeys feature surprisingly little in *Clever Claws*.
70 Mike says that's because it's already well-known that they're intelligent. Orang-utans do get a mention, however. We see a mother helping her family cross a river full of crocodiles in Borneo. She's watched humans and so borrows a boat and
75 paddle so that her little ones can enjoy a safe crossing. Now that's what you call intelligence!

4A Personal challenges

Vocabulary ▶ CB pages 52–53

1 Topic: personal life and experience
Choose the correct word in each sentence.

1 I *have been / was born* in 1960 in a small town in Wales.

2 When I was five years old, my parents died and I became an *orphan / orphanage*.

3 Life was not easy during my early *childish / childhood* and I was often miserable.

4 As I didn't have many friends, I often felt very *on my own / lonely*.

5 During my teenage years, I *was brought up / was grown up* by foster parents.

6 Although my foster parents were not *well out / well off*, they looked after me well.

7 In my *final teens / late teens* I left home and started work in a supermarket.

8 My workmates were all older than me, but we *got on / got off* very well.

9 I didn't *win / earn* much money, so it was sometimes difficult to make ends meet

10 A lot of families lived in *poorly / poverty* in my hometown, so I worked hard and was very ambitious.

11 I managed to *put by / put off* a little money each month.

12 I dreamt of having my own business and living a life of *luxury / luxurious*.

13 One day, I had the *possibility / opportunity* to go on a managerial training course; I loved it.

14 Now I am manager of the supermarket and engaged to a girl from quite a *wealth / wealthy* family.

15 Our *wedding / marriage* will take place next month.

16 I'll probably never *get / achieve* my ambition of being a millionaire. It doesn't seem so important anymore.

2 Phrasal verbs

a Mark the correct word in each pair.

1 As night fell, we set *out / about* on our journey across the desert.

2 Although it was raining heavily, I forced myself to keep *up / on* running.

3 If you want to run the marathon, you'll have to give *over / up* smoking!

4 The expedition ran *into / through* trouble when their jeep broke down.

5 This hot weather really wears me *off / out*. I don't have any energy left at all.

6 A: 'We've lost our map!'
B: 'Well, we'll have to do *without / off* it, won't we?'

7 We need to stop at a garage. We're running *out / up* of petrol.

8 John is always complaining. I don't know how you put up *with / by* him.

b Read the email and replace the words in brackets with phrasal verbs from Exercise 2a in the correct form. Add any other necessary words.

New Message

Hi Gerry

I've just reached midway point on my marathon cycle ride around Australia! I can hardly believe it! As you know, when I **(1)**............................. (*started*) on the ride I was feeling really optimistic. Well, I **(2)**............................. (*encountered*) difficulties after just a couple of days when the brake cable on my bike broke. Fortunately, there was no traffic so I managed to **(3)**............................. (*survive without*) brakes until I reached the next town and got them fixed! It's been really hard to **(4)**............................. (*tolerate*) the heat though. It's absolutely **(5)**............................. (*exhausted me*). When I almost **(6)**............................. (*had no water left*) in the desert, I got pretty scared – I seriously thought about **(7)**............................. (*stopping*). But as you can see, I've managed to **(8)**............................. (*continue*) cycling. Knowing that I'm doing it for charity keeps me going.

More news soon!

Thomas

---

3 Exam practice: word formation (Paper 3 Part 3)

Read the text below. Use the word given in capitals at the end of some of the lines to form a word that fits in the space in the same line. There is an example at the beginning (0).

ULTRA MARATHONS

If you've ever run a marathon, like those held (0)......annually...... in places like   **ANNUAL**
London and New York, then you'll know that this is an (1)...........................   **EXTREME**
(2)........................... thing to do. If you're going to finish the 26-mile course,   **CHALLENGE**
then you need to do months of (3)........................... to ensure the necessary   **PREPARE**
level of (4)........................... . Spare a thought then for people who go in for   **FIT**
what are known as ultra marathons. These are longer than (5)...........................   **TRADITION**
city marathons and are run over difficult terrain, often in (6)...........................   **HOSPITABLE**
places like deserts where (7)........................... may have to run across sand or   **COMPETE**
stones, in weather conditions ranging from baking (8)........................... to   **HOT**
torrential rain. For example, the 135-mile Badwater Marathon is a real test of
(9)........................... , taking runners from the lowest point in (10)...........................   **ENDURE**
North America to the highest, passing through Death Valley on the way.   **CONTINENT**

Language development 1

Narrative tenses ▶ CB pages 54 –55, GR pages 188–189

1 Narrative tenses
Put the story into the correct order. Mark the correct verb form in each pair.

☐ 1   a   My girlfriend has a lovely black kitten called Max.

☐   b   I *went / was going* to her house, of course, to help her find Max.

☐   c   There was Max! He *lay / was lying* fast asleep in his basket!

☐   d   When she opened the door, I could see from her eyes that she *had cried / had been crying*.

☐   e   She phoned me yesterday to say that she *lost / had lost* him.

☐   f   We *had / were having* a hot chocolate when we heard a sound.

☐   g   20 minutes later we still *didn't find / hadn't found* Max, so we went back inside.

☐   h   She told me on the phone that she *looked / had looked* everywhere.

☐   i   It was cold in the garden and it *rained / was raining* heavily.

☐   j   We *went / had gone* out into the garden to look for Max together.

2 Time conjunctions

a Match the sentence halves to make logical sentences. They form a short story.

A

1 One day I *was leaving* the house **when**
2 **By the time** Sue arrived,
3 **As soon** as I saw her face,
4 The postman arrived with a letter **as**
5 She didn't continue her story **until**
6 I began to laugh **once**

B

a she *was telling* me about her boyfriend, Robert.
b I *had opened* the letter.
c I *had recovered* from the shock of reading Sue's wedding invitation.
d I *had been waiting* impatiently for an hour.
e my sister Sue *phoned* to say she was on her way to see me.
f I *knew* she had something to tell me.

b Combine the sentence pairs, using the time conjunctions in bold. Put the verbs in brackets in the appropriate tense. Do not change the order of the sentences.

1 We (arrive) at the party. Everyone (go) home. **by the time**

   ....

2 I (watch) a horror film on television. The lights suddenly (go) out. **when**

   ....

3 The air hostess (count) all the passengers. The plane (take) off. **once**

   ....

4 I (never live) on my own. I (go) to university. **before**

   ....

5 Peter (hear) the good news. He (telephone) his wife. **as soon as**

   ....

6 We (wait) for an hour and a half. The train eventually (arrive). **when**

   ....

7 The customs officer (search) all our luggage. He (allow) us to go. **after**

   ....

8 I (stay) at my grandfather's house. I (discover) an old photograph album. **while**

   ....

9 Sarah (not go) back to work. She (recover) from the flu. **until**

   ....

10 My sister (read) her exam results. She (burst) out laughing. **when**

   ....

3 Key word transformations

Complete the second sentence so that it has a similar meaning to the first sentence, using the word given. Do not change the word given. You must use between two and five words, including the word given.

1 We arrived at the cinema too late for the start of the film. **already**
   The film .... the time we arrived at the cinema.

2 On hearing the good news, everyone at the office gave a cheer. **when**
   Everyone at the office gave a cheer .... the good news.

3 A fire broke out on board the plane shortly after it left the ground. **just**
   The plane .... off when a fire broke out on board.

4 James was surprised by their friendliness. **expected**
   James .... be so friendly.

5 I had hardly opened the front door when the phone rang. **soon**
   The phone rang .... the front door.

6 We didn't set off for the mountains until midday. **when**
   It .... off for the mountains.

7 He read the whole letter before saying anything. **until**
   He didn't say .... the whole letter.

8 I met somebody I knew on my flight to Athens last week. **while**
   I met somebody I knew .... flying to Athens last week.

9 Sue was excited because it was her first visit to India. **never**
   Sue was excited because *she never visit* .... India before.

10 The train journey took six hours, so we were really tired when we got to Madrid. **for**
   We were really tired when we got to Madrid because we .... six hours by train.

Writing Story (Paper 2 Part 2)

▶ CB pages 56–57, WR page 201

Exam strategy

When you write a story, think about how it will develop **before** you start writing. Your story should lead naturally from the given sentence. Don't try to make it too complicated. Make sure you:

- write in paragraphs
- use vivid vocabulary to make the story more interesting
- check your use of tenses when you have finished.

1 Understand the task

Read the task below and answer the questions.

1 Who is going to read the story?
2 Who is the main character? What pronoun should you use?
   a *I*   b *she*

You have been asked to write a story for a student magazine.

> Your story must begin with the words:
> *Gillian was cold and hungry and completely lost.*

Write your **story** in **120–180** words.

2 Check and improve a sample answer

a Read the story a student has written. The story should have five paragraphs. Mark where a new paragraph should begin.

b Match each paragraph of the story to its function (a–e).

Function	Paragraph
a describes an important action or event	....
b sets the scene of the story	....!......
c develops the story further and moves towards the conclusion	....
d reflects on the events of the story as a whole/how the main character feels about what happened	....
e supplies some important background details	....

c **Mark examples of the past simple and past perfect tenses in the story. Which tense is used:**

1 to give background information? ....
2 to move the story forward? ....

d Find words and phrases in the story which could be replaced by the following more vivid or descriptive expressions.

EXAMPLE: exhausted <u>tired</u>

1 exploring ....
2 freezing ....
3 plump ....
4 with a warm smile on her face ....
5 gazed ....
6 dipped ....
7 burst into tears ....
8 jumped up ....
9 fallen in love with ....

> Gillian was cold and hungry and completely lost. She looked around at the tall dark trees. Where was the village she had left that morning? She sighed and continued to follow the footpath through the woods. It was Gillian's first visit to Wales. At first, she had liked the wild beauty of the place. It frightened her now, though, because she didn't know where she was. After a while, she came to a shallow stream. She took off her boots and put her feet in the cold water. Then she started to cry. She had been walking for hours and felt too tired to take another step. Suddenly, she heard a voice: 'Hello, can I help?' She looked up. A fat, cheerful woman was standing in front of her, smiling. She was holding a dog on a lead. Gillian got up and hugged the woman. She was safe! When they got back to the village, Gillian realised how lucky she had been. She would never again go walking alone in the mountains of Wales.

3 Do the task

Write your own story in your notebook.

Listening Sentence completion (Paper 4 Part 2)

1 **Before you listen**

  a Read the instructions for the listening task below. Answer these questions.
     1 How many speakers will you hear?
     2 What is the topic?

  b Read the sentences 1–10. Try to predict the type of information you are listening
     for to complete each gap. Will any of the answers be
     a) numbers   b) adjectives   c) names of sports?

  c Mark the main ideas in each sentence. (The first one has been done for you.)
     Think about each statement. Do you agree or disagree?

2 🎧 **Listening for specific information**

  a Listen once and complete the gaps. Were your predictions correct?

  b Listen again to check your answers.

> You will hear part of a radio programme in which a famous sportsman is being interviewed about the
> training for various types of challenging physical activities. For questions **1–10**, complete the sentences.
>
> Malcolm has achieved sporting success as a [_____ **1**].
>
> Malcolm says that fundraising for [_____ **2**] can be just as demanding as competitive sport.
>
> Malcolm says that mountain climbing, desert running and [_____ **3**] are all sports requiring training.
>
> Malcolm tells us that his weight is around [_____ **4**].
>
> Malcolm believes that adults can find a comparable level of [_____ **5**] to youngsters.
>
> Malcolm believes having a [_____ **6**] is as important as having a goal.
>
> Malcolm recommends making progress in small stages to avoid feeling [_____ **7**].
>
> Malcolm says that training becomes boring if it lacks [_____ **8**].
>
> Malcolm advises us to work towards [_____ **9**] goals in order to enjoy training.
>
> Malcolm admits that training can sometimes be a [_____ **10**] activity.

4B Sport

Vocabulary ▶ CB pages 58–59

▶ CB pages 58–59

Exam strategy

In Paper 5, Speaking, Part 1, the examiner may ask you what kind of sports you and your friends are interested in. In Parts 3 and 4, you may have to compare different sports and discuss why people do them or what kind of people they might appeal to. Make sure you know the necessary vocabulary.

1 Topic: describing sports

a Write these sports in the correct column in the table. Which are team sports (T)? Which are individual sports (I)?

snowboarding   windsurfing   tennis   ice hockey
karate   water skiing   hang gliding   climbing
basketball   running   scuba diving
parachute jumping   rugby   high jump   golf

Category	Sport
Risk (extreme) sport	hang gliding (I)
Track and field event	
Water sport	
Winter sport	
Martial art	
Ball games	

b Which sports from Exercise 1a are these comments describing? Mark the word(s) which help you decide.

> The first time I jumped off the side of the hill, I was scared stiff.

1 ....

> It's hard to keep your balance as the boat pulls you out of the water. At the beginning I was always falling over.

2 ....

> You need to practise the kicks and punches every day if you want to make progress.

3 ....

> You don't need a lot of equipment – just a pair of trainers and a good racket.

4 ....

> It's important to wear a helmet to protect your head from falling rocks.

5 ....

> The equipment can be expensive – you need a mask and flippers and a wet suit.

6 ....

> You stand on a kind of ski and use your whole body to make turns and jumps. It's quite difficult to keep your balance at first.

7 ....

> It's much more dangerous than ice-skating. You have to wear protective clothing like a helmet, knee pads and gloves.

8 ....

2 Informal expressions

Read the text below and decide which answer A, B or C best fits each space.

> 66 I'm not really (1)............. sport, but I love skiing. I took it (2)............. while I was living abroad. It was my friends who (3)............. me into doing it; they were all keen skiers. They just kept (4)............. at me until I agreed to (5)............. it a go. I hadn't expected to enjoy it so much – I absolutely loved it from the (6)............. go. The sense of speed is exhilarating, and of course there's the wonderful scenery. I admit I was (7)............. stiff the first time, but pretty soon I just wanted to carry (8)............. skiing all day. 99

1	A	for	B	into	C	about
2	A	up	B	on	C	down
3	A	spoke	B	told	C	talked
4	A	across	B	on	C	over
5	A	give	B	put	C	have
6	A	word	B	minute	C	time
7	A	frightened	B	scared	C	terrified
8	A	on	B	in	C	through

3 Sports quiz
Answer the following questions by choosing the correct answer A, B, C or D.

1 What word is used to describe the area where a game of tennis is played?
   A pitch   B court   C course   D ring

2 What word is used in football results to mean that a team didn't score any goals?
   A zero   B nought   C nil   D nothing

3 The main difference between badminton and tennis is that in badminton
   A there is no net in between the players.
   B the players do not use rackets.
   C the players do not use a ball.
   D the players wear protective masks.

4 A *regatta* is a sporting event at which there are races between
   A teams of climbers.
   B rowing or sailing boats.
   C light aircraft.
   D vintage cars.

5 What is the name of the sport in which a bow is used to shoot arrows at a target?
   A fencing   C wrestling
   B archery   D judo

6 Which sport was invented in Scotland and involves hitting a ball with a club?
   A golf   C hockey
   B cricket   D lacrosse

7 In baseball or cricket, one team beats the other by scoring more:
   A sets.   B goals   C laps.   D runs.

8 Where are you likely to hear the word *jockey* used?
   A a horse race
   B a golf championship
   C a skiing event
   D a boxing match

9 Which word is **not** used in football?
   A tackle   B pass   C shoot   D serve

10 What is the name of the person who supervises a game of tennis?
   A umpire   C coach
   B referee   D spectator

Language development 2 Quantity
▶ CB page 61, GR page 183

1 Countable and uncountable
Complete the sentences with *a, some* or *any* (If no article or determiner is needed, write Ø.)

1 a Can I have .... glass of water, please?
   b Don't drop that vase! It's made of ....
      glass, not plastic.

2 a I'm going to buy my little brother ....
      football for Christmas.
   b I think it is better to play .... football
      than watch it on television.

3 a Could you put .... chocolate on top
      of my cappuccino, please?
   b Would you like .... chocolate?
      Go on – they're delicious!

4 a Did you enjoy the party? You certainly look as if
      you had .... good time!
   b I would like to help you, but I don't have
      .... free time at all.

5 a Could you buy me .... paper? I want
      to see what's going on in the world.
   b They've used a new kind of plastic for the cycle
      helmet. It's as light as .... paper, but
      much stronger.

2 Determiners
a **Five of these sentences contain mistakes with determiners. Find and correct the mistakes. If a sentence is correct, put a tick (✓) by it. You only need to change one word each time.**

EXAMPLES: I don't think there will be much interest in tonight's football match. ✓

There is a large ~~number~~ of sports information on the Internet. ......amount......

1 There isn't many news about David Beckham at the moment. ....

2 We have no money at all for new sports equipment. ....

3 How much players were injured during the game? ....

4 Football fans caused a great deal of damage to the stadium. ....

5 We don't have very many time to prepare for the championship. ....

6 There are always plenty of spectators at the London Marathon. ....

7 They only have a small amount of tickets left for the final game. ....

8 How many money will the new tennis courts cost? ....

b Complete this extract from an email with *few/a few* or *little/a little*.

Sorry I haven't been in touch. I've been training very hard for the championship and I've had very
(1)........~~sho~~ *little* time to relax or enjoy myself recently. My trainer is extremely strict, and he insists I train every day. I have managed to get away on
(2)........~~so~~ *a few* occasions, though. I think it's important to take **(3)**........~~as~~ *a little* time off now and then. You can't train all the time, can you?
Last weekend I went into town and did some shopping, although, to be honest, I have very
(4)........ *little* money to spare. And yesterday,
(5)........ *A few* fans came to see me. They were very impressed when I told them about my training routine. Very **(6)**........ *few* people realise how difficult training for a big event can be.

3 Key word transformations.

Complete the second sentence so that it has a similar meaning to the first sentence, using the word given. Do not change the word given. You must use between two and five words, including the word given.

1 The players spent a lot of time training for the big game.
deal
The players spent .... time training for the big game.

2 Not many fans attended the match on Saturday.
very
The match on Saturday was attended .... fans.

3 My brother is not very interested in sport.
much
My brother doesn't show .... sport.

4 First-class sports equipment is often very expensive.
lots
You often need to spend .... to buy first-class sports equipment.

5 There is a complete lack of sports facilities at our college.
no
Our college has .... all.

6 The government spends very little money on sports education.
small
The government only spends .... money on sports education.

4 Exam practice: open cloze
(Paper 3 Part 2)

Read the text below and think of the word which best fits each space. Use only **one** word in each space. There is an example at the beginning **(0)**.

THE JOY OF ICE-SKATING

A lot of people have a go
(0)............*at*............ ice-skating in their teenage years and many will remember slipping over – to the great amusement of friends and family. For **(1)**........................... majority of people, therefore, ice-skating is remembered as a bit of a laugh, or possibly as a skill they couldn't master, and very **(2)**...........................
ever go back and attempt to take
(3)........................... the sport seriously. This is a shame, because once they have overcome their nerves, and built **(4)**........................... a bit of confidence, people discover
(5)........................... ice-skating is great exercise as **(6)**........................... as being enjoyable and fun.

Most major cities in the UK now have ice-skating rinks, and so a
(7)........................... more people could rediscover the sport. Most rinks have an introductory package for new ice-skaters which includes either group **(8)**........................... individual lessons. There are various types of ice-skating, but many newcomers to the sport choose ice-dance
(9)........................... it is the most sociable activity on ice. Skaters find that the thrill of moving around so gracefully is like **(10)**...........................
else they have ever experienced. Of course, such grace doesn't come overnight, **(11)**........................... with regular practice, it can be achieved. A couple of hours' individual tuition with a teacher, plus five hours' practice each week is roughly the level **(12)**........................... commitment needed to make progress.

Reading Gapped text (Paper 1 Part 2)

1 Before you read

Read the instructions for the reading task and the title and subheading of the article opposite. Which of the following topics do you think the article will talk about?

1 The future of sponsorship.
2 The advantages of sponsorship.
3 How commercial sponsorship of sports started.
4 The disadvantages of sponsorship.

2 Skimming

Skim the article. Match the topics in Exercise 1 to the paragraphs in the text. Which topic is not mentioned?

3 Gapped text

a Read the first paragraph of the text and look at sentence H. Which words in the text link to the highlighted words in sentence H?

1 they = the organisers of the tennis tournament
2 the company =
3 the privilege =

b Read the rest of the text carefully. Make sure you understand the main information.

c For each gap, do the following.

- Read the text before and after the gap and think about the type of information which is missing.
- Look for a sentence that talks about this topic area.
- Choose the correct answer by checking the grammatical and lexical links between the base text and the key sentence. Look out for pronouns, synonyms, etc.
- Cross off each sentence as you use it, but be prepared to look again when you check your answers.

d Read the text again with your answers to check that it makes sense.

You are going to read a text about the commercial sponsorship of sport. Seven sentences have been removed from the text. Choose from the sentences **A–H** the one that fits each gap (**1–6**). There is one extra sentence which you do not need to use.

A People also complain that sponsors have too much influence on the sport in return for their financial backing.

B Many loyal local fans also believe that their needs are being ignored in favour of more profitable television audiences.

C Sporting agents believe that the injection of money and commercialism into sport from various sources has helped everybody.

D Although this may appear harmless, the pressures they face can be intolerable.

E By 1992, this new business had an annual turnover of over £30 million.

F But there is a downside: much is demanded of the top stars in return for their high earnings.

G Increased public awareness of sports has, in turn, helped to stimulate demand for certain products.

H It was only in the 1970s that they realised they could be charging the company for the privilege instead.

HELP

➤ **Gap 2**
Which sentence above refers to an *increased overall income*?

➤ **Gap 3**
What is the topic of this paragraph? Which sentence above introduces this topic?

➤ **Gap 4**
What is the topic of this paragraph? Which sentence above introduces this topic?

Business calls the shots

Sport has undoubtedly made huge financial gains from business sponsorship, but at what cost to the fans and players?

Many sporting organisations only began to understand how valuable commercial sponsorship might be in the last decades of the twentieth century, when individual players and their agents started finding their own sponsors. The organisers of the famous Wimbledon Tennis Tournament, for example, had been paying the sports equipment manufacturer, Slazenger, to supply balls and equipment since 1902. Slazenger had been getting hundreds of thousands of pounds' worth of free publicity from the live television coverage of the event, but the organisers of the tennis tournament were getting nothing in return. **1** ⬚

Wimbledon also began to put its name on a range of merchandise which it sold to fans – including clothing, towels, china and stationery. **2** ⬚ Because of their increased overall income, the organisers of the tournament were able to donate millions to the British Lawn Tennis Association and so help develop the sport in the country where the tournament is held.

3 ⬚ Players have gained financially, with earnings reflecting the true value of their abilities; sports administrators have cashed in on television's wish to broadcast major events; businesses have gained publicity for their products and found top sports stars willing to promote them, and lastly, the public's desire to see top matches and wear a range of sporting goods has been satisfied.

4 ⬚ Top tennis players have to play more and more events across the world. Three-times Wimbledon winner Boris Becker was referring to the top ten players at the end of one exhausting season when he said 'Everyone is badly injured, or is having a nervous breakdown.'

Meanwhile, agents are now signing up potential stars at even earlier ages – some are as young as ten years old. **5** ⬚ Child stars Andrea Jaeger and Tracy Austin were both forced out of the game after receiving permanent injuries while still in their teens. At least Ms Austin had earned $5 million before her injury.

6 ⬚ A sportswear manufacturer might, say, insist that a player it sponsors competes in a minor tournament in its home town. Meanwhile, the demands of television often influence sporting decisions. The timing of major sporting events, such as cup finals, key matches or Olympic events are set to coincide with peak viewing times or to avoid clashes with popular programmes. In 1994, the football World Cup was held in the USA because it was the country which offered the organisers the best commercial opportunities, even though it had no organised football league, and the game is relatively unknown there. US television companies even discussed altering the length of the playing periods in order to get in more advertising.

But whatever the arguments, commercialisation has given many sports a higher profile. **7** ⬚ Sometimes, of course, the public finds that these goods are also the most expensive, so they end up paying for the sponsorship anyway. But then, as the saying goes, 'You pay your money, you take your choice.'

5A Human science

Vocabulary ▶ CB pages 66–67
▶ Colloquial English page 122

1 Word formation

a Complete the table.

Subject	Person	Adjective
1	2	scientific
3..................	geneticist	4 ....
5..................	psychologist	6 ....
7..................	8	linguistic
9..................	10	archaeological
astronomy	11	12 ....

b Now complete the word formation rules by adding: *subject, person* or *adjective.*

- The suffix *-ist* or *-er* is often used for a(n)
  ....

- The suffix *-ics* or *-y* is often used for a(n)
  ....

- The suffix *-ic*, or *-ical* is often used for a(n)
  ....

c Use the word given in capitals at the end of each sentence to form a word that fits in the space.

1 100 students were asked to take part in a .... experiment. **PSYCHOLOGY**

2 The study of .... has made it possible to clone animals. **GENETIC**

3 Copernicus is one of the most famous .... who has ever lived. **ASTRONOMY**

4 The speed of a child's .... development depends on many factors. **LINGUIST**

5 The area around Stonehenge, in the southwest of England, is of great .... importance. **ARCHAEOLOGY**

6 Modern .... theories about the universe often seem strangely similar to the beliefs of ancient cultures. **SCIENCE**

2 ∩ Pronunciation

a Look again at the words in the table in Exercise 1a and listen to the recording. Mark the stressed syllable in each word.
EXAMPLE: scien<u>tif</u>ic

b Listen again and practise saying the words aloud.

3 Expressions
Replace the words in bold in the sentences with a phrase from the list below.

- as a consequence of
- hard to put down
- to great effect
- getting better and better
- packed with
- the latest
- in the widest sense
- at the forefront of

1 According to **the most recent** theories, the universe is expanding rapidly.

2 We understand the 'genetic code' better today, **due to** the hard work of many scientists around the world.

3 Stephen Hawking's book *A Brief History of Time* is **full of** interesting facts and theories.

4 *Language Play* by David Crystal is **a book you cannot stop reading.**

5 The Roslin Institute in Scotland is **one of the leading organisations doing** research into cloning.

6 Scientific techniques which tell us the age of archaeological finds are **improving steadily.**

7 Scientific research at many universities benefits the community **generally**: members of the public, artists, writers and academics.

8 Einstein used his knowledge of mathematics and physics **very effectively.**

4 Adjective + noun collocations

a Match each adjective in A to a set of nouns in B. The adjective must collocate with all the nouns in the set.

A		B	
1	original	a	belief/responsibility/experience
2	fascinating	b	ideas/news/information
3	eye-catching	c	book/insight/discovery
4	influential	d	reading/breeze/colour
5	ideal	e	idea/design/plan
6	personal	f	present/holiday/solution
7	up-to-date	g	photo/dress/advertisement
8	light	h	theory/scientist/organisation

b Complete the sentences with one word from column B. Use each word once only.

1 Jack loves music, doesn't he? The ideal birthday .... for him would be an iPod, I think. It's a great little gadget.

2 It's my personal .... that very young children should not be allowed to use mobile phones.

3 Astronomers have made a fascinating .... ! There is evidence of life on Mars.

4 The .... of the new car is extremely original. It looks quite different from other cars on the road.

5 The Internet is extremely useful for getting up-to-date news or .... about any product on the market.

6 Darwin's .... of evolution was extremely influential. It changed the whole course of science.

7 Yesterday was a perfect day for walking – very sunny with a light ....

8 The .... for the new shampoo is really eye-catching. You can't miss it!

5 Exam practice: multiple-choice cloze (Paper 3 Part 1)

Read the text below and decide which answer, **A**, **B**, **C** or **D** best fits each space. There is an example at the beginning (**0**).

0 A fact **B** deed **C** detail **D** point

THE DISCOVERY OF DNA

The (**0**).....A..... that genetic information in animals and plants is carried by something (**1**)............. DNA is now regarded as (**2**)............. knowledge. Before the 1950s, however, (**3**)............. was known about DNA or how it worked. One of the (**4**)............. moments in science occurred in 1953, when Francis Crick and James Watson at Cambridge University discovered the structure of DNA. They said that DNA was (**5**)............. to two spiral staircases going up and down at the same time. Scientists all over the world (**6**)............. this 'double helix' model immediately. The discovery was, of course, the result of years of hard work, and Crick and Watson were not the only scientists who had been (**7**)............. out research in an attempt to find out what DNA (**8**)............. like. Maurice Wilkins and Rosalind Franklin at King's College, London, had also been (**9**)............. on the problem. They used x-ray analysis of DNA, (**10**)............. Crick and Watson preferred to build models. One day, without (**11**)............. a word to her, Wilkins showed Franklin's results to Watson, and it was those results which helped him to discover the real structure of DNA. In 1962, Watson, Crick and Wilkins were (**12**)............. the Nobel Prize for their work. Rosalind Franklin, who had died four years earlier, was not even mentioned at the ceremony.

	A		B		C		D	
1	called	**B**	known	**C**	referred	**D**	described
2	normal	**B**	general	**C**	usual	**D**	ordinary
3	few	**B**	hardly	**C**	tiny	**D**	little
4	greatest	**B**	largest	**C**	tallest	**D**	broadest
5	same	**B**	similar	**C**	alike	**D**	resembled
6	accepted	**B**	agreed	**C**	admitted	**D**	allowed
7	making	**B**	doing	**C**	holding	**D**	carrying
8	looked	**B**	appeared	**C**	existed	**D**	compared
9	thinking	**B**	trying	**C**	working	**D**	seeking
10	however	**B**	whereas	**C**	unlike	**D**	despite
11	telling	**B**	dropping	**C**	giving	**D**	saying
12	presented	**B**	awarded	**C**	donated	**D**	celebrated

Language development 1

Future forms ▶ CB pages 68–69, GR pages 189–190

1 Present simple, present continuous, *will* or *be going to*?

Mark the most appropriate verb form in each pair.

1 What time *does the bank close / is the bank closing* in the afternoon?

2 A: There's no milk in the fridge.
   B: OK. *I'm getting / I'll get* some from the supermarket.

3 Those magazines I ordered arrived a month late. *I'm complaining / I'm going to complain* to the manager of the shop!

4 Get away from that ladder! *It's going to / It'll* fall down – look at the strength of the wind.

5 *Will you do / Are you doing* anything this evening? If not, do you want to go out?

6 I wouldn't go near Julia's dog, if I were you. *He's going to / He'll* bite you.

7 I can't go to the cinema with you on Friday because *I meet / I'm meeting* Paul.

8 Haven't you written your composition yet? What *are you telling / are you going to tell* Professor Stevens on Thursday?

9 *Are you going to / Will you* help me? I can't lift this heavy table on my own.

10 I believe that Jerry Bond *will win / is winning* the local elections.

2 Future simple, future continuous or future perfect?

Complete the sentence with the most appropriate form of the verb in brackets.

1 I am sure that scientists .... (*discover*) life on another planet one day.

2 I can't believe I've been promoted! This time next week, I .... (*work*) in a smart office in New York.

3 Don't worry – I .... (*finish*) writing my report by Friday. I'll give it to you then.

4 Don't call me tomorrow. I .... (*paint*) the house all day.

5 On Saturday, we .... (*be*) married for 20 years. It's amazing, isn't it?

6 Have we run out of coffee? I .... (*go out*) now and get some.

7 It is no trouble to take you to the airport – I .... (*go*) that way anyway.

8 I don't think you'll see your friends. They .... (*leave*) before you get back.

3 Time clauses

Complete the sentences with the correct form of the verbs in brackets.

1 I promise I .... (*let you know*) as soon as I .... (*find out*) the answer.

2 After you .... (*finish*) classes, ... (*we/go*) to the cinema?

3 .... (*you/want*) a cup of coffee before you .... (*leave*)?

4 As soon as everyone .... (*be*) here, we .... (*start*) the seminar.

5 When the exams .... (*be*) over, my group .... (*have*) a big party to celebrate.

6 When the rain .... (*stop*) why .... (*we/not/go*) for a walk?

4 Degrees of certainty

Read the text and decide which future form A, B or C best fits each space.

In a hundred years' time, I'm absolutely certain that astronauts (1)............ on Mars. By then, they (2)............ a space colony there as well. Who knows? It's quite likely, of course, that human beings (3)............ other planets as well by that time – Jupiter perhaps. Within a century, it's almost certain that people (4)............ on the moon.

As regards medicine, it (5)............ very different in a hundred years from now. We (6)............ a lot more about DNA. I'm sure that doctors (7)............ genetic information to diagnose diseases on an everyday basis. By then it's possible they (8)............ ways to use the same genetic data to stop people from getting ill. What an absolutely amazing prospect!

1 **A** will have landed   **B** might land   **C** might have landed
2 **A** are going to build   **B** could build   **C** might have built
3 **A** will visit   **B** are visiting   **C** will have visited
4 **A** will be living   **B** are going to live   **C** are living
5 **A** will be   **B** will have been   **C** could have been
6 **A** will have known   **B** will know   **C** could know
7 **A** are going to use   **B** are using   **C** will be using
8 **A** may find   **B** may have found   **C** could be finding

5 Exam practice: open cloze (Paper 3 Part 2)

Read the text below and think of the word which best fits each space. Use only one word in each space. There is an example at the beginning (**0**).

SCIENCE AS A CAREER

For years, British universities have been worried because fewer (**0**)........and........ fewer students are choosing to do degrees in scientific subjects. These days, students (**1**)............ do well at science and maths at school are more attracted (**2**)............ careers in areas such (**3**)............ information technology and electronics rather (**4**)............ in pure scientific research.

Many people think that when they are choosing which course to study, students do a kind of 'cost-benefit analysis'. In (**5**)............ words, they ask themselves (**6**)............ the effort of doing the course will be matched by future career prospects. Unfortunately, (**7**)............ students work very hard to get science degrees, they won't necessarily get a big salary if they go for a career in science afterwards. But there's nothing new in this. Scientists through the ages have rarely been well-paid, and (**8**)............ my opinion earning lots of money shouldn't really be the motivation for scientists either.

(**9**)............ attracted me to science was the thought of discovering some new law of nature (**10**)............ nobody had ever seen before. In short, catching (**11**)............ glimpse of things that are bigger than we humans. That (**12**)............ be much more satisfying than designing computer games or vacuum cleaners, mustn't it?

Writing Email (Paper 2 Part 1)

▶ CB pages 70–71, WR pages 197–198

Exam strategy

Before you start writing, make a plan for your answer. Think about the best way of organising the points you have to include in your email.

1 Understand the task

Read the task below and answer the questions.
1 Who are you writing to?
2 What style should you use?
3 Why are you writing?
4 What points MUST you include? Mark them.

You are the secretary of the Science Club at your college. You have seen an advertisement for the St Aubrey Astronomical Observatory and decided to organise a group visit. You have written some questions you would like to ask. Read the advertisement and your questions carefully. Then write an email to the Director of the observatory explaining what you want to do and asking for the information you need.

Public
Open Day

On Saturday, June 18th
we are open all day to the public!
*
Come and look around

Talk to the staff about what they do
See the powerful St Aubrey telescope
*
For further information, please email or
phone Dr John Good (Director).

group of 20 students – a problem?
best time to visit?
can we try out the telescope?
photos allowed?

Write your **email** in **120–150** words. You must use grammatically correct sentences with accurate spelling and punctuation in a style appropriate for the situation.

2 Plan your email

Decide how to order the key points in the task and complete this paragraph plan.
Paragraph 1: introduce myself, give reason for writing
Paragraph 2: mention ……….. and ask …………..
Paragraph 3: ……..……….…………..
Paragraph 4: ……..……….…………..
Paragraph 5: conclusion

3 Organise a sample answer

a Read the jumbled sentences of a student's email below. Decide which paragraph 1, 2, 3, 4 or 5 each sentence should go in. The last paragraph is only one sentence. (The first one has been done for you.)

Dear Dr Good

☐ a Could you also let me know the best time for us to visit?

☐ b However, there are some questions I would like to ask you beforehand.

[1] c I am secretary of the Science Club at Erasmus College.

☐ d Firstly, since all our members are interested in coming to the observatory, there would be about twenty of us.

☐ e Would so many students be a problem?

☐ f I saw your advertisement for the St Aubrey Open Day and would like to organise a group visit.

☐ g I understand, of course, that photography may not be allowed.

☐ h I would also like to know if we will be allowed to look through the St Aubrey telescope?

☐ i We have heard so much about it and would love to try it out!

☐ j I look forward to hearing from you.

☐ k They want to know whether they can take photographs inside the observatory.

☐ l Finally, several students are keen photographers.

Yours sincerely,

Richard Zimler

Richard Zimler

b Write the email out in your notebook. Put the sentences within each paragraph in the appropriate order.

Listening Sentence completion
(Paper 4 Part 2)

1 Before you listen

a Read the instructions for the listening task below. What is the topic? Try to remember what you know about this topic.

b Read sentences 1–10 and try to predict what kind of information is missing.

1 Which answer do you think will be a number?

2 Which answers do you think will be proper names?

3 Which answer do you think will be part of the face?

4 Which answers do you think will be adjectives?

Remember to look at the words **before** and **after** the gap.

2 ⌒ Listening for specific information

a Listen to the recording once, and complete the sentences.

b Listen again to check and complete your answers.

You will hear an interview with a woman who's written a book about face-reading, the skill of judging a person's character from the shape of their face. For questions **1–10**, complete the sentences.

FACE READING

The skill of face-reading is believed to have come from ⬚ **1** originally.

The title of Lillian's book is ⬚ **2** .

Lillian explains that the face contains approximately ⬚ **3** muscles.

Lillian says that when people look in a ⬚ **4** , they usually manage to look their best.

Lillian says that people often feel ⬚ **5** when they see themselves on video.

Experts say that the left side of the face is regarded as more ⬚ **6** by most people.

Lillian says that successful ⬚ **7** are often people with wide cheekbones.

Lillian says that the shape of a person's ⬚ and **8** may show how determined they are.

Lillian advises women against using too much ⬚ **9** at interviews.

Lillian suggests ⬚ and **10** when listening to people at interviews.

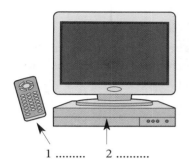 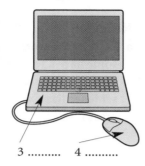   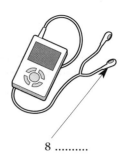

1 ....   2 ....   3 ....   4 ....   5 ....   6 ....   7 ....   8 ....

Vocabulary ▶ CB pages 72–73

Exam strategy

Inventions and their usefulness or importance is a common topic in Paper 5. In Part 3, for example, you may be asked to talk about a number of different inventions and decide which three you could not live without or which have changed our lives the most. Collect useful vocabulary in your vocabulary notebook.

1 Topic: modern inventions

a Label the pictures above with words and phrases from the list. There are some words you do not need to use.

remote control   broadcast   keyboard   download text message   lens   earphones   channels   call website   software   DVD player   images   focus optical mouse   ring tone   viewfinder   zap

b Complete the sentences with a word or phrase from the list in Exercise 1a.

1 Some people change the .... of their mobile several times a week.

2 You need the right computer .... in order to create digital photos at home.

3 With cable TV, the number of .... which are available to viewers is enormous.

4 You don't need to .... my camera. It does it automatically.

5 I found a really good .... yesterday about sharks and whales. I'll email you the address if you like.

6 Last night's interview with the President was .... live from the White House.

7 I love my MP3 player. I .... songs every morning from the Internet and listen to them while I'm on the bus.

8 You can edit the .... you've taken with your camera using your computer.

9 I'll put my mobile where I can hear it. I'm expecting a .... from my brother.

10 Using the remote control, it is easy to .... from channel to chaennel.

2 Agreeing and disagreeing

Two students, Peter and Ingrid, are discussing this question: 'What do you think is the most important thing ever invented?'

Read the extract from their discussion and put the sentences in the correct order. Then look at the words in italics and mark the correct word in each pair.

1 a **Peter:** I think the computer is the most important thing ever invented. If you have a computer, you can do so many things that you couldn't do before. Computers and the Internet have changed the way people live.

☐ **b** **Ingrid:** Yes. You *are / have* right. I hadn't thought of that. I'm not sure if fire is a thing that we invented, though. It's a natural phenomenon. People discovered it. *Aren't / Don't* you agree?

☐ **c** **Ingrid:** I couldn't agree *much / more*. Without writing we wouldn't be able to live like we do today. The whole of our civilisation is based on things which are written down. Maybe it is the most important thing which has ever been invented.

☐ **d** **Ingrid:** Yes, that's *true / truth*. But I don't think computers have changed our lives as much as cars. The car is a more important invention, *to / in* my opinion. It's easy to live without a computer but you can't live without a car, can you?

☐ **e** **Peter:** Yes, I suppose *so / that*. Well, writing then – writing was invented. That was a really important invention, I think.

☐ **f** **Peter:** No, I suppose *no / not*. Most people depend on them nowadays. Life would be *much / more* slower and more difficult without them. But I think other things are more important. What *for / about* fire, for example? I mean, that's something that changed the history of the whole human race.

3 Commonly confused words

Complete the sentences with the correct word. Use each word once only.

1 **machine / engine**
   a This car has a very powerful .... , so you'll have to drive carefully.
   b To operate the coffee .... , just put your money in here and press the button.

2 **electric / electrical**
   a We need to buy a new .... cooker as soon as possible.
   b All the .... equipment in this room needs to be replaced.

3 **appliance / device**
   a A vacuum cleaner is a(n) .... which almost every household possesses.
   b My car has a(n) .... which checks whether everyone is wearing a seat belt.

4 **mechanic / technician**
   a My father works as a .... in the microbiology unit of the hospital.
   b A .... looked at my car the other day and said that I should get a new one.

5 **invent / discover**
   a I am sure that astronomers will .... much more about distant galaxies in the future.
   b Do you think someone will .... a flying car one day?

6 **fix / correct**
   a Can we find someone to .... the video? It doesn't work properly.
   b I've noticed a number of errors in this report. Can you .... them, please?

Language development 2

Reflexives; structures with question words

▶ CB page 76

1 Reflexives

a **Look at the sentences below. Some are correct and some have a word which should not be there. If a sentence is correct, put a tick (✔) by it. If a sentence has a word which should not be there, cross it out.**

EXAMPLES: I usually get ~~myself~~ up at seven o'clock in the morning.
Nobody came to repair the TV, so I fixed it myself. ✔

1 I wonder myself whether he'll be able to fix my car.

2 You'll hurt by yourself if you are not careful!

3 He went to the dance on his own.

4 They talked to themselves one another all evening.

5 Did you feel yourself nervous when you talked to the Prime Minister?

6 My brother managed to learn about computers by himself.

7 John and Alice met each one another on holiday last year.

8 I enjoyed myself at the party last night.

4 Exam practice: word formation (Paper 3 Part 3)

Read the text below. Use the word given in capitals at the end of each line to form a word that fits in the space in the same line. There is an example at the beginning (0).

THE RISK OF NEW TECHNOLOGY

Sometimes a new invention, or the **(0)** introduction of a new	INTRODUCE
piece of technology fails to make the **(1)**........................... on our	IMPRESS
lives that people thought it would. Home **(2)**........................... is	ENTERTAIN
one area where there is a constant stream of new	
(3)........................... , only a few of which will become universally	PRODUCE
(4)........................... and a part of our everyday lives. This is a	SUCCESS
cause of great **(5)**........................... to designers and manufacturers	ANXIOUS
who invest large sums of money in the research and	
(6)........................... of new technologies. For example, in the period	DEVELOP
(7)........................... after digital television systems first went on	IMMEDIATE
(8)........................... , relatively few people bought them. Many	SELL
people were quite **(9)**........................... with their existing television	SATISFY
(10)........................... , but it was also because the new systems	RECEIVE
were so expensive.	

b Complete the sentences using the correct form of the verbs in the list and any other words that are necessary.

blame   like   look   cut   write   relax
concentrate   know

EXAMPLE: This knife is extremely sharp. I've just
.........cut myself......... .

1 The accident was not your fault. Don't
.... for what happened.

2 I'm not going to help you with your letter. You can
....

3 Tom and Simon are very good friends. They've
.... for ages.

4 You look exhausted. Why don't you
.... more?

5 Maria stood in front of the mirror and
.... for over five minutes.

6 Melina's grades are very poor. She really needs to
.... on her schoolwork this term.

7 Alexia and Nick will probably refuse to work together. They don't .... , I'm afraid.

2 Structures with question words

a Match the sentence halves in A and B to make logical sentences.

A		B	
1	John didn't know	a	**how** to operate your new electric typewriter.
2	Susan couldn't understand	b	**what** to do when his computer crashed.
3	The instructions tell you	c	**what** to say when they asked you about it.
4	The police were not sure	d	**why** her car wouldn't start.
5	I know exactly	e	**where** the robbers they were chasing had gone.
6	I'm surprised you knew	f	**why** you have come to see me.

b Complete the dialogues using a structure with a question word and the verb in brackets in the correct form.

1 A: Do you have a problem?
   B: Yes. I don't know .... (use) this new coffee machine.
   A: It's easy. Let me show you.

2 A: What are you looking for?
   B: I've lost my new pen. I can't remember .... (put) it.
   A: I think I saw it next to the telephone.

3 A: You look worried.
   B: Yes, I'm not sure .... (do) about my exam results. They're terrible!
   A: I think you should talk to Professor Thom.

4 A: Are you upset about something?
   B: Yes, I am. Ivan was rude to me this morning. I can't understand .... (speak) to me like that.
   A: Maybe he was just in a bad mood.

3 Key word transformations

Complete the second sentence so that it has a similar meaning to the first sentence, using the word given. Do not change the word given. You must use between two and five words, including the word given.

1 Was the party enjoyable last night?
   yourself
   Did .... the party last night?

2 Are you badly hurt?
   hurt
   Have .... badly?

3 I didn't need any help to repair my bicycle.
   repaired
   I .... own.

4 A lot of students can't use the university's new computers.
   know
   A lot of students don't .... the university's new computers.

5 I can't remember Mike's instructions.
   forgotten
   I .... told us to do.

6 Paul didn't know the right person to ask for technical advice.
   sure
   Paul wasn't .... for technical advice.

7 Nobody came with me to the cinema yesterday.
   myself
   I .... to the cinema yesterday.

8 In the interview, I couldn't think of anything to say about my hobbies.
   know
   In the interview, I didn't .... about my hobbies.

9 Luke and Paul are having a very long conversation.
   talking
   Luke and Paul have .... other for ages.

10 Is this your own drawing or did someone help you?
   yourself
   Did .... or did someone help you?

Reading Gapped text (Paper 1 Part 2)

1 Before you read

Look at the title and subheading of the article opposite. Answer these questions.

1 Does *too clever for their own good* have a positive or negative meaning?

2 What pieces of electronic equipment do you use regularly? Make a list.

....

3 Which ones on your list do you find especially difficult to use? Tick them.

2 Scanning and skimming

a Scan the text to find what electronic equipment it mentions. Compare with your list in Exercise 1.

b Skim the text. What is the main message of the article?

   a Companies should pay more attention to what customers want when they design new products.

   b Many new products don't function properly because they are too complicated.

3 Gapped text

a Read the first paragraph and sentence H (in gap 1). Which words in sentence H link to the highlighted sections in the first paragraph?

   1 The Emperor = He

   2 Mozart's new Music =

   3 sensing this =

b Read the rest of the text carefully. Make sure you understand the main information.

c For each gap, do the following.

   • Read the text before and after the gap and think about the type of information which is missing.

   • Look for a sentence in the box which talks about this topic area.

   • Choose the correct answer by checking the grammatical and lexical links between the base text and the key sentence. Look out for pronouns, synonyms, etc.

   • Cross off each sentence as you use it, but be prepared to look again when you check your answers.

d Read the text again with your answers to check that it makes sense.

You are going to read a magazine article about technology. Seven sentences have been removed from the article. Choose from the sentences **A–H** the one which fits each gap. There is one extra sentence you do not need to use.

A And that's because technological development is led by engineers, whose job involves endlessly dreaming these up and adding them to products.

B In reality people say all sorts of things in response to a list of questions, but rarely what they really think.

C And having bought one, which of us actually has the patience to go through the detailed instruction booklets that comes with it?

D It's probably the same list of essential pieces of equipment, since most of them are difficult to use.

E There are, however, reasons to be hopeful, if evidence from companies in the airline and motor industries is anything to go by.

F People who invent useful things are good at solving technical problems, but often they are not so good at explaining things to non-technicians.

G Indeed, there's a whole industry sector that specialises in such trials.

H He says he likes it, but doesn't seem very convinced – something's not quite right.

In search of simplicity

Have you ever felt that some pieces of electronic equipment were just too clever for their own good?

In the film Amadeus, there's a lovely scene in which Emperor Joseph II of Austria is asked what he thinks of Mozart's music. It's a tense moment for Mozart, the unknown young composer. What does
5 the emperor make of Mozart's new music? **1** **H** 'What do you mean, Sir?' Mozart asks sensing this. 'Too many notes,' replies the emperor. That feeling, that there is too much to understand all at once, is a familiar one to users of many modern technology
10 products. Think of a software programme with all its detailed menus and screens, or e-commerce sites with form after form to fill in, or the complicated telephone in your pocket with all those buttons, icons and messages. Too many functions, too many
15 screens — too many notes.

The 'too many notes' problem is a symptom of a larger one in technological innovation because a good idea can easily turn into a bad product. For example, think about the products considered to be
20 the great technological successes of the twentieth century: the photocopier, fax, video recorder, PC, mobile phone. Now think of the technology that frustrates you as a consumer. **2**

Yet it's not that these products don't function
25 properly. Companies put technical products through all sorts of tests before they come onto the market. **3** But what they are testing is whether the product works. What they should be testing is how it works, and how it could work better for the
30 consumer.

There seems to be some confusion about what makes a good product, as opposed to good technology. People seem to believe that the more a piece of equipment can do, the better it is. Most
35 software packages and most pieces of electronic equipment have too many functions. **4**

In a typical home, for example, there are many devices that tell the time: cookers, radios, answering machines, TVs and hi-fi systems, as well as clocks
40 and wristwatches. Some of them need to know the time to perform their other functions, but others don't — the clock was just added for the sake of it.

Another problem is that companies are not good at getting the right information from the people who
45 will use their products. For example, a lot of faith is put in market-research interviews. **5** To understand consumer behaviour, designers of domestic appliances are now getting help from people called ethnographers, who spend their time
50 observing how people actually behave, which can be of great importance in the design of a genuinely useful new product.

A further reason for the failure of technology is the lack of cooperation between the engineers and
55 those who do the marketing in many companies. **6** Marketing staff, therefore, find it hard to follow what engineers are talking about, so tend to put too much emphasis on the familiar aspects of new technology when promoting the products.

60 Until companies realise that the technology they are producing is not what customers actually want, they'll no doubt continue to persuade us to buy new pieces of equipment which will disappoint us. **7** They have found that when designers and
65 marketing people do talk together at an early stage in the development of a product, then equipment is less likely to end up containing unwanted functions that get in the way.

6A Music and TV

Vocabulary ▶CB pages 80–81
▶Colloquial English page 122

1 Word formation
a **Use the word given in capitals at the end of each sentence to form a word that fits in the space.**

1 Even as a little girl, Madonna's .... was to become a famous singer.
AMBITIOUS

2 It wasn't easy to find a .... for the band's lead singer when she fell ill with a throat infection. **REPLACE**

3 To become a top musician, you need both skill and considerable ....
CONFIDENT

4 World music is steadily gaining in .... among young people.
POPULAR

5 Jamie Cullum's .... to become a great jazz performer was apparent at an early age. **DETERMINE**

6 Many people were impressed by the .... of singer George Harrison during his final illness. **BRAVE**

7 Bjork is well-known for the .... and originality of her songs. **CREATE**

8 Some great performers often experience feelings of .... and depression in their personal lives. **LONELY**

b **Put the nouns from Exercise 1a in the correct column in the table. Then add two more nouns you know to each column.**

-ence	-ity	-ion	-ment	-ness	-ery

2 ◠ Pronunciation
a **Look at the words below and listen to the recording. Mark the stressed syllable in each word. (The first one has been done for you.)**

1 am**bi**tion determination satisfaction fascination

2 creativity popularity dependability adaptability

b **Complete the pronunciation rule by ticking (✓) the correct answer a, b or c.**
When a word ends in -tion or -ity we stress:
a the suffix.   b the second syllable.
c the syllable before the suffix.

3 Prepositional phrases
Mark the correct preposition in each pair.

1 A year ago, our folk rock group *Caravan* was *in / under* danger of splitting up.

2 The group's lead guitarist and vocalist, Rick, was *in / at* hospital for over six months.

3 Performing without Rick was *away from / out of* the question.

4 Quite *by / at* chance, we heard of another musician who could replace him.

5 We contacted Paddy *at / by* email, asking him if he would like to join the group.

6 Paddy's agent telephoned *on / in* his behalf and suggested we organise a jam session.

7 Paddy turned out to be a brilliant musician and already knew a lot of our songs *at / by* heart.

8 Two months later, the new band's first performance *in / at* public was a huge success.

4 Verb + noun collocations
a **Complete the text with a word from the list below.**

records album role opportunity debut impact
audition scholarship offer performance

J. Lo! Jennifer Lopez was born in 1970 in New York. Having decided at an early age to become a musical theatre actress, she <u>gave</u> her first **(1)** .... when she was just 16. Then, at 17, she won a **(2)** .... to a well-known Manhattan dance school.

In 1990, Jennifer went for an **(3)** .... for a minor part in the TV series *In living Colour* and was successful. She was then given the **(4)** .... to appear as a backup dancer in Janet Jackson's video *That's the Way Love Goes*.

Five years later, Jennifer Lopez made her big screen **(5)** .... in *The Money Train*. This film opened more doors for her, but it was the film *Selena*, in which she played the leading **(6)** ...., that turned her into a superstar.

In 1999, Jennifer took up an **(7)** .... from Sony and moved into music. As all her fans know, she has made a huge **(8)** .... on the musical scene since then. In 2002, she released the **(9)** .... *J to tha L-O: The Remixes*, which became one of the most successful remix albums ever.

Is that all? Well … Jennifer Lopez also owns a a restaurant in California, a clothing line (*JLO*) and a popular line of perfumes. When she ventured into the perfume industry, the appropriately-named *Glow by J.Lo* broke all **(10)** .... in sales.

b **Mark the verb which is used with each noun you have used in Exercise 4a. The first one has been done for you.**

5 Key word transformations

Complete the second sentence so that it has a similar meaning to the first sentence, using the word given. Do not change the word given. You must use between two and five words, including the word given.

1 Joanna is now at the top of her profession. **risen**
Joanna .... the top of her profession.

2 The lead dancer performed exceptionally well this evening. **gave**
The lead dancer .... this evening.

3 Gary is obviously the best singer in the group. **stands**
Gary .... the best singer in the group.

4 When on tour, musicians often miss their home. **feel**
Many musicians tend to .... when they're on tour.

5 Everyone was surprised at how popular the band's first album was. **by**
Everyone was surprised .... of the band's first album.

6 Jennifer didn't accept the role in the new musical. **down**
Jennifer .... the role in the new musical.

7 The lead vocalist gets impatient very easily when she's rehearsing a new song. **lacks**
The lead vocalist .... when she's rehearsing a new song.

8 In April, the band left London to begin their World Tour. **set**
The band's World Tour began when they .... London in April.

9 Lucas has always been full of ambition. **very**
Lucas has always .... person.

10 Despite rumours, the bass guitarist does not intend to leave the band. **has**
Despite rumours, the bass guitarist .... the band.

Language development 1 Relative clauses

▶ CB pages 82–83, GR pages 186–187

1 Defining or non-defining relative clauses?

a Decide if the sentences below contain defining or non-defining relative clauses. Write *D* (defining) or *ND* (non-defining). Add any missing commas.

EXAMPLE: The Rolling Stones, who were one of the most popular groups of the 1960s, still give live concerts today. **ND**

1 We're taking the plane that leaves Heathrow at six o'clock. ....
2 Jennifer Lopez's perfume *Glow* which was launched in 2001 quickly became the number one perfume in over nine countries. ....
3 Look! The pianist who played at the concert last night is sitting over there! ....
4 Where are the tickets for *Cats* that I bought this morning? ....
5 Jennifer Lopez whose success as a singer has been phenomenal has no plans yet to stop acting. ....
6 I'll arrange an interview with someone who can help you. ....
7 The song which we enjoyed most at the Eurovision Song Contest was the Hungarian one. ....

b In two sentences in Exercise 1a, the relative pronoun could be omitted. Find them and cross out the relative pronoun.

2 Relative clauses

Read the article below. Rewrite it in your notebook, adding the missing information (a–h) in the gaps 1–8. Use relative clauses and make any changes necessary.

EXAMPLE: Karaoke, whose popularity has spread throughout the world in recent years, originated in Japan.

Karaoke (1) .... originated in Japan. *Kara* is an abbreviation of the word (2) ...., and *oke* is short for *okesutura* or orchestra. Usually, a recorded song consists of both vocals and a musical accompaniment. However, recordings of songs (3) .... are called karaoke.
For almost thirty years, Japanese people (4) .... have been picking up microphones and 'singing karaoke'. Family karaoke sets (5) .... are extremely popular in Japan. Apparently, they also help children (6) .... to learn to read more quickly.
In Japan (7) .... noise can be a problem. So special places for people (8) .... started to appear in the towns and countryside. The first 'karaoke box' appeared in a rice field near Kansai as early as 1984.

a they wanted to sing karaoke
b houses and flats are often built very close together there
c they consist only of the accompaniment
d they display the words and scenes of a song on a monitor
e its popularity has spread throughout the world in recent years
f they have reading problems
g it means empty in Japanese (karappo)
h they have always enjoyed singing after work and at parties

3 Reduced relative clauses

a Shorten these sentences, using present or past participles.

EXAMPLE: The people ~~who live~~ in the flat above mine are actors. ......living......

1 The musical *Moulin Rouge*, which starred Nicole Kidman and Ewan McGregor, was a huge success at the box office. ....

2 Many songs which were written more than 10 years ago seem very dated nowadays.

....

3 One day I saw a busker who was playing four instruments at the same time.

....

4 Jennifer Lopez's second album, *J.Lo*, which was released in 2001, went straight to the top of the charts. ....

5 All the money which is earned from ticket sales goes to charity. ....

b Read two extracts from student articles. Mark the relative clauses which can be shortened. Rewrite them in your notebook.

EXAMPLE: The rock concert held last night ...

A

The rock concert, which was held last night in the main hall of the college, was a great success. I'm sure everyone who went last night will not forget it for a long time. During the performance, Jeff Stone, who was constantly cheered and applauded by his fans, amazed the audience by his skill as a musician. He played a number of old favourites, which included Red Rose and Road to Heaven, and sang a number of songs from the band's latest album. At one point, the people who were sitting in the front seats jumped up and started to dance in the aisles.

B

The classical concert on April 6th was disappointing. Beethoven's seventh symphony, which was performed by the University Orchestra, lacked passion throughout. In fact, the musicians who were playing in the strings section of the orchestra appeared to be positively bored. The conductor, James Oliver, who has led the orchestra for the past two years, surprised the audience by his unorthodox interpretation of the symphony.

4 Relative clauses and prepositions

Combine the following sentences in two ways – formal and informal.

EXAMPLES: That's the man. I bought the tickets from him.
Formal: *That's the man from whom I bought the tickets.*
Informal: *That's the man I bought the tickets from.*

1 That's the person. I spoke to her on the phone earlier.
Formal: ....
Informal: ....

2 Bill is the sound technician. We work for him.
Formal: ....
Informal: ....

3 They are redecorating the hall. The concert will take place in it.
Formal: ....
Informal: ....

4 Is this the tape? You recorded the album on it.
Formal: ....?
Informal: ....?

5 Are these the tickets? We paid so much money for them.
Formal: ....?
Informal: ....?

5 Exam practice: open cloze (Paper 3 Part 2)

Read the text below and think of the word which best fits each space. Use only one word in each space. There is an example at the beginning (0).

An Opera Director's Upbringing

My mother loved music and she certainly encouraged me (0) ...in.... my choice of career. She had a number of records (1) .... I played over and over again from quite (2) .... early age. These included classical recordings as (3) .... as traditional folk music and the pop songs of the time. It was good because I discovered all kinds of music, but my mother never gave me the impression that one sort was better (4) .... another. I just learnt to love each type of music for (5) .... it was. The thing which really influenced my future career, (6) .... , was the public lending library near our home. Before the days of the Internet and cheap paperbacks, everybody in the UK used (7) .... use public libraries, and the one near our house had a record collection (8) .... addition to books. In the school holidays, I would borrow whole operas which came in boxed sets, complete (9) .... a booklet containing all the words and the musical score. I learnt to play the piano and I used to sing along too, even (10) .... I wasn't much of a singer! It soon became obvious to everyone that I would go to university to study music. Of course, (11) .... I got there and met students from other backgrounds, I realised how exceptionally lucky I (12) .... been.

Writing Review (Paper 2 Part 2)

▶ CB pages 84–85, WR page 205

Exam strategy

You write a review of something you have experienced. For example, it could be a review of a film that you have seen or a book you have read. Make your review as interesting as you can and address your readers directly. It is very important to express your personal opinion of what you experienced.

1 Understand the task

Read the task below and answer the questions.

1 Where will the review appear? Who will read it?
2 What is the aim of the review?
3 What MUST you include?
4 What style will you use?

Write your **review** in **120–180** words in an appropriate style.

REVIEWS NEEDED!
Could you write us a review of a concert you went to recently? Pop, rock, folk, classical – it doesn't matter! Write about the concert, including information about who the musicians were and what they played. Say whether the concert was a success or not. **The best reviews will be published next month.**

---

2 Compare two sample answers

Look at the table below, which lists the features of a good review. Then read Review 1 and 2 and complete the table. Which review is better?

A good review:	Review 1	Review 2
has an eye-catching title.		
has an interesting opening paragraph, which tells the reader what exactly is being reviewed		
is divided into paragraphs, each focusing on one aspect of the subject of the review		
is written in an appropriate style and involves the reader by addressing him/her directly		
describes clearly what the writer experienced, including important details		
gives the reader a clear impression of the personal opinion (good or bad) of the writer		
uses varied and interesting language		
finishes with a strong sentence, which summarises what has been said		

3 Correct the sample answers

a Correct the errors in each review which the teacher has identified. (See Unit 1, page 9 for a key to the correction symbols.)

b Write your own answer to the task in your notebook.

REVIEW 1

THE FLAMING LIPS DON'T DISAPPOINT THEIR BRITISH FANS.

It was obvious from the start that the Flaming Lips concert at the Brighton Centre was going to be different. When Wayne Coyle floated over the heads of the audience inside a huge plastic bubble, everyone knew this is ⟨T⟩ a night to remember.

The Flaming Lips are putting ⟨T⟩ on shows like this since the band was formed in 1983 in Oklahoma. They love to surprise their fans with special effects and surrealistic costumes. Wayne Coyle, the band's charismatic vocalist, loves to give people a good time.

In Brighton, the Flaming Lips played that old favourite Yoshimi Battles the Pink Robots, as well as The Yeah Yeah Yeah Song. The audience danced and sang along with the band, going wild with excitement when the Flaming Lips began to play Mr Ambulance Man.

The concert was a huge success. When I left, it seemed that the world had suddenly become more interesting – and more fun. If you love rock music, go and see them. They won't be in Britain for long! [180 words]

REVIEW 2

I like music and I love going to concerts. Last month I went to two concerts.

A band I really like is the White Stripes. You have heard ⟨GR⟩ of them? They are an exciting band from Detroit in America. The White Stripes play back-to-basics blues. They have a hugely ⟨Ww⟩ number of rock fans from all over the world. The band consists of Jack and Meg White, and they are using ⟨T⟩ just guitar and drums to accompany the most ⟨GR⟩ their songs. The White Stripes are from Detroit. They suddenly became famous in 2001. Before that, nobody knew anything about them. Meg and Jack always wear red, white and black clothes when they perform. Three really famous White Stripes songs are Aluminium, Blue Orchid and The Hardest Button to Button. Recently, these songs were rewritten for orchestra. I read at ⟨Ww⟩ a student magazine that the Royal Ballet is going to dance to these songs at the Royal Opera House in London. I am wondering ⟨T⟩ what the audience will think? They normally go and see Swan Lake!

I would like to go to that concert. [180 words]

Listening Multiple-choice
questions (Paper 4 Part 4)

1 Before you listen
a Read the instructions for the listening task below, and the questions. Mark key words and think about what the speaker will be talking about.
b What do you think the subject and purpose of the TV programme was?

2 🎧 Multiple-choice questions
a Listen to the recording once. For each question, note the answer as you listen. (The questions follow the order of the text.) Then choose the best option A, B or C.
b Listen again to check and make sure the other options are not possible.
c Was your prediction in Exercise 1b correct?

3 🎧 Vocabulary: idiomatic expressions
Listen to the recording again, and complete the spaces in these extracts from the tapescript.
1 But fortunately, they called back and gave me a number at the television company where I could call them and that's when I realised it was ....
2 To be honest, I thought it was all ....
3 But the worst .... was having to film what's called a video diary every evening saying how the lessons had gone and how I was feeling.
4 The artist wants you to think, you know, which can be .... !
5 … I realised that a part of me was coming out in the painting. It reduced me ....
6 Lots of people were surprised when three out of four experts failed .... which paintings were mine. But I was ....
7 They only seemed to be interested in how much it would .... in the future.

You will hear an interview with Peter Harris, a painter and decorator who took part in a television programme in which he learnt to be an artist. For questions 1–7, choose the best answer A, B or C.

1 How did Peter become involved in the television programme?
   A His employer told him about it.
   B A television company approached him.
   C Some friends suggested it to him. [1]

2 How did Peter feel when he went to the local art gallery?
   A foolish in front of his friends
   B unimpressed by the quality of the things he saw
   C confident that he'd be able to produce some abstract art [2]

3 What did Peter find most difficult about his training?
   A There was no fixed programme.
   B His lessons were filmed for television.
   C He had to comment on it afterwards. [3]

4 What did Peter discover about abstract art?
   A It's not so serious as people think.
   B Some of it is actually not very good.
   C It's not meant to be easy to understand. [4]

5 How did Peter feel when he realised he'd painted a wheelchair?
   A It affected him quite deeply.
   B He became angry with himself.
   C The experience was rather frightening. [5]

6 How did Peter feel about the final programme in the series?
   A surprised to have fooled the experts
   B satisfied with what he had achieved
   C disappointed not to have done better [6]

7 What does Peter say about selling his paintings?
   A He dislikes some of the buyers.
   B Other painters were jealous of him.
   C His family doesn't approve of the idea. [7]

Art and entertainment

Vocabulary ▶ CB pages 86–87
▶ Colloquial English page 123

Exam strategy
In Paper 5 Part 2, you may be asked to compare two photographs showing different types of art or music and say which you prefer. It is important to use relevant vocabulary and to say as much as you can about the topic. You won't make a good impression if you cannot speak for one minute.

1 **Topic: talking about the arts**
What kind of art is each person (1–5) describing? Choose from the list. Mark the words which helped you to decide. There are two words you do not need to use.

film   art exhibition   musical   ballet   play
TV show   street performance

1 'The first picture was taken at a(n) .... I can see a lot of paintings on the walls, and in the middle of the room there are some statues as well. Some people are looking at the works of art on display. The man in the foreground looks very serious and he seems to be writing things in a notebook. Maybe he is an art critic or something like that.'

2 'In this picture, I can see some people who are doing some kind of .... They are in the town square, I think. They are wearing very colourful clothes. One of them is playing a violin and the woman in the foreground looks as if she is reading something aloud – or perhaps she is singing, I don't know. There is a hat on the ground in front of them, where people are putting money.'

3 'This photo shows a .... , but it's strange because the photo wasn't taken in a theatre. The actors are performing in a big old building – it's a kind of warehouse, I think. There is no stage and the lighting is not very good. The audience is really big though and they seem to be having a good time.'

4 'These two photos both show different kinds of .... In the first photo, there are some people in a TV studio chatting to the presenter about something – maybe politics or current affairs. They look very serious! In the other photo … I can see two teams in the studio, so it's probably a quiz show. I hate quiz shows – usually I change the channel!'

5 'Personally, I would prefer to see the .... , especially if the director is well-known and there are some big names in the cast. I do go to the theatre now and then, but I prefer the cinema. When the plot is exciting, you just forget all your problems.'

2 **Definitions**
Find words in the wordsquare to match the definitions below.

C	O	M	P	O	S	E	R
A	E	E	L	M	I	V	E
S	O	Q	C	W	S	N	V
T	S	I	H	N	T	B	I
V	C	L	A	P	A	H	E
O	R	M	P	U	G	P	W
D	I	E	T	C	E	L	X
U	P	B	E	P	R	O	S
P	T	E	R	F	O	T	T

1 The names of all the actors in a film or play. ....

2 The words of a film or play that an actor has to learn. ....

3 The writer of a piece of classical music. ....

4 An article written by a critic giving his/her opinion of a film or play. ....

5 The story of a film or novel. ....

6 The audience do this to show they have enjoyed a performance. ....

7 A book is divided into a number of these. ....

8 A raised platform in a theatre where plays are performed. ....

3 **Adjective + noun collocations**
a **Match each set of adjectives in A to a noun in B. All the adjectives in the set must collocate with the noun.**

A		B	
1	detective/romantic/historical	a	plot
2	talented/young/eccentric	b	statue
3	live/open-air/free	c	painting
4	ethnic/commercial/abstract	d	novel
5	oil/famous/valuable	e	concert
6	huge/marble/bronze	f	soap opera
7	complicated/clever/gripping	g	art
8	Brazilian/popular/low-budget	h	artist

b **Complete the sentences with an adjective from column A.**

1 I read .... novels because I like trying to guess who the murderer is.

2 The plot of his last novel was so .... that I got really confused.

3 I don't know why soap operas are so .... in my country. They're always dubbed as well!

4 I'm not keen on .... art because it doesn't represent the real world.

5 My favourite work of art is Michelangelo's .... statue of David in Florence.

6 The state should do more to encourage .... young artists.

7 The problem with .... rock concerts is you have to dress for the weather.

8 I prefer watercolours to .... paintings.

4 Exam practice: multiple-choice cloze (Paper 3 Part 1)

Read the text below and decide which answer **A**, **B**, **C** or **D** best fits each space. There is an example at the beginning **(0)**.

0 **A** time **B** day **C** date **D** age

ART ONLINE

At one **(0)** ...A... , only the largest, most powerful companies had real works of art hanging in their boardrooms. They usually chose expensive paintings by well-known artists whose work smaller companies couldn't **(1)**............ . And when a smaller company wanted to **(2)**............ in a more modest work of art, this could **(3)**............ up quite a lot of time. As an expensive consultant was **(4)**............ out of the question, a **(5)**............ of staff had to visit various art galleries and choose something in the **(6)**............ that their colleagues would like it.

But things have changed because now art has **(7)**............ online. There are websites to help companies find the right picture or piece of sculpture. Most employees who buy art for their workplaces do not know a great **(8)**............ about it. So one of the main aims of the website is to **(9)**............ them in their choice. They describe the type of work they want, for example traditional or modern, and what budget is available. This information is then **(10)**............ in a search engine, and a selection of art **(11)**............ up on the screen. Workers back at the company can **(12)**............ the selection and email their comments.

1 A assist	**B** appeal	**C** achieve	**D** afford
2 A bargain	**B** purchase	**C** invest	**D** profit
3 A keep	**B** take	**C** hold	**D** run
4 A accurately	**B** likely	**C** eventually	**D** probably
5 A member	**B** fellow	**C** person	**D** individual
6 A hope	**B** trust	**C** aim	**D** wish
7 A joined	**B** gained	**C** turned	**D** gone
8 A load	**B** deal	**C** lot	**D** extent
9 A show	**B** teach	**C** guide	**D** learn
10 A entered	**B** presented	**C** enrolled	**D** introduced
11 A brings	**B** comes	**C** bears	**D** lays
12 A regard	**B** notice	**C** view	**D** spot

Language development 2
Adjectives and nouns + prepositions; *be used to/get used to* + *-ing* ▶ CB page 90

1 Key word transformations
Complete the second sentence so that it has a similar meaning to the first sentence, using the word given. Do not change the word given. Use between two and five words, including the word given.

1 Opera does not interest Tania.
   interested
   Tania .... opera.

2 He has the ability to become a great musician. **capable**
   He .... a great musician.

3 The Institute of Art and the College of Art are not connected. **connection**
   There .... the Institute of Art and the College of Art.

4 Whose job is it to choose the actors' costumes? **responsible**
   Who .... the actors' costumes?

5 We need to solve this problem quickly.
   solution
   We need to find .... this problem.

6 Charles never forgets people's names.
   good
   Charles is very .... people's names.

7 You cannot compare these two artists.
   comparison
   There .... these two artists.

8 The number of students at the college suddenly increased. **increase**
   There was .... the number of students at the college.

9 I find it very difficult to understand the work of that artist. **difficulty**
   I have great .... the work of that artist.

10 I am sure it was a disappointment to you that you missed the concert.
   disappointed
   I'm sure you .... the concert.

2 *be used to/get used to* + *-ing*

a TV magician and street entertainer David Blaine, once spent spend two and a half days in a block of ice; on another occasion, he lived for 44 days without food in a Plexiglas pod in London. Match the sentence halves in A and B to make logical sentences about his life.

A

1 When David Blaine was a child he

2 When he was only 19, his mother died. David couldn't

3 He moved to Manhattan, where he

4 In David Blaine's TV show *Street Magic*, he

5 Before his 'ice performance', he trained hard so that his body

6 Although most magicians still wear formal evening clothes when they perform, David Blaine

7 Although he eats meat, he

B

a usually prefers to eat fish.

b used to perform his tricks for ordinary people on the pavements of Manhattan.

c used to live with his mother in a very poor part of New York.

d used to do card tricks for celebrities in nightclubs.

e usually wears a simple jacket and T-shirt.

f get used to living on his own afterwards.

g would get used to being in a very cold environment.

b **Find and correct the mistakes with *used to* in these sentences.**

1 Since David Blaine is now a celebrity, he is used to be approached by people on the street in America

2 He stopped appearing in public with his friend, Leo DiCaprio, because he couldn't to get used to the way people always called him 'Leo's friend'.

3 David Blaine is used to be spending a lot of time preparing for his difficult and often dangerous feats.

4 He recently tried to hold his breath underwater for longer than the world record of 8 minutes 58 seconds. In training for this, he had to getting used to slow down his heartbeat so that his body used less oxygen.

5 Although it was very unpleasant at first, David Blaine is now use to being attacked in the press by other illusionists and entertainers.

3 Exam practice: open cloze (Paper 3 Part 2)

Read the text below and think of the word which best fits each space. Use only one word in each space. There is an example at the beginning **(0)**.

THE APPEAL OF ART

I was never very interested **(0)** ..in.. art as a teenager. The famous paintings by classical artists of the past were obviously quite good, but the subject matter didn't appeal **(1)** ...... me. In our local art gallery, **(2)** ...... instance, they had lots of portraits of people looking very stiff and formal. I'd never heard of most of these people, so they didn't really hold **(3)** ...... attention. There were other pictures: a **(4)** ...... pretty landscapes and some showing scenes from classical myths and legends, which were more interesting because something was clearly happening in them. I was never quite sure **(5)** ...... it was, however, because I didn't know the stories in **(6)** ...... first place.

There was also one room full of modern art. We used to laugh at the paintings in there because they seemed to be things **(7)** ...... any child could do. We couldn't make any sense of them at **(8)** .... So when I started going out with a girl **(9)** ...... was studying at art college, it came as quite a pleasant surprise **(10)** ...... she told me that she didn't like the stuff in our art gallery either. Her idea of art was things known **(11)** ...... 'installations'. These are sculptures made out **(12)** ...... everyday objects like old bicycle frames and saucepan lids. Now this may sound strange, but at that point art suddenly started to mean something to me!

Reading Multiple-choice questions
(Paper 1 Part 1)

1 Before you read
Read the instructions for the reading task, and the title of the article opposite. Think about what the article might be about.

2 Skimming
Skim the text. Answer these questions, which focus on the main idea of each paragraph.
Paragraph 1: What is unusual about the museum described in the article?
Paragraph 2: How has the museum and the local area changed?
Paragraph 3: What happened two years ago and why?
Paragraph 4: What is the aim of the evening events at the museum?
Paragraph 5: What was the result of introducing these events?

3 Multiple-choice questions
a First, read the questions 1–8. (You will need to turn the statements in 2, 7 and 8 into questions.) Don't look at the options A–D yet.

b Find the place in the text where the information is contained. Find your own answer to the question and mark the relevant piece of text.

c Now read options A–D and choose the one closest to your answer. Read the piece of text carefully to check that your answer is right and that the other options are definitely wrong. Look for phrases in the text and in the option that express the same idea.

You are going to read a newspaper article about a museum in New York. For questions **1–8**, choose the answer **A**, **B**, **C** or **D** which you think fits best according to the text.

1 What has attracted the man called Bryan to the museum this evening?
- **A** the chance to meet new people
- **B** the type of music being played
- **C** the range of entertainment on offer
- **D** the fact that it costs nothing to get in

2 In the past, the museum attracted few visitors because of
- **A** the poor quality of the exhibitions it put on.
- **B** the negative way it was described in reviews.
- **C** the part of the city where it was located.
- **D** the limited space it had for exhibitions.

3 What does 'them' in line 27 refer to?
- **A** museums
- **B** guidebooks
- **C** visitors
- **D** exhibitions

4 What did Arthur Lehman decide to do when he became director of the museum?
- **A** concentrate on art from Brooklyn
- **B** change the type of things exhibited
- **C** improve the appearance of the building
- **D** get local people interested in the museum

5 What has pleased Arthur Lehman most about 'Free Saturdays'?
- **A** Young people are showing an interest in art.
- **B** Other museums are now trying to copy the idea.
- **C** The idea has made money for the museum.
- **D** The music and dancing has been particularly popular.

6 What does the word 'vindicate' in line 66 mean?
- **A** prove that something is right
- **B** disagree with something
- **C** make us think about something
- **D** be an exception to something

7 The man called Jean-Michel is given as an example of somebody who
- **A** had heard about the museum from friends.
- **B** was profoundly affected by the art he saw.
- **C** hadn't actually visited the museum for years.
- **D** didn't come with the intention of looking at the art.

8 In the last paragraph, the writer shows that she
- **A** is unsure about the real value of 'First Saturdays'.
- **B** admires what the museum has managed to do.
- **C** doubts that the scheme will have long-term success.
- **D** is surprised by the way visitors have reacted to the art.

For the art, turn left at the dance floor

It is Saturday night at the Brooklyn Museum of Art in New York, a large important-looking nineteenth-century building. Since six o'clock, entry to the museum has been free of charge. People are shouting in the galleries, but the
5 guards, who seem to be unusually relaxed, take no notice. On the ground floor, in the galleries devoted to African art, children are playing hide-and-seek while their parents sip beer from plastic cups. Some teenage girls wander by, leaving a
10 trail of perfume, and head through the sculpture exhibition to a temporary dance floor where a DJ is playing reggae music. Watching the scene is Bryan, a young teacher from a local school. What brings him out tonight? 'I'm here for the
15 reggae, of course,' he says. 'When I heard they were playing that I thought, "I have to be there," and obviously a lot of people feel the same way.' Besides the DJ, the museum has laid on gallery talks, a Martin Scorsese film, a puppet
20 show and a samba band.

The Brooklyn Museum of Art wasn't always so trendy. For decades, it put on excellent exhibitions that few came to see. Guidebooks described the enormous building as 'an
25 undiscovered treat'. Had it been over in the city's fashionable Upper East Side, of course, the museum would have been packing **them** in. Even when they put on dull exhibitions, New York's top museums can count on a steady
30 stream of visitors – mostly tourists. But Brooklyn, one of New York's toughest districts, isn't on the standard tourist route. When the museum was built, it was in a wealthy suburb, but these days the surrounding streets are home to recent
35 immigrants, mostly poor folk from the Caribbean.

Two years ago, in an effort to revive itself, the museum appointed a new director, Arnold Lehman, who was born in Brooklyn. Lehman was convinced that the museum should forget
40 about trying to attract visitors from the other side of town and try to appeal instead to people from the surrounding area. 'The neighbourhood's changed,' he explains, 'but this is where the museum is, and we can't – and won't – pretend
45 we're somewhere else.'

The free evening events, called 'First Saturdays', are Lehman's way of reaching out to people. They are certainly popular: the crush of visitors has forced the museum to move the
50 dance floor from the entrance hall to the car park. Lehman is delighted with the result: 'It's remarkable to hear people say, "I live four blocks away, and I've never been in this building before". The great thing for me is when
55 you see teenage boys looking at art in the galleries without being handcuffed to their parents,' he says. What's more, the annual number of visitors to the museum has roughly doubled, from 250,000 to half a million since
60 the scheme was introduced. Similar institutions across the country are now calling, wanting to know how much it costs 'to throw a good party'. The answer, incidentally, is about $25,000 per event. 'And worth every dime,' says Lehman.

65 Tonight, a woman called Akesha, who seems to **vindicate** the new direction the museum has taken, is standing on the edge of the dance floor. Akesha walked to the museum from her home, but hasn't been here since primary
70 school, when a teacher organised a trip to see an exhibition. 'The free concert is why I came,' she admits, 'but I must come back and look round the museum.' Others who come to dance find their way into the galleries almost by
75 accident – like Jean-Michel, who lost his friends in the crush of dancers and thought he might as well take a look at the art. The real achievement of First Saturdays is, therefore, both more significant and more profound than the
80 increased visitor numbers suggest. Most people visit art museums because they want to have a special 'artistic' experience. The Brooklyn Museum of Art has introduced thousands of people to the idea that museum-going can be a
85 perfectly ordinary part of their lives.

7A Fast food

Vocabulary ▶ CB pages 94–95

1 Food quiz
Answer the following questions by choosing the correct answer A, B, C or D.

What do you know about food?

1 What word is used to describe rubbing cheese, fruit, etc. against a rough surface in order to break it into small pieces?
   A slice   C grate
   B chop   D shred

2 What word is used to mean that food is cooked slowly in water that is gently boiling?
   A roast   C bake
   B simmer   D fry

3 What do you add to food when a recipe tells you to season it?
   A salt and pepper
   B olive oil
   C tomato ketchup
   D vinegar

4 If you eat a *dessert* after your main course, you eat something:
   A sweet   C sour
   B bitter   D spicy

5 When you are eating food, what should you do before you swallow it?
   A digest it
   B sip it carefully
   C gobble it up
   D chew it well

6 Which of these kinds of food is rich in vitamin C?
   A meat and poultry
   B rice and pasta
   C fruit and vegetables
   D oil, butter and margarine

7 Why would you say that you need to *count your calories*?
   A You have to heat the oven to a certain temperature.
   B You need to calculate the weight of some meat.
   C You are on a diet.
   D You have to boil an egg.

8 Which word is used to describe old bread which has become hard?
   A rancid   C rotten
   B mouldy   D stale

9 Which spice is used to make Indian and Mexican food hot?
   A cinnamon   C nutmeg
   B chilli   D saffron

10 What would someone mean if they said that some meat had *gone off*?
   A It is undercooked.
   B It is overcooked.
   C It has just been taken out of the oven.
   D It is bad and cannot be eaten.

11 What is the substance called which makes bread rise?
   A yeast   C calcium
   B starch   D flour

12 Which ingredients might you find in a fresh salad?
   A beef, pork or chicken
   B lettuce, cucumber and tomatoes
   C lentils or beans
   D rice or noodles

2 Phrasal verbs

a Match the verbs in A to phrases in B.

A		B	
1	come across	a	something you don't want
2	find a way round		
3	come up with	b	something different
4	run		
5	get rid of	c	weight
6	turn to	d	something unexpectedly
7	cut down on		
8	put on	e	the amount of food you eat
		f	a solution or idea
		g	a business
		h	a problem or difficulty

b Two students, Yvonne and Pablo, are discussing the value of fast food. Complete the dialogue with verbs from column A above in the correct form.

Yvonne: I don't think fast food is good for you at all. I'm sure that if we (1)................................ fast food restaurants, we'd be much healthier. Nobody would miss them.

Pablo: I don't agree, Yvonne. My father (2)................................ a small fast food restaurant and people go there every day to eat. Teenagers meet their friends there for lunch.

Yvonne: Exactly. They're in fashion at the moment. People will (3)................................ something else when they think that burger restaurants are not cool places to be anymore. Maybe salad bars.

Pablo: No. I think that fast food restaurants are here to stay. Someone will have to (4)................................ a really brilliant idea if they want young people to stop eating hamburgers. Anyway, I don't see why they are so bad.

Yvonne: They're bad for you because they don't contain healthy ingredients. I (5)................................ an article in a magazine the other day which said that they only put poor quality meat in hamburgers.

Also if you eat a lot of junk food you (6)................................ a lot of weight. It's a big problem in the USA today. Researchers are trying to (7)................................ it by going to schools and encouraging children to (8)................................ the amount of fast food they eat.

3 Exam practice: multiple-choice cloze (Paper 3 Part 1)

Read the text below and decide which answer **A**, **B**, **C** or **D** best fits each space. There is an example at the beginning **(0)**.

0 **A** imagine **B** think **C** dream **D** believe

TOMATOES – THE PERFECT FRUIT

It is difficult to **(0)** A a world without tomatoes. High in the Andes mountains of modern-day Peru, the local inhabitants have been cultivating and eating tomatoes since prehistoric **(1)**............ , but the food has only become **(2)**............ in the rest of the world **(3)**............ recently. These days, the bright red fruit **(4)**............ an important role in the cooking of many cultures and is a key ingredient in many types of fast food, providing both taste and colour to dishes that **(5)**............ would be rather ordinary.

The tomato **(6)**............ to the nightshade family of plants, many members of which are poisonous. When they were first **(7)**............ into North America, therefore, tomatoes were viewed with **(8)**............ and people tended to use them as table decorations **(9)**............ than as food. In Europe, the tomato was first grown in Italy in 1555, although it wasn't **(10)**............ with pasta until much later. The first recipe for tomato ketchup dates from 1727 and in the 1800s, tomatoes began to be used more **(11)**............ in sauces and soups. These days, as well as tasting good, tomatoes are known to contain substances which are good for our health. Nutritionists **(12)**............ out, however, that many processed tomato products also contain additives such as salt and sugar which can reduce the beneficial effects of the fruit.

	A	B	C	D
1	ages	periods	times	dates
2	popular	favourite	preferred	general
3	effectively	relatively	apparently	eventually
4	forms	meets	does	plays
5	nonetheless	otherwise	instead	meanwhile
6	admits	possesses	fits	belongs
7	imported	arrived	appeared	presented
8	doubt	threat	suspicion	danger
9	except	better	apart	rather
10	joined	combined	added	accompanied
11	greatly	broadly	wholly	widely
12	point	prove	mark	show

Language development 1

Permission and necessity; advice and recommendation ▶ CB pages 96–97, GR pages 190–191

1 Permission, necessity, advice and recommendation

a Rewrite the sentences in your notebook, using *can, must, have to, should, ought to.* Use negative verb forms where appropriate.

EXAMPLE: It's a good idea to eat lots of fresh fruit and vegetables.
You ought to eat lots of fresh fruit and vegetables.

1 You are allowed to take your own wine to that restaurant.
2 It's not a good idea to eat junk food every day.
3 We aren't allowed to sit here because the table is reserved.
4 It isn't necessary for Alice to come with us if she doesn't want to.
5 I think you had better leave your coat in the cloakroom.
6 Is it necessary for us to book a table at that restaurant?
7 It's advisable not to eat too much before going to bed.
8 Parking your car just outside the restaurant is prohibited.
9 Are we permitted to sit at any table we want?

b Complete the email. Use only one word in each space. There may be more than one possibility.

---

000   New Message

Hi Ruth

I saw Dr Ingrims last week and he said
that I **(1)**........................... to lose at least
ten kilos. Since then, I've been on a strict
diet. I **(2)**........................... eat chicken
and fish in small amounts, but, of course,
I am not **(3)**........................... to eat red
meat at all. He also told me that I
(4)........................... avoid cheese,
although it didn't matter if I ate a little
now and then. I suppose I had
(5)........................... get used to living on
fresh salads, hadn't I? Actually, I forgot
my diet yesterday and ordered a Chinese
takeaway. I know that I **(6)**...........................
not have eaten Chinese food, but I felt I
(7)........................... got to eat something I
really liked. It was wonderful! Perhaps I
needn't **(8)**........................... felt so guilty
afterwards – it was a chicken dish, after all
– but I think I **(9)**........................... to have
been a bit more sensible. From now on,
it's just lettuce and carrots!

Love, Liza

---

2 Key word transformations

Complete the second sentence so that it has a similar meaning to the first sentence, using the word given. Do not change the word given. Use between two and five words, including the word given.

1 It wasn't necessary for us to take a taxi. **have**
We .... take a taxi.
2 You can't smoke in the non-smoking area. **allowed**
You .... in the non-smoking area.
3 You really should wear a warmer coat. **better**
You .... a warmer coat.
4 It's very important to remember to tip the waiter. **not**
You .... to tip the waiter.
5 You are under no obligation to accept his offer. **have**
You .... his offer.
6 It was a mistake going to that restaurant last night. **should**
We .... to that restaurant last night.
7 They made me book the table a week in advance. **had**
I .... the table a week in advance.
8 Don't go to that part of town after dark! **must**
You .... to that part of town after dark!

3 Exam practice: open cloze (Paper 3 Part 2)

Read the text below and think of the word which best fits each space. Use only **one** word in each space. There is an example at the beginning **(0)**.

IRN-BRU

Scotland is probably the only country in the world **(0)**........where........ the top-selling soft drink is not Coca-Cola. A local product called Irn-Bru, made **(1)**........................... the small family company AG Barr, continues to sell **(2)**........................... larger quantities than any of its big multinational competitors. Irn-Bru is a sweet, brightly coloured fizzy drink **(3)**........................... a taste that reminds some people of bubble gum and **(4)**........................... of the pink mouthwash you get at the dentist. **(5)**........................... so many other fast-food products, you either love it or **(6)**........................... you hate it.

Yet at the time of **(7)**........................... conception, about one hundred years ago, there was nothing particularly original about 'Iron-Brew', as it was then called. There were many similar soft drinks **(8)**........................... the market, many with the same name. But Barr's Irn-Bru had the big advantage of **(9)**........................... manufactured in Glasgow, a city which had a population of one million, and it quickly became extremely popular. What's more, Barr was one of the first businessmen to understand **(10)**........................... value of celebrity endorsement. As early as 1905, the world champion wrestler Alex Munro was advertising the drink, and it continues to benefit **(11)**........................... clever marketing today. Young Irn-Bru drinkers are encouraged to think that they don't **(12)**........................... to follow the trend in order to be cool.

Writing Email (Paper 2 Part 1)

▶ CB pages 98–99, WR pages 197–198

1 Understand and plan the task

a Read the task below. Mark the points you have to include in the email.

b How many paragraphs will you write? Make a plan in your notebook.

You work at Westbury Language School. You have invited a famous historian to talk to your students. Read the email she sent you and the notes you have made, together with the map of Westbury. Then write an email in reply, using all your notes.

New Message

Bristol Hotel

You did not mention the hotel you have booked me into. Could you tell me how to get there from the station? — check map

I intend to arrive in the morning and will give my talk in the afternoon. Do you have any suggestions as to what I could do in Westbury before I come to your school? — Castle?

Finally, I'd like you to give me a few more details about the restaurant meal you have planned for the evening. — Give details

I am very much looking forward to seeing you on 12 May.

Best wishes

Matilda White

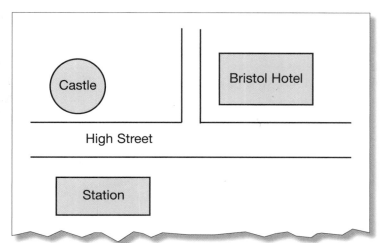

Castle

Bristol Hotel

High Street

Station

Write an **email** of between **120** and **150** words. You must use grammatically correct sentences with accurate spelling and punctuation in a style appropriate to the situation.

2 Check and improve a sample answer

a Read the letter a student has written and tick (✓) the points which have been included. What important information is missing?

Information about ....

b Look at the map and write sentences to include the missing information. Mark where this information should go in the email.

....
....
....

c Read the email again and find a phrase which:

1 makes a suggestion.

....

2 refers to a question.

....

New Message

Dear Ms White

Thank you for your email. Here are the answers to your questions.

I have booked you into the Bristol Hotel, which is a pleasant hotel near the station.

If you want to go sightseeing in the morning, why don't you visit Westbury Castle? It's close to your hotel and I am sure you will find it very interesting.

Finally, you asked me about the meal in the evening. I have booked tables at a popular local Indian restaurant, which serves both meat and vegetarian dishes. I will pick you up at your hotel and we can meet the students at the restaurant.

I look forward to seeing you in Westbury.

Yours sincerely

Julia Jacobs

Listening

Extracts: multiple choice
(Paper 4 Part 1)

1 Before you listen

a Look at the listening task opposite. How many extracts will you hear?

b For each extract, read the context sentence, the question and the three options A, B and C. Think about the situation, who will be talking and what they will be talking about. Mark key words in each question.

2 🎧 Extracts

a Listen to each extract. Focus on the speaker's main idea – don't worry if you don't understand every word. You will hear each extract twice.

b Choose one of the options after listening the first time. If you don't know an answer, have a guess and go on to the next question.

c Listen again to check your answers. Make sure the other options could not be correct.

You will hear people talking in eight different situations. For questions **1–8**, choose the best answer **A**, **B** or **C**.

1 You hear the beginning of a radio programme about food. What does the presenter say is most surprising about the website he's describing?
   A the number of recipes available
   B the way that different flavours have been combined
   C the fact that one ingredient appears in so many of the recipes | 1 |

2 You hear an old woman talking about vegetarianism. What is she doing when she speaks?
   A supporting the principles of vegetarianism
   B doubting the seriousness of many vegetarians
   C explaining why she has become a vegetarian | 2 |

3 You hear part of an interview with a woman who is in favour of organically-grown food. What opinion is she expressing?
   A Only food grown locally should be labelled as organic.
   B It's best to avoid the organic sections of supermarkets.
   C Even commercially produced organic food is a good thing. | 3 |

4 You hear part of a radio discussion about travel guidebooks. What does Graham find disappointing about the book called *The Ultimate Guide*?
   A the range of information included
   B the quality of the illustrations
   C the clarity of the descriptions | 4 |

5 In a radio play, you hear two people talking about pizza. Where is this scene taking place?
   A in their home
   B in a restaurant
   C in a supermarket | 5 |

6 You hear part of a radio programme about looking for a job on the Internet. Which group of people is being described?
   A unemployed people
   B people dissatisfied with their jobs
   C part-time workers looking for full-time jobs | 6 |

7 You hear a radio news report about a scientific conference. What is the main aim of the experiment described?
   A to attract attention to an idea for a new product
   B to demonstrate the power of marketing
   C to get funding for a new area of research | 7 |

8 You hear the owner of a large restaurant talking about her work. What is her main aim in running the restaurant?
   A encouraging competition between the chefs
   B ensuring a standardised product for the customers
   C involving all the staff in checking the quality of the food | 8 |

Vocabulary ▶ CB pages 100–101
▶ Colloquial English page 123

1 Topic: the clothes you wear
Read the comments different people made about what they usually wear and decide which answer A, B or C best fits each space.

A 'I tend to wear fairly elegant clothes during the week – (1)............................ jackets, straight skirts or trouser suits. The first (2)............................ my clients get of me is very important. Now I don't feel right in (3)............................ clothes, so even at the weekends I still wear the same kind of thing.'

1	A	fitted	B	shaped	C created
2	A	appearance	B	impression	C picture
3	A	easy	B	relaxing	C casual

B 'When I'm not at school, there's no point in dressing up in (1)............................ clothes. They just get dirty. I wear (2)............................ bottoms and a T-shirt. I've also got three different football (3)............................ – Manchester United, England and Barcelona.'

1	A	smart	B	sharp	C official
2	A	tracksuit	B	trouser	C suit
3	A	uniforms	B	kits	C costumes

C 'At the moment, the (1)............................ is to wear very short or very long skirts with trainers or shoes with (2)............................ heels. Interesting or unusual patterns in (3)............................ colours are popular this season too. I wouldn't dream of wearing anything that wasn't (4)............................ fashion. I wear patterned or (5)............................ tights with my school uniform.'

1	A	habit	B	design	C trend
2	A	high	B	tall	C extended
3	A	bright	B	full	C powerful
4	A	on	B	at	C in
5	A	wrinkled	B	striped	C lined

D 'I like clothes, but I'm not a fashion victim. Now I've got kids I want to be comfortable, so I don't wear (1)............................ skirts any more. However, that doesn't mean that I live in jeans and baggy (2)............................ all the time. I don't like (3)............................ clothes. I go for well-cut clothes in (4)............................ like silk or cotton.'

1	A	firm	B	close	C tight
2	A	scarves	B	hats	C sweaters
3	A	careless	B	scruffy	C disordered
4	A	fabrics	B	substances	C cloths

2 Commonly confused words
Complete the sentences with the correct word(s). Use each word once only.

1 number / size / figure
a Yes, we have that dress in black. What .... are you?
b We only have a limited .... of tracksuits in stock.
c She has such a wonderful .... because she's always at the gym.

2 suit / fit / match
a That hat doesn't .... you. It's too old-fashioned.
b I need a white handbag to .... my new white dress.
c I must have put on weight. These trousers don't .... me any more.

3 dress / get dressed / wear
a Come on, ...! You can't stay in bed all day!
b How do you normally .... for work?
c You can't possibly .... that skirt to the party. It's dirty.

4 try on / put on / have on
a It's raining heavily outside, so .... your raincoat.
b Can I .... the coat in the shop window? How much is it?
c Are you sure you saw Peter? What kind of jacket did he ....?

5 take off / undo / loosen
a Do you want to .... your coat and put it over there?
b In the summer, I have to keep my tie on. I usually .... it a bit though.
c Can you help me .... the buttons on the back of my dress?

6 uniform / costume / suit
a What .... are you going to wear to the fancy-dress party?
b As a soldier, you have to wear a .... at all times.
c When I worked for that company, I refused to wear a ....

3 Exam practice: word formation (Paper 3 Part 3)

Read the text below. Use the word given in capitals below the text to form a word that fits in the space in the same line. There is an example at the beginning **(0)**.

FANCY DRESS

At some point in our lives most of us will receive an **(0)** ___invitation___ to a fancy-dress party. What would your **(1)** _____ be? Clearly, some people get very excited at the prospect of dressing up in **(2)** _____ clothes, and they will immediately start thinking about their **(3)** _____ of costume. These people will **(4)** _____ invest quite a lot of money and effort in making sure that they make the best possible **(5)** _____ on the night. Others are likely to be less **(6)** _____ with the idea of changing their normal appearance and these people might get **(7)** _____ about what to wear for quite different reasons. Nobody wants to look **(8)** _____ , so don't go as James Bond if you don't have the style and **(9)** _____ to carry it off. Much better to wear the silliest **(10)** _____ imaginable and go prepared to join in the fun.

(0)	INVITE	**(6)**	COMFORT
(1)	REACT	**(7)**	ANXIETY
(2)	USUAL	**(8)**	FOOL
(3)	CHOOSE	**(9)**	ELEGANT
(4)	PROBABLE	**(10)**	FIT
(5)	IMPRESS		

Language development 2
Speculation and deduction ▶ CB page 103

1 Speculation and deduction: present
a For each sentence below, decide if the speaker means:

A I'm certain it's true.
B I'm certain it's not true.
C I'm not sure if it's true.

EXAMPLE: I think the library might be closed today. ___C___

1 That dress you want must be very expensive if it has a designer label. _____
2 She hasn't answered the phone, so she might not be at home. _____
3 She must be Greek because her name is Papadopoulos. _____
4 They didn't come tonight. They could be watching TV, I suppose. _____
5 Peter can't be ill because I saw him playing tennis this morning. _____
6 They are laughing a lot next door. They must be having a good time. _____
7 The ticket couldn't be that expensive. I expect they've made a mistake. _____

b Complete the sentences using *might, might not, may, may not, must* or *can't* and the verb in brackets. You need to use the continuous form (modal verb + *be* + *-ing*) in two of the sentences.

EXAMPLE: John didn't come to class today. He ___might be___ (*be*) ill, I suppose, or just bored.

1 This scarf _____ (*belong*) to Stella. She hates black.
2 Tell Maria which restaurant you plan to take her to on her birthday. She _____ (*like*) Chinese food.
3 You've been working hard all day. You _____ (*be*) exhausted!
4 John _____ (*have*) that book already. Why don't you give him a ring to check?
5 This bag is very cheap. It _____ (*be*) a genuine Gucci handbag.
6 There's a lot of music and laughter coming from next door. They _____ (*have*) a party.
7 I wonder why they are so late? They _____ (*try*) to find somewhere to park, I suppose.

2 Speculation and deduction: past

Rewrite the following sentences using *might (not) have, must have* or *can't have*.

1 I'm sure Claudia was upset when she discovered that someone from the party had taken her coat.
Claudia ....

2 It's possible that the person who took it didn't realise it was the wrong one.
The person who took it ....

3 I'm quite sure Anna didn't take it because I saw her go home early.
Anna ....

4 Rachel is the same size as Claudia, so maybe she took it.
Rachel is the same size as Claudia, so she
....

5 It was a fur coat, so it's certain it was worth a lot of money.
It was a fur coat, so it ....

6 I'm sure her father wasn't very pleased when she told him about it.
Her father ....

3 Choosing the correct present or past form.

Some of the sentences below contain errors with modal verbs. Tick (✔) the correct sentences. Correct the ones with mistakes.

EXAMPLE: Why is Peter wearing a pullover on such a hot day? He must ~~to~~ be very hot.

1 You shouldn't phone Alex at this time, because he could be asleep.

2 Mr Dickens looks very smart these days. He must find a new job.

3 Simon's car is not here, so he must have left for work.

4 Tina can't have been paid £200 for that dress – it doesn't even fit her!

5 The neighbours are shouting at each other again. They must have another argument!

6 It can't have been raining all night because the road is almost dry.

7 Keith is late, isn't he? He may be do overtime at the office, I suppose.

8 Emma looks very unhappy after her shopping trip. She may not found a wedding dress that she liked.

4 Exam practice: multiple-choice cloze (Paper 3 Part 1)

Read the text below and decide which answer (**A, B, C** or **D**) best fits each gap. There is an example at the beginning (**0**).

A DESIGNER'S TASTE

I am a fashion designer by (**0**) ...A..... Each year I produce my own (**1**) .... of new clothes for young people to wear, which I present to the world in a fashion show in London. Although I like the outfits that I design, and I feel very proud when my shows get good (**2**) .... in the press, the clothes are quite (**3**) .... the things I would choose to wear myself. (**4**) .... , some people think it's surprising that the clothes I find most comfortable are not currently fashionable at all. I get (**5**) .... pleasure, for example, out of what are (**6**) .... 'vintage clothes', especially those designed by the great fashion houses of the past. I (**7**) .... a big thrill from imagining who might have worn them in the past and what their history might be. Some of my coats and dresses are quite valuable, so they must have been worn by quite famous people, but I don't know this for (**8**) .... Although they are really a piece of history, in my (**9**) .... vintage clothes should be worn, not hung on the wall or put in a museum. Some people have the (**10**) .... that I buy old clothes so that I can use them as a (**11**) .... of inspiration for my own work. But this is not the (**12**) .... It's just a hobby really.

0	**A**	profession	**B**	work	**C**	employment	**D**	job
1	**A**	arrangement	**B**	collection	**C**	gathering	**D**	composition
2	**A**	replies	**B**	revisions	**C**	reviews	**D**	receipts
3	**A**	unlike	**B**	dissimilar	**C**	different	**D**	opposite
4	**A**	Elsewhere	**B**	Despite	**C**	Otherwise	**D**	Indeed
5	**A**	large	**B**	great	**C**	wide	**D**	deep
6	**A**	titled	**B**	known	**C**	called	**D**	referred
7	**A**	have	**B**	take	**C**	find	**D**	get
8	**A**	sure	**B**	real	**C**	true	**D**	fact
9	**A**	belief	**B**	feeling	**C**	opinion	**D**	attitude
10	**A**	impression	**B**	conclusion	**C**	judgement	**D**	assumption
11	**A**	spring	**B**	means	**C**	source	**D**	way
12	**A**	matter	**B**	case	**C**	issue	**D**	event

Reading Gapped text

(Paper 1 Part 2)

1 Before you read

Look at the title and subheading of the article opposite. Think about the topic and decide if these statements are *True* or *False* for you.

1 We judge other people according to the way they look.
2 It's a good idea to look at people in magazines and try to dress the same way.
3 It's important to choose the right clothes for different occasions.
4 Most people have a favourite style of clothing.
5 We should not be frightened to try new colours even if we are not sure we like them.
6 It doesn't matter if our clothes are a size too big.
7 What we say is more important than how we look.

2 Skimming

Skim the text and look at your answers in Exercise 1 again. Did you agree with the writer of the article?

3 Gapped text

a Read the first paragraph and sentence H (in gap 1). Which words in sentence H link to the highlighted section before the gap?
Which ideas in sentence H are contrasted in the highlighted sections after the gap?

b Read the rest of the text carefully. Make sure you understand the main information.

c For each gap, do the following.
  • Read the text before and after the gap and think about the type of information which is missing.
  • Look for a sentence in the box which talks about this topic area.
  • Choose the correct answer by checking the grammatical and lexical links between the base text and the key sentence. Look out for pronouns, synonyms, etc.
  • Cross off each sentence as you use it, but be prepared to look again when you check your answers.

d Read the text again with your answers to check that it makes sense.

4 Vocabulary: phrasal verbs and idiomatic expressions

Match the verbs and expressions from the text in A to the definitions in B.

A	B
1 pick up on (option H)	a take or choose something quickly
2 dwell on (line 22)	b influence or control
3 dictate (line 31)	c notice
4 catch someone's eye (line 48)	d think or talk for too long about something unpleasant
5 grab (line 67)	e make someone notice something

You are going to read a magazine article about personal appearance. Seven sentences have been removed from the article. Choose from the sentences **A–H** the one which fits each gap. There is one extra sentence you do not need to use.

A Look at these items and ask yourself what they have in common.

B A better idea is to stand in front of a full-length mirror and be honest with yourself about what you see.

C Sometimes we buy these ill-fitting clothes without thinking.

D But once you've got used to this change, it will be easier to make those difficult decisions.

E It may be fun to cross these sometimes, but do take care not to go too far all at once.

F However, there's no need to abandon your individual taste completely.

G You'll look better and you'll feel a better person all round.

H Other people then pick up on this outward confidence and respond positively towards us.

HELP
➤ Sentence A
Look for what 'these items' could be.
➤ Sentence B
Look for a bad idea in the text to contrast this with.
➤ Sentence E
Look in the text for something which you 'cross'.

Make your image work for you

Our appearance conveys a message to everyone we come into contact with.
Maybe it's time to pay a bit more attention to it.

When we meet people for the first time, we often make decisions about them based entirely on how they look. And, of course it's
5 something which works both ways, for we too are being judged on our appearance. When we look good, we feel good, which in turn leads to a more self-assured
10 manner. **1** **H** Undoubtedly, it's what's inside that's important, but sometimes we can send out the wrong signals, and so get a negative reaction, simply
15 by wearing inappropriate clothing or not spending enough time thinking about how others will see us.

For example, people often make the mistake of trying to look like someone else; perhaps someone they've seen in a magazine, but this is usually a
20 disaster as we all have our own characteristics. **2** There is no need to dwell on your faults when you do this as we all have good points and bad points – think instead about the best way to emphasise the good ones.

25 When selecting your clothes each day, think about who you're likely to meet, where you're going to be spending most of your time and what tasks you are likely to perform. Clearly, on a practical level, some outfits will be more appropriate to different sorts of
30 activity and this will dictate your choice to an extent. **3** After all, if you dress to please somebody else's idea of what looks good, you may end up feeling uncomfortable and not quite yourself.

35 But to know your own mind, you have to get to know yourself. What do you truly feel good in? There are probably a few favourite clothes that you wear a lot – most people wear 20 per cent of their wardrobe 80 per cent of the time. **4**

40 Are they neat and tidy, loose and flowing? Then look at the things hanging in your wardrobe that you don't wear and ask yourself why. Go through a

few magazines and catalogues and mark
45 the things that catch your eye. Is there a common theme?

Some colours bring your natural colouring
50 to life and others can give us a washed-out appearance. Try out new ones by all means, but remember
55 that dressing in bright colours when you really like subtle neutral tones, or vice versa, will make you feel self-conscious and uncomfortable. You know deep down where your own taste boundaries lie.
60 **5**

So, you've chosen an outfit that matches your style, your personality, your shape and your colouring. But is it really the right size? If something is too tight or too loose, you won't
65 achieve the desired effect, and no matter what other qualities it has, it won't improve your appearance or your confidence. **6** For example, some people who dislike shopping grab the first thing they see, or prefer to use mail-order
70 or the Internet. In all cases, if it doesn't fit perfectly, don't buy it, because the finer details are just as important as the overall style.

Reappraising your image isn't selfish because everyone who comes into contact with you will
75 benefit. **7** And if in doubt, you only need to read Professor Albert Mehrabian's book *Silent Messages* to remind yourself how important outward appearances are. His research showed that the impact we make on each other depends
80 55 per cent on how we look and behave, 38 per cent on how we speak and only 7 per cent on what we actually say. So, whatever stage you are at in your life, whatever role you play, isn't it time you made the most of yourself?

8A Relationships

Vocabulary ▶ CB pages 108–109

1 Vivid vocabulary

a Complete the diagrams with these words and expressions from the text on CB page 109.

- stare at someone
- give someone a nod
- clutch something
- get to your feet
- dash
- tap someone on the shoulder
- give something a kick
- slip (on a wet surface)
- push something into someone's hand

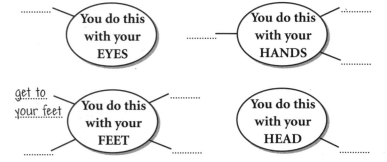

You do this with your EYES

You do this with your HANDS

get to your feet

You do this with your FEET

You do this with your HEAD

b Now add these words and expressions to the diagrams in Exercise 1a.

- wink at someone
- shake someone's ...
- grab something
- tap your ...
- shake your ...
- trip over something
- glance at someone
- wave at someone
- jump up

c Complete the spaces with verbs from Exercise 1a and b in the correct form. Use only one word in each space. Then put the story into the correct order.

- □ a He turned round, looked at her and (1)............... his head.
- [1] b On the bus home one day, Rachel noticed an art student nervously (2)............... his portfolio.
- □ c The student was looking out of the window, so she (3)............... him lightly on the shoulder. 'Remember me?' she said.
- □ d She knew it was rude but she couldn't help (4)............... at him: he seemed so familiar.
- □ e Hearing the words sun and beach in one of the songs, she suddenly remembered. She took off the headphones and (5)............... up.
- □ f The bus stopped suddenly and Rachel (6)............... his arm. 'We met on holiday in Spain,' she said. 'We said we'd never forget each other!'
- □ g The student (7)............... at Rachel once or twice, but showed no sign of recognition.
- □ h She put on her Walkman and started to (8)............... her feet to the rhythm of the music.

2 Collocations

Write an appropriate verb from the list in each space below. It must collocate with all the words and phrases in the set. Use each verb once only.

fall   have   be   break   get   celebrate   go   make

1 .... engaged/married/divorced/on well with someone
2 .... in love/excited/happy/confused
3 .... in love/asleep/out with a friend (over something)
4 .... a wedding anniversary/a birthday/ an engagement
5 .... a date/a relationship/a baby/an argument/problems
6 .... friends/up with someone (after an argument)/plans/a mistake
7 .... out with someone/on a date/on a honeymoon
8 .... off an engagement/up a relationship/up with someone

3 Topic: relationships

a Read the comments below. Complete the sentences with words from the list. Use plural forms where necessary.

best friend   partner   acquaintance   workmate   fiancée   colleague   flatmate   relative

1 My family is very big – two brothers, three sisters and lots of cousins. I have some .... in Australia, but we're not very close. We send each other cards on special occasions, that's all.

2 I share an apartment with another student from the university. My .... is a bit older than me but we have a lot in common. I don't think I could share with someone who was totally different from me.

3 I don't know Tracy very well, so she's an .... rather than a friend. I get the impression that she looks down on me because my family isn't as well off as hers.

4 I've known my .... ever since we were children. I've always adored her. I felt so happy when we got engaged six months ago. The wedding's going to be next month.

5 I work in a small office. I have known most of my .... for over five years and we see eye to eye on most things.

6 Yvonne was my .... at school. We did absolutely everything together. *I really admired her* – she knew exactly what she wanted in life and was willing to work hard to get it.

7 Unfortunately, Dennis was my .... in yesterday's tennis match. *I can't stand him* – he's so rude and uncooperative. Roger and Bill beat us really easily.

8 During the summer holidays I had a job picking fruit on a farm. It was hard work, but my .... were friendly and *I grew very fond of them*.

b Look at the words in italics in each sentence in Exercise 3a. Tick (✓) the expressions which describe positive feelings and put a cross (✗) for those that describe negative feelings.

c In your notebook, write short descriptions of members of your family and friends.

4 **Exam practice: multiple-choice cloze** (Paper 3 Part 1)

> Read the text below and decide which answer **A**, **B**, **C** or **D** best fits each space. There is an example at the beginning (**0**).
>
> **0 A** got   **B** held   **C** set   **D** joined

MY MOST EMBARRASSING MOMENT

When I was 18, I (**0**) .....A..... a job with a television company. I was in a small office with three other girls, and there was a boy working upstairs we all (**1**)............ . He seemed very cool and sophisticated because, (**2**)............ us, he actually got to meet the stars. None of us thought we (**3**)............ a chance with him, but we used to try to (**4**)............ him up whenever he paid a (**5**)............ to our department. Then one day, (**6**)............ unexpectedly, he invited me to a big charity dinner at an expensive hotel. I couldn't believe my (**7**)............. . All the big stars were going to be there, so I had to look my best. I (**8**)............ spending a fortune on a new dress, shoes and hairstyle.

As we walked into the hotel, cameras were flashing and I felt like a real celebrity. We went up a long, wide flight of stairs, just like in a (**9**)............ from the movies. But as we (**10**)............ the top, one of my new leather-soled shoes slipped on the red carpet. I fell backwards and went head over (**11**)............ down the stairs, landing in a heap at the bottom. I was unhurt, but (**12**)............ shaken and extremely embarrassed. My partner took one look at me and decided he had better take me home!

1 A	approved	**B**	fancied	**C**	regarded	**D**	appealed
2 A	opposite	**B**	instead	**C**	different	**D**	unlike
3 A	stood	**B**	kept	**C**	ran	**D**	carried
4 A	speak	**B**	chat	**C**	talk	**D**	gossip
5 A	tour	**B**	trip	**C**	stay	**D**	visit
6 A	more	**B**	even	**C**	quite	**D**	much
7 A	break	**B**	fortune	**C**	chance	**D**	luck
8 A	brought about	**B**	called for	**C**	ended up	**D**	went through
9 A	part	**B**	scene	**C**	play	**D**	show
10 A	managed	**B**	achieved	**C**	arrived	**D**	reached
11 A	elbows	**B**	knees	**C**	heels	**D**	feet
12 A	badly	**B**	poorly	**C**	toughly	**D**	hardly

Language development 1
Reported speech
▶ CB pages 110–111, GR pages 193–194

1 **Reporting exact words**
The following sentences have mistakes with the *verb tense* (T) or *word order* (WO), or the *wrong word* (WW) is used. Correct the mistakes and write T, WO or WW.
EXAMPLE: Tina told me that she ~~has spent~~ three months at a college in the UK last year. ..spent (T)..

1 I asked her why had she gone there. ....

2 She replied that she wants to improve her English. ....

3 I asked her if she will go to London with me in the summer. ....

4 She said that she had spent some time there the last year and wasn't keen. ....

5 I asked her why didn't she want to go there again. ....

6 She said me that it had rained all the time she was there. ....

7 I said that we could bring umbrellas with us. ....

2 **Reporting verbs**
a Mark the correct verb in each pair.
1 My teacher *advised / recommended* me to go abroad to study.

2 Peter *told / said* to me that he wanted to get married and settle down.

3 I *denied / refused* to tell Paul what I had done the previous evening.

4 Julia *admitted / informed* that she had been out with Ben.

5 My mother *blamed / accused* me of breaking her favourite vase.

6 My girlfriend *insisted / agreed* to come to the airport with me.

7 Sandra *threatened / warned* to tell Richard what I had said.

8 Tania *suggested / persuaded* going for a pizza after the film.

b Match the sentences (1–10) to an appropriate reporting verb in a–j and rewrite them in reported speech.

☐ 1 Would you like to come to my house for lunch?
a 2 I'm really sorry I missed your birthday party.
☐ 3 I will definitely be at the wedding.
☐ 4 Don't go out with Ken because he's dangerous!
☐ 5 I'll help you write the invitations.
☐ 6 If you go to the Oasis Club again, I'll tell your father.
☐ 7 I really didn't invite your ex-boyfriend to my party.
☐ 8 Why don't you ask Dave out on a date?
☐ 9 I think you should break off your engagement.
☐ 10 You told me a lie!

a Anna invited __me to go to her house for lunch__ .
b Ruth suggested ....
c Denise offered ....
d Eve denied ....
e Keith threatened ....
f Maureen advised ....
g Sue apologised ....
h Rob accused ....
i Richard promised ....
j Maria warned ....

3 Key word transformations

Complete the second sentence so that it has a similar meaning to the first sentence, using the word given. Do not change the word given. Use between two and five words, including the word given.

1 'I won't tell anyone what you did,' George said.
   promised
   George .... what I had done.
2 'I'll buy the theatre tickets,' Peter said. **insisted**
   Peter .... the theatre tickets.
3 'Can I have a piece of cake?' Doug asked. **whether**
   Doug asked .... another piece of cake.
4 'Why didn't you arrive on time, John?' Sally asked.
   why
   Sally asked John .... on time.
5 'You've broken my watch, Simon!' Alan said. **accused**
   Alan .... watch.
6 'Don't leave the mountain footpath, Paul!' Patricia said. **warned**
   Patricia .... leave the mountain footpath.
7 'Would you like to go to a rock concert this weekend, David?' Maria asked. **invited**
   Maria .... go to a rock concert that weekend.
8 'We haven't reserved you a seat, I'm afraid,' the airline representative said. **admitted**
   The airline representative ....
   reserved me a seat.
9 'I'm sorry about the mistake I made,' John said.
   apologised
   John .... a mistake.

10 'Let's go to the cinema,' Alice said. **suggested**
   Alice .... a film.

4 Exam practice: open cloze (Paper 3 Part 2)

Read the text below and think of the word which best fits each space. Use only **one** word in each space. There is an example at the beginning **(0)**.

BLIND DATE

I first met my girlfriend Charlotte through what
(0)............ is .... known as a dating agency. We had each sent in our personal details
(1)............................. inclusion in the agency's database. The agency decided that we were a good match **(2)**............................. paper and put us in touch with each **(3)**............................. . Our first meeting took **(4)**............................. in a restaurant in London. It was **(5)**............................. people call a blind date, and **(6)**............................. of us had ever been on **(7)**............................. before, although we didn't realise this at the time.

My first impression was that Charlotte looked very nice, much prettier **(8)**............................. in her photo, and she was smartly dressed. She told me she had come straight from the office and there hadn't been time to change into something more casual. At first, it was quite difficult to find something to talk about apart **(9)**.............................
our jobs. But then Charlotte asked me what my hobbies **(10)**............................. and we found we had quite a few interests in common.

Although I had gone on the date with an open mind, I didn't really expect it to lead to a long-term relationship. So I wasn't sure
(11)............................. to suggest meeting again or not. In the end, I found enough courage to ask Charlotte and I'm glad I **(12)**............................. , because we've been going out regularly ever since.

Writing Essay (Paper 2 Part 2)

▶ CB pages 112–113, WR page 203

Exam strategy

It's important to plan an essay in advance, so that the argument is organised in the most logical way. Don't include too many points but make sure you:
- support your points with reasons or examples
- use linking words to show the connection between your ideas.

1 Understand the task

a Read the task below and answer the questions.
1 Who will read the essay?
2 What style should you use?

b Note down two advantages of living at home and two disadvantages.

Advantages	Disadvantages
....	....
....	....

> After a class discussion on how young people learn to be independent, your teacher has asked you to write a composition, giving your opinions on the following statement.
>
> *Young people should live with their parents for as long as they want.*
>
> Write your **essay** in **120–180** words in an appropriate style.

2 Read a sample answer

a Read the following essay which a student wrote. For each space (1–6), cross out the one linking expression A, B or C, which is not possible.

1	**A** However	**B** Furthermore	**C** Nevertheless
2	**A** Therefore	**B** For instance	**C** For example
3	**A** Despite this	**B** As a result	**C** Consequently
4	**A** However	**B** On the other hand	**C** Even so
5	**A** Similarly	**B** In other words	**C** That is to say
6	**A** Nevertheless	**B** As a consequence	**C** On the other hand

b Read the composition again and complete the paragraph plan the writer followed.

Paragraph 1: Introduction ....

Paragraph 2: Advantages of living at home
Advantage(s): ....
Example(s): ....

Paragraph 3: ....
Disadvantage(s): ....
Example(s): ....

Paragraph 4: Conclusion ....

Nowadays, it is common for young people to continue to live with their parents until their mid- or late-twenties. (1)................ , many people think that this is not a good idea and that children should be encouraged to leave home much earlier.

There are many reasons why young people want to continue to live with their parents. The main reason is that they feel comfortable at home. (2)................ , they do not need to cook, wash their clothes or pay rent. This last point is important, because life today has become very expensive. (3)................ , it is difficult to live well if you do not earn a high salary.

(4)................ , many young people say that they only became mature when they left home. Living away from their parents when they went to college or started work forced them to be independent. (5)................ , they had to start to think for themselves and to face problems without the help of their parents.

In my view, young people should be able to stay with their parents if they want to. (6)................ , they should understand that leaving home would be very good for them.

3 Features of an essay

Read the list of features that a good essay should have. Which features does the sample answer have? Tick (✓) them.

A good essay:

is divided into three or four paragraphs. ☐

has an introduction that makes a general statement about the topic. ☐

supports the main points with details. ☐

uses linking words to connect the ideas. ☐

states the writer's view in the conclusion. ☐

uses a neutral style consistently. ☐

is between 120 and 180 words. ☐

4 Do the task

Write your own answer to the task in your notebook.

Listening Multiple matching
(Paper 4 Part 3)

1 Before you listen
a Read the instructions for the listening task opposite. What are the speakers going to talk about?

b Read the statements A–F carefully and mark the key information in each.

2 🎧 Multiple matching
a Listen to the recording and focus on each speaker's main point. Match the main points with the closest option (A–F).

b Listen again to check your answers. Make sure that the ideas expressed in the recording match the options exactly.

3 🎧 Paraphrasing
Listen again. Complete the phrases in the recording that express the key words in each statement A–F.

A *the way people regarded us*:
… but people just .... us together
… people still got us .... , which
used to .... me a lot.

C *frequent disagreements*:
we used to .... at least once a day.
We even had .... , too.

D *similar tastes*:
Emily and I were very much in ....
with each other. … We'd have the same
.... about most things … because
we were a ....

E *glad not to spend too much time*:
… we tried to keep .... each other's
....

F *let me down occasionally*:
… she didn't always .... my
.... …

You will hear five women talking about what it was like to grow up with a twin sister. For questions **1–5**, choose from the list **A–F** the statement which best matches what each person says. Use the letters only once. There is one extra letter which you do not need to use.

A The way people regarded us used to annoy me.	Speaker 1	1
B I always felt I was being compared to my sister.	Speaker 2	2
C I had frequent disagreements with my sister.	Speaker 3	3
D My sister and I had very similar tastes.	Speaker 4	4
E I was glad not to spend too much time with my sister.	Speaker 5	5
F My sister used to let me down occasionally.		

8B Hobbies

Vocabulary ▶ CB pages 114–115

1 Word formation

Exam strategy

In the word formation task (Paper 3 Part 5), you should not only decide what part of speech the word is (e.g. adjective, noun, verb, etc.), but also whether it is plural or negative.

Read these extracts about hobbies. Use the word given in capitals at the end of each sentence to form a word that fits in the space. You may need to make some words negative or plural.

1 Reading .... magazines, you'd think that celebrities like film stars, top models, etc. spend their whole non-working lives at parties. **WEEK**

2 But according to a new book, this is often far from the .... **TRUE**

3 We don't expect rock stars to enjoy doing things like collecting stamps, that people generally regard as really .... hobbies. **BORE**

4 Being a celebrity is all about image, and their fans have certain .... of these people. **EXPECT**

5 Jarvis Cocker, lead singer of rock band Pulp, spends a lot of time birdwatching – and he's not .... because quite a few rock stars collect things like old coins and matchboxes. **USUAL**

6 During my research I saw some very .... film stars doing crossword or jigsaw puzzles. **GLAMOUR**

2 Talking about hobbies

Exam strategy

In Paper 5 Part 1, the examiner may ask if you have any hobbies and how you became interested in them. Make sure you are familiar with the vocabulary you would need to describe your hobby effectively.

a **What hobby is each speaker opposite describing? Choose from the list below. There are two hobbies you do not need to use. Mark the words which help you decide.**
knitting   stamp collecting   train spotting
board games   chess   gardening
making models   birdwatching

b **In your notebook, write a short description of a hobby you have, or have had in the past.**

> I started doing it when I was a child. I used to buy plastic kits. The only thing you needed was a tube of glue and some paints. Nowadays, I make all the parts myself from wood or metal.

1 ....

> I've had this hobby all my life. You don't need any special equipment – just albums to put your collection in and a magnifying glass. I love all the different colours and designs from around the world.

2 ....

> It's exciting when you see species you know are rare. You have to try to get as close as you can without making a sound. A good pair of binoculars is essential.

3 ....

> Since we moved to a bigger house, I've been doing a lot of it. It keeps me fit. I have a number of tools, such as forks and spades, and a lawn mower, which I use every weekend.

4 ....

> You have to keep a record of everything that comes into the station. It can get a bit cold waiting on platforms all day, so you need a warm coat or anorak.

5 ....

> My sister and I have six or seven different ones. It's much better than playing cards. I love the moment when you throw the dice – you never know what's going to happen.

6 ....

3 Paraphrasing

What items of clothing or equipment in Exercise 2a are these students describing?

1   I really like cutting the grass in the garden with – it's a sort of machine, but I don't know what's it's called in English. ....

2   When I was a kid, I loved to throw the two – you know, they're like little wooden boxes. I got really excited if I got two sixes. ....

3   I used to spend all my time sticking pieces of wood together with – a liquid – like toothpaste. ....

4   Every weekend I put on my – what's it called? – it's like a short coat – it stops you getting cold and wet – and go with friends to the airport. ....

5   My father bought me a – you know, a big round glass which makes things bigger – and I looked at everything through it. ....

6   On my birthday I was given a – I don't know what the word is – you use it for looking at things which are far away – you use both eyes like this. ....

4 Phrasal verbs and expressions

Mark the correct word in each pair in the text.

Do you want an exciting new hobby?

Do you **(1)** *spend / pay* a lot of time watching TV in the evenings? When you need to wind **(2)** *up / down* at the end of a hard day, do you put your **(3)** *feet / legs* up in front of 'the box'? It's not very creative, is it?

Why not take **(4)** *up / out* a new and exciting hobby? The ancient Japanese art of origami – folding paper to make attractive objects – is a fascinating way of **(5)** *passing / occupying* the time. All you need are some coloured paper squares, a pair of scissors and our easy-to-follow, step-by-step guide.

If you are keen **(6)** *at / on* making things with your hands, then origami is for you! Groups of enthusiasts are springing **(7)** *up / over* everywhere. Reach for the telephone and **(8)** *make / give* us a call now!

0118 4960009

Language development 2

Ways of expressing ability ▶ CB page 118

1   *can, could, be able to*

Read the text and complete the spaces with the correct form of *can, could* or *be able to*. You may need to make the verb negative.

Vanessa Freeman talks about her new-found passion – scuba diving.

I (1) .... swim since I was a teenager and scuba diving is something I've always wanted to do. So last summer I went on a four-day Ocean Frontiers training course in the Cayman Islands. I had a fantastic time! I'd encourage anyone who is interested in (2) .... dive to go on this course.

On the first day, we met our diving instructor, Neil, who showed us a video and gave us a test. I (3) .... answer all the questions, because I'd carefully studied the training manual they'd sent me before the course.

After lunch, we went to the swimming pool so that we (4) .... start to put the theory into practice. Neil showed us all the equipment and told us to breathe normally under the water. At first, I panicked and (5) .... breathe at all, but it soon became much easier.

In the pool, we learnt several skills. One of the most difficult was achieving 'buoyancy'. It is very important for divers (6) .... float in the water, so we spent a lot of time learning how to do this.

In the days that followed, we went diving in the sea. It was truly amazing. We soon found that we (7) .... move around easily in the sea, gazing at the colourful sea life around us.

'In the future, you (8) .... dive anywhere in the world you want,' Neil told us at the end of the course. 'Time has been short, so I (9) .... show you how to take photos underwater or how to dive in a wreck. But those are things you (10) .... learn whenever you want. You are now certified divers. Congratulations!'

2 Other ways of expressing ability

Complete each sentence using the verb in brackets and an appropriate verb from the list. Make any changes necessary.

win   use   beat   climb   play   light   speak   ~~ride~~

EXAMPLE: I'd love to cycle around Europe but I
.... don't know how to ride .... a bike. (*not know*)

1   Although it was very windy on the beach, we
.... a fire. (*manage*)

2   Although his opponent was a better chess player, Jason .... him in the first game. (*succeed*)

3   Can I come with you to Paris? I'll be useful because I .... French. (*know*)

4   Dave is an inexperienced mountaineer; I don't think he   .... the South Face next month. (*manage*)

5   Sue was an excellent dancer and
.... all the prizes at the competition. (*succeed*)

6   Gill had a bad cold, but she still
.... the violin beautifully on Saturday evening. (*manage*)

7   I wanted to take some photos yesterday, but I
.... my father's new digital camera. (*not know*)

3 Key word transformations

Complete the second sentence so that it has a similar meaning to the first sentence, using the word given. Do not change the word given. Use between two and five words, including the word given.

1   I was unable to go to my sister's wedding because I had flu. **could**
I had flu so .... to my sister's wedding.

2   Can you take part in the chess tournament next week? **able**
Will .... part in the chess tournament next week?

3   Eve is a strong swimmer, but she can't swim across that lake. **capable**
Although Eve is a strong swimmer, she
.... across that lake.

4   Amanda is not a very good pianist. **know**
Amanda doesn't .... the piano very well.

5   My sister was the best singer in the college choir. **could**
Nobody in the college choir
.... than my sister.

6   I can probably fix your car, even though I don't have the right tools. **able**
I might .... your car, even though I don't have the right tools.

7   How were you able to make such a tiny model train? **manage**
How .... such a tiny model train?

8   My brother managed to pass his driving test first time. **succeeded**
My brother .... his driving test first time.

9   I couldn't take any photos at the party because my camera was broken. **able**
Since my camera was broken I .... any photos at the party.

10 Despite the wind and rain, the climbers were able to put up their tent. **managed**
Despite the wind and rain, the climbers
.... their tent.

4 Exam practice: open cloze (Paper 3 Part 2)

Read the text below and think of the word which best fits each space. Use only **one** word in each space. There is an example at the beginning (**0**).

COLLECTING THINGS

A new book (**0**).......... has .... just come out with the title *To Have and to Hold*. On the cover, it calls itself a history of collecting and collectors, but actually it goes much further (**1**).................. that. As well as telling us about great collectors of the past, it also investigates the reasons why people collect things.

In past centuries, only wealthy people (**2**).................. afford to travel and most collections started out with just a (**3**).................. strange objects which had been bought on trips abroad. In the days before photography and television, this was the only (**4**).................. people could see objects from other cultures. Gradually, museums were established so that ordinary people would be (**5**).................. to see these treasures too.

These days, everyone seems to be (**6**).................. collector. The book describes collectors (**7**).................. the 'archaeologists of the present' and it contains some fascinating interviews. (**8**).................. instance, there's the man (**9**).................. has 50,000 items of food packaging stored in his home, and the teenager willing to spend large sums of money on the rare *Star Wars* toy that (**10**).................. complete her collection. In explaining (**11**).................. we collect things, however, the book sees no difference (**12**).................. great art collectors and teenagers collecting items related to their favourite pop stars. The social and psychological explanations for collecting, it says, are much the same.

Reading
Multiple matching (Paper 1 Part 3)

1 Before you read
Look at the title and subheadings of the article opposite. Answer these questions.
1 What job does each person do?
2 What kind of hobby do you think each person has?

2 Skimming
Skim the text to check your ideas in Exercise 1.

3 Multiple matching
a Look at the example (0) in the exam task opposite. Mark the part of text D that tells you this is the answer.

b For each question, do the following.
- Read the question carefully and mark key words so that you know what you are looking for.
- Scan the texts quickly to find the section which deals with the idea in the question. Look for parallel phrases and parts of sentences.
- When you have found the relevant part, read it carefully to make sure it has exactly the same meaning as the question. (The same topics and vocabulary may appear in more than one text, so be careful that the meaning matches the question exactly.)
- When you find the answer, mark it and write the question number on the text, so that you can check it later.
- If you can't find the information, put a question mark next to the question and go back to it later. When you've answered all the questions, you can look again at the parts of the texts where you haven't found answers.

You are going to read a magazine article about four people and their hobbies. For questions **1–15**, choose from the people (**A–D**). Some of the people may be chosen more than once. There is an example at the beginning (**0**).

Which person says that their hobby

is too expensive to do in some places?	**0**	**D**
has to conform to certain fixed regulations?	**1**	
used to be associated with a particular type of person?	**2**	
produces different results depending on the location?	**3**	
fits in well with other commitments?	**4**	
has become easier thanks to recent improvements in the equipment?	**5**	
involves him/her in learning by watching experts in the activity?	**6**	
is associated with a certain type of clothing?	**7**	
sometimes provokes negative reactions in people?	**8**	
has not always interested him/her so much?	**9**	
has advantages over another similar hobby?	**10**	
requires the clever combination of certain materials?	**11**	
also provides some of his/her income?	**12**	
requires participants to have formal qualifications?	**13**	
grew out of a regular family custom?	**14**	
is a thrilling experience when it goes well?	**15**	

HELP
➤ **Question 1**
Which hobby is likely to involve *regulations*? Look for another word with the same meaning. Remember that the text will not use the same words as the question.
➤ **Question 4**
A *commitment* is something you have to do, which stops you doing something else. Which text mentions this?

Me and my passion

Four people talk about their hobbies

A Katie Holleran: accountant

When you mention windsurfing to people, they generally imagine suntanned 20-year-olds. But the sport
5 has matured since it started in the 1960s, and so have its participants. Any reasonably fit person can do it, and age isn't a barrier. Beginners
10 need enough strength in their arms to pull themselves back up onto the board after falling off. At first, you do spend a lot of time in the water, but it's worth it for the feeling of excitement you get when
15 you're moving along successfully – that's fantastic.

In the early days, sails and boards were made of heavy materials like polyethylene, and the sport was very physical. But improved technology has changed all that. And you don't have to live by the sea – 50 per
20 cent of windsurfing takes place on inland lakes and reservoirs. I used to have a boat, but with that you always need other people to help you. And you're not allowed to take a boat on some lakes, whereas you can windsurf anywhere.

B Kevin Shaw: builder

25 It's become a tradition in our household that I make an Indian curry every Monday evening. I wanted to learn how to make my
30 dishes more authentic, so I signed up for a cookery course at a top Indian restaurant in London. Every time I go, I learn something
35 new and I'm now building up quite a repertoire of curry recipes.

Andy, the head chef, is also a qualified teacher, which is a big advantage of the course. He explains how the herbs, spices, oils and rice used in Indian cooking are
40 combined by experts to get subtle variations in flavour. It's perfectly possible to have dishes which contain exactly the same ingredients, but you end up with something totally different depending on the methods used in the part of the country where it's prepared.
45 After all the theory, we go down to the kitchen to observe Andy and his team of highly-qualified chefs in action and then, of course, we get to sample the dishes we've learned to cook.

C Karen Hallstrom: salesperson

50 When I tell people I race vintage cars from the 1920s and 1930s, one question they're sure to ask is: 'Do you wear 1920s outfits too?'
55 'No,' is the polite version of my answer. I have to wear fireproof overalls and a helmet in order to meet modern safety laws, I'm
60 afraid. Things have changed

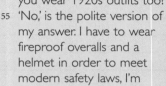

in other ways since the old days, too. To be allowed to race my cars, I had to pass both written and practical tests. That wasn't difficult, but then vintage cars aren't a novelty to me: they were part of my upbringing. I used
65 to spend hours, bored stiff, with my fingers stuck in my ears while my father watched races at the local motor-racing track. I said it was the last thing I'd ever do. But when I was a bit older, I too fell in love with cars, first driving a vintage model at age 17. Then, later, a boyfriend
70 with a boat got me interested in sailing, much to the horror of my family! But it didn't last, and somehow I've always come back to cars.

D Joe Campilos: office worker

I'm lucky because, within reason, I can choose what
75 hours I do at the office and this means I have time to combine it with my real passion, which is jazz music. Every weekend, and
80 sometimes on Fridays as well, we play on the street. Not in the main square, as you need to buy a licence

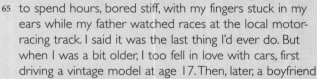

for that and it's a bit pricey, but in various places around
85 the city where there are no regulations.

People sometimes complain because they think we're beggars, but that's not fair. Although we do accept money, because it's the accepted custom, that's not why we're there. It's really a kind of advertisement – if
90 somebody likes what they hear, then they can hire us. We get to do weddings, parties, that sort of thing, which gives us a bit of extra pocket money. Sometimes jazz clubs approach us, too. But it's never fame and fortune – and to tell you the truth, I like my life just the way it is.

81

MODULE 9 The consumer society

9A A matter of conscience

Vocabulary ▶ CB pages 122–123

1 Topic: charity work

a Complete the table.

Verb	Noun
donate	1 ....
distribute	2 ....
3	suffering
be poor	4 live in ....
5	a volunteer (= person)
6	information
support	7 ....
collect	8 ....
9	funds/funding
10	a contribution

b Match the verbs in A to the nouns in B to form common collocations.

A
1 take
2 raise
3 set up
4 collect
5 distribute
6 make
7 relieve
8 receive

B
a a donation (from)
b a charity/an organisation
c a contribution (to)
d measures/action
e poverty/suffering
f funds (for)
g money (in the street)
h leaflets/food/medicines

c Complete the advertisement with words from Exercises 1a and b in the correct form.

Will you help?

We are looking for (1).................. to help us (2)..................
funds for a new **Golden Age** Home for the old and homeless.
We can't offer you money, but we can offer you the chance to
(3).................. the suffering of many unfortunate older people.
By giving us a little of your time each week, you will be
(4).................. a valuable contribution to society.

The first **Golden Age** Home was (5).................. in
Cambridge in 1960. It was the idea of a group of students who
wanted to help old people living in real (6).................. . They
were not content just to talk about the problem – they were
determined to (7).................. action. Since then the organisation
has received thousands of pounds in (8).......................... from
the public and runs three homes in different cities. We need
YOU to go into the streets to (9).................. more money for
us. We also need you to (10).................. leaflets which both
inform people of the work we are doing and explain the need
for their help.

If you are aged between 18 and 50, please telephone
the following number: **01632 960008**

2 Phrasal verbs

a Match the sentence halves in A and B and mark the correct particle in each phrasal verb.

A
1 Don't expect her to make a donation! She's saving *up / on* for
2 Charity organisations, like other businesses, need to keep *off / up* with
3 I'll soon be able to pay *up / back*
4 We've recently set *up / off*
5 The Oxfam shop in our town is so busy it needs to take *up / on*
6 He went to the bank to take *out / off*
7 They are so well off, they were able to pay *for / off*
8 She took out her pen and wrote *down / out*

B
a the money I borrowed from you.
b some new members of staff.
c some money for his business trip.
d new developments in technology.
e a luxury cruise to the Bahamas.
f a business which employees only homeless people.
g a cheque for £5,000.
h their new car in cash.

b Write examples to show the meaning of the other verb + particle combination in each pair above. Use your dictionary to help you.

3 Topic: money
Put the letters in brackets in the correct order to complete the incomplete words.
1 I had to with draw.................. (*wrad*) £500 from my current ac.......................... (*tnouc*) to pay for my computer.
2 When Bob in.......................... (*tedireh*) money from his uncle, he decided to in.......................... (*stev*) half of it in property, and don.......................... (*eat*) the rest to an animal sanctuary.
3 Some friends of mine made a lot of money on the stock ma.......................... (*trek*) recently. I followed their advice and bought some sh.......................... (*ears*) myself.
4 A man who had a painting he thought was worth.......................... (*sels*) sold it at an au.......................... (*ticon*) yesterday for £20,000. He gave all the money to a charity for the blind.

82

5 My uncle runs a small mail order business, but the company's annual turn.................... (*rove*) has gone down. He is afraid that if the economy doesn't improve, he'll go bank.................... (*trup*).

6 The cost of li.................... (*ngiv*) has gone up dramatically. The government says that the rate of in.................... (*iaftlon*) is only 6 per cent, but I think it's more like 12 per cent.

4 Exam practice: multiple-choice cloze (Paper 3 Part 1)

Read the text below and decide which answer **A**, **B**, **C** or **D** best fits each space. There is an example at the beginning **(0)**.

0 A treated   **B** dealt   **C** handled   **D** faced

THE ROUGH GUIDE STORY

When Mark Ellingham went to Greece in the late 1970s, he couldn't find a guidebook he liked. There was nothing available which **(0)**....A.... Greece as a twentieth-century, living culture, and which didn't **(1)**............ you feel inadequate for not having a lot of money. So Mark, together with his partner, Natania Jansz, and John Fisher, set out to write his own guidebook. *The Rough Guide to Greece*, published in 1982, was a **(2)**............ success.

After Greece, this small **(3)**............ of recent college graduates wanted to write a guide to Sri Lanka, which was where Natania's family came from. **(4)**............ , their publishers talked them **(5)**............ doing Spain and Portugal. By the time they had written those, they had a series. Today there are almost 200 *Rough Guide* titles **(6)**............ the market.

Nowadays, the *Rough Guides* no longer seem **(7)**............ 'rough'. The early books were written on very **(8)**............ money for readers who were assumed to be in the same **(9)**............ . But the books **(10)**............ to a much wider **(11)**............ of readers than was originally anticipated, so they began to **(12)**............ information about more upmarket hotels and restaurants.

1 A cause   **B** result   **C** make   **D** lead
2 A bright   **B** great   **C** strong   **D** loud
3 A team   **B** crew   **C** gang   **D** committee
4 A Although   **B** Despite   **C** Though   **D** However
5 A up   **B** to   **C** into   **D** through
6 A to   **B** on   **C** at   **D** in
7 A absolutely   **B** particularly   **C** specifically   **D** definitely
8 A much   **B** few   **C** small   **D** little
9 A boat   **B** vehicle   **C** place   **D** house
10 A attracted   **B** influenced   **C** appealed   **D** affected
11 A range   **B** collection   **C** set   **D** number
12 A take   **B** put   **C** choose   **D** include

Language development 1
Conditionals

▶ CB pages 124–125, GR pages 191–192

1 Zero, Type 1 and Type 2 conditionals

a Mark the correct verb form in each pair.

1 If Stella *opens / will open* a boutique in the High Street, she'll make lots of money.

2 If the economy doesn't improve, lots of businesses *will close / would close* down.

3 If you were sensible, you *will put / would put* that money in the bank.

4 Sue is so generous, she always gives money if someone *asks / will ask* her.

5 George may go to prison unless he *pays / will pay* his taxes.

6 The organisation *was / would be* more effective if it was sponsored by the government.

7 If the employees of a company *are / were* happy, they work harder.

8 We might sell our business if it *makes / would make* another loss this year.

9 If you *were / would be* in John's position, what would you do?

10 If the public *don't give / didn't give* money to homeless people, they would face great hardship.

b Look at each sentence again and decide if the condition is:

A always true   **B** possible or likely
C unlikely or imaginary

2 Conjunctions

Complete the sentences with the conjunctions in the list. There may be more than one possibility, but use each conjunction once only.

unless   as long as   even if   provided that   if

1 I think I'll be able to stay in business, ... the bank lends me the money I need.

2 You can ask your boss for a rise, but you won't get one. .... you beg him, he won't give you one!

3 We'll make a nice profit this year .... people continue to buy our books.

4 Amanda's well-qualified, but .... she makes more effort she'll end up unemployed.

5 Rick will pass his driving test easily .... he keeps a cool head.

3 Type 3 conditionals

Complete these conditional sentences, using the verbs in brackets in the correct form.

1 If I .... (*invest*) money in that company last year, I .... (*make*) a considerable profit.

2 If people .... (*support*) small local businesses more, so many of them .... (*not/close down*).

3 If my brother .... (*not/sell*) those shares last month, he .... (*lose*) £5,000.

4 Keith .... (*not/set up*) his own business if he .... (*listen*) to his friends.

5 If Julia .... (*not/leave*) her purse at home, she .... (*give*) some money to the busker.

6 Colin .... (*give*) you some valuable financial advice if you .... (*ask*) him.

7 Oliver .... (*not/be able*) to buy all the equipment he needed if he .... (*not/borrow*) £200 from his father.

8 I .... (*buy*) a ticket for the concert, if I .... (*know*) that all the money was to be sent to famine victims in Ethiopia.

4 Mixed conditionals

Write mixed conditional sentences beginning with *If*, using the information given.

EXAMPLE: Sheila went to Peru on holiday. She owns a language school in Lima today.

If Sheila hadn't gone to Peru on holiday, she wouldn't own a language school in Lima today.

1 I did not go into business with my best friend. I am not rich and successful today.
If ....
....

2 Friends supported me when I lost my home and job. I am not a beggar on the street today.
If ....
....

3 My brother did not take the advice of his teachers. He has apartments in New York and London today.
If ....
....

4 Julia is a really good journalist. She won the *Journalist of the Year* Award recently.
If ....
....

5 Large numbers of people are homeless today. The government did not help the survivors of the earthquake.
If ....
....

5 Key word transformations

Complete the second sentence so that it has a similar meaning to the first sentence, using the word given. Do not change the word given. Use between two and five words, including the word given.

1 I didn't know about her birthday, so I didn't send her any flowers. **some**
If I had known about her birthday, I .... flowers.

2 He is very rich today because he bought shares in an oil company. **be**
If he hadn't bought shares in an oil company, he .... today.

3 If you obey the college rules, you will not have any problems. **long**
You will not have any problems, ... the college rules.

4 You don't get good marks because you don't study hard. **harder**
If you studied .... better marks.

5 Listen carefully or you won't know what to do. **if**
You won't know what to do .... carefully.

6 Anna speaks such good German because she lived in Hamburg for ten years. **so**
If Anna hadn't lived in Hamburg for ten years, she .... well.

7 Unless you make some serious mistakes, I'm sure you'll do well in the interview. **provided**
I'm sure you'll do well in the interview, ... make any serious mistakes.

8 You feel so tired every day because you go to bed late. **earlier**
If you went to bed .... so tired every day.

9 No matter how hard you work, you'll never earn much money as a lawyer. **even**
You'll never earn much money as a lawyer, ... really hard.

10 Without a law degree, you won't get that job in Paris that you want. **unless**
You won't get that job in Paris that you want .... a law degree.

Writing Email (Paper 2 Part 1)

▶ CB pages 126–127, WR pages 197-198

1 Understand and plan the task

a Read the task below and mark the points you have to include in your email.

b Make a paragraph plan.

Paragraph 1: ....

Paragraph 2: ....

Paragraph 3: ....

Paragraph 4: ....

Paragraph 5: ....

You bought a video camera from a company over the Internet but soon regretted doing so. Read the online advertisement for the camera and the notes you have made. Then write an email to the Sales Manager, using all your notes, to complain about the advertisement. Ask for a refund and mention that that future advertisements should be less misleading.

Amazing New Video Camera – Only £140!

Order your new Handycam digital video camera now!

- High quality video camera with leather case.   *case was dirty and scratched*

- Extremely easy to use.   *just the opposite!*
  Delivered to your door within 24 hours.   *3 days actually*

- Any problems? Phone us on 01632 960008 and we'll do our best to help!   *girl I spoke to was extremely rude!*

- Your emails are always welcome!

Phone us now on
01632 960008

Write an **email** of **120–150**. You must use grammatically correct sentences with accurate spelling and punctuation in a style appropriate for the situation.

2 Check and improve a sample answer

a Read the email a student wrote, and tick (✓) the points you marked in the task as they are mentioned. Does the email include all the information?

b How many paragraphs does the email have? Compare the organisation with your plan.

New Message

I want to complain about your advertisement for the Handycam video camera.

I ordered the camera from your company last week. (1) .... you say that delivery takes less than 24 hours, I got the camera three days later. I couldn't believe my eyes when I noticed that the leather case was dirty and scratched.

In your advertisement, you (2) .... mention that the Handycam video camera is easy to use. (3) ...., it took me two hours to read the instructions and I still could not use the camera. When I telephoned for help, the girl I spoke to was very rude.

If I had known your advertisement was a load of lies, I would never have ordered the camera. I expect an apology and my money back now. (4) ...., I feel that you should change future advertisements so that they are not so misleading.

I look forward to hearing from you.

Yours faithfully

Alex Vidal

---

c Complete the spaces in the email with a linking word from the list. There are two you do not need to use.

in fact   also   furthermore   although   despite   consequently

d The email includes 5 words or expressions which are too informal. Find and replace them with the more appropriate formal expressions a–f. There is one expression that you do not need to use.

a an immediate refund of £140

b am writing to complain

c would like to point out that

d received

e so inaccurate

f to my great surprise

e Write the improved email out again in your notebook.

Listening Multiple-choice questions (Paper 4 Part 4)

1 Before you listen
Read the instructions for the listening task below, and the questions. Mark key words and think about what you will hear. What do you think Mandy did with the money she won?

2 🎧 Multiple-choice questions

a   Listen to the recording and choose the best option as you listen. (The questions follow the order of the text.)

b   Listen again to check your answers and make sure the other options are not possible.

c   Was your prediction in Exercise 1 correct?

You will hear a radio interview with a woman who won a lot of money in a lottery. For questions **1–7**, choose the best answer **A**, **B** or **C**.

1   What does Mandy say about her winning lottery ticket?

   A   It was the first one she'd ever bought.

   B   She had a feeling it was going to win.

   C   She was persuaded to buy it by a friend. `1`

2   How did Mandy's father react to the news that she'd won?

   A   He was too shocked to speak.

   B   He became rather over-excited.

   C   He rushed to tell her the news. `2`

3   Mandy now feels that she made a mistake when

   A   she allowed her win to be publicised.

   B   she trusted the people at the TV station.

   C   she told her story to a newspaper reporter. `3`

4   How did Mandy feel about the way certain people reacted to her win?

   A   disappointed with close friends

   B   unsure of strangers

   C   annoyed by her family `4`

5   What does Mandy say about her friend Louise?

   A   She refused to accept the gift Mandy bought her.

   B   She became rude and unfriendly towards Mandy.

   C   She couldn't help resenting Mandy's good fortune. `5`

6   How did the begging letters affect Mandy?

   A   She wished she'd never won the lottery at all.

   B   She became angry with the people who sent them.

   C   She realised that it wasn't right to have so much money. `6`

7   What does Mandy feel about the money now?

   A   glad that she's given it all away

   B   content with the lifestyle it's given her

   C   sorry that she didn't use it more wisely `7`

Vocabulary ▶ CB pages 128–129

1 Topic: ways of shopping

a Look at the pictures (A–D). Which method of shopping do the statements below refer to? Write A, B, C or D next to each statement.

1 There are big trolleys to put your shopping in. ....
2 You can find all the shops you need in one place. ....
3 The fruit and vegetables you buy are often very dirty. ....
4 You don't have to leave your living room to shop. ....
5 There is usually a place where people can sit and relax, with a fountain or some exotic plants. ....
6 Before you can buy anything, you have to send the company your credit card number. ....
7 There are usually several checkouts where you can pay, so you don't have to queue for long. ....
8 If it's raining, you can go from shop to shop without getting wet. ....
9 Sometimes they don't let you pick the fruit or vegetables you want yourself. ....
10 You have a lot of choice. If you want coffee, for example, there may be 20 different types of coffee on the shelf. ....
11 What they send you may be different from what you ordered. ....
12 You sometimes have to be careful that they don't try to cheat you or give you the wrong change. ....

b Look at each statement spent again and decide whether it is an advantage (✓) or a disadvantage (✗) or it doesn't matter (–).

2 Commonly confused words
Complete the sentences with the most appropriate word or phrase A, B, C or D.

1 I asked the assistant for a bottle of herbal shampoo but she said they were ....
  A in stock **B** out of stock **C** on sale   **D** for sale
2 The assistant said that she couldn't give me a refund without a ....
  A receipt   **B** recipe   **C** prescription **D** ticket
3 In the sale, I paid £20 instead of £50 for my new camera, so it was an absolute ....
  A reduction **B** discount **C** opportunity **D** bargain
4 How much is this shampoo? I can't see the .... anywhere.
  A price   **B** fee   **C** cost   **D** payment
5 Small shops usually treat their regular .... better than supermarkets.
  A patients **B** clients   **C** customers **D** shoppers
6 What .... of washing-up liquid do you normally buy?
  A mark   **B** make   **C** brand   **D** label
7 In our local street market, there's a .... which sells delicious hot potatoes.
  A counter   **B** stall   **C** table   **D** store
8 If you buy clothes from a mail-order company, you choose what you want from a ....
  A prospectus **B** brochure **C** directory **D** catalogue
9 You can pay for your new computer in monthly .... if you wish.
  A doses **B** parts   **C** instalments **D** cheques
10 I wanted to buy a small radio so I went to a shop which sells electrical ....
  A produce **B** goods   **C** purchases **D** exports

Language development 2

Number and concord; *it/there* ▶ CB page 132

1 Singular or plural verb?

a Decide if the underlined words need a singular or plural verb. Mark the correct verb form in each pair.

1 I think that 120 euros *is / are* a lot of <u>money</u> to pay for a shirt.

2 Some <u>people</u> only *buys / buy* clothes with a designer label.

3 The <u>furniture</u> we bought at that shop *was / were* not very well made.

4 <u>Economics</u> *is / are* my favourite subject at college.

5 The <u>police</u> *thinks / think* that Tom stole that camera from a shop.

6 <u>Everybody</u> in my village *has / have* to go shopping in the nearby town.

7 The <u>majority</u> of my friends *spends / spend* more than £20 a week on clothes.

8 Local <u>politics</u> *doesn't / don't* interest me at all, I'm afraid.

9 My father moved his shop to another building because the old <u>premises</u> *was / were* unsuitable.

10 These new <u>trousers</u> *is / are* far too tight for me.

11 A <u>number</u> of new shops *has / have* opened in town recently.

12 The <u>United States</u> *has / have* just passed a new law about advertising.

b Put the nouns in Exercise 1a into the correct column in the table.

Nouns + singular verb	Nouns + plural verb

c Complete this shop notice with the correct form of *be* or *have*.

> The police **(1)** .... suggested that we introduce closed circuit television on the premises of this store. As most staff **(2)** .... aware, a total of £3,000 worth of stock **(3)** .... stolen last month as a result of shoplifting. Although a group of teenagers **(4)** .... been arrested in connection with this theft, the problem continues. Whilst recognising that 90 per cent of our customers **(5)** .... honest people, we feel that urgent measures need to be taken. More than one shop in this neighbourhood **(6)** .... had to close as a result of such losses. The police authorities **(7)** .... advised us that the installation of cameras in the shop will have immediate results. Each member of staff **(8)** .... asked to support us in this matter.

2 Three big spenders

a Read the information about three celebrities who love shopping and spending money.

Victoria Beckham (Posh Spice)

Birth name: Victoria Caroline Adams

Date of birth: April 17, 1974

Place of birth: UK

Occupation(s): singer, songwriter, fashion designer

Marital status: married David Beckham, the football player (1999)

Family details: has three sons (Brooklyn, Romeo and Cruz)

Other information: David Beckham once bought her an entire Versace collection of clothes; their wedding reception probably cost more than £500,000

Britney Spears

Birth name: Britney Jean Spears

Date of birth: December 2, 1981

Place of birth: USA

Occupation(s): dancer, singer, actress, songwriter, author

Marital status: married Jason Alexander (2004 – marriage lasted 55 hours); married Kevin Federline (2004–2007)

Family details: father was a building contractor, mother was a teacher; has two sons (Sean and Jayden)

Other information: made headlines once when in Europe by sending her private jet back to the USA to pick up the ingredients of a Coffee Bean and Tea Leaf ice-blended frozen drink. Total cost of drink – $40,000!

Courtney Cox

Birth name: Courtney Bass Cox

Date of birth: June 15, 1964

Place of birth: USA

Occupation(s): dancer, actress,

Marital status: married David Arquette (1999)

Family details: has a daughter (Coco)

Other information: has a beach house said to be worth $10 million; one room of the house is devoted to karaoke

b   In your notebook, write sentences comparing the three celebrities. Use the information on the cards and the prompts below. Put the verbs in the correct tense. Begin your sentences with one of these phrases.

- All of them ... .
- None of them ... .
- One of them ... .
- Both X and Y ... .
- Neither X nor Y ... .

EXAMPLE: love / shopping
All of them love shopping.

1   Britney Spears / Courtney Cox / be born / USA.
2   be born / the 60s
3   have / children
4   come from / UK
5   Victoria Beckham / Courtney Cox / be happily married
6   Victoria Beckham / Britney Spears / have / more than one child
7   Victoria Beckham / Britney Spears / have / daughter
8   be / film director
9   be / fashion designer
10 Britney Spears / Courtney Cox / be / dancers.

c   Write more sentences of your own using the information.

3   *it* or *there*?

There are mistakes with the use of *it* and *there* in some of the sentences. Tick (✓) the correct sentences. Correct the ones with mistakes.

EXAMPLE: I was late for a doctor's appointment yesterday because it~~it~~ was a lot of traffic. ......*there*......

1   I don't want to watch this programme anymore. It's really boring. ....
2   A: I need to buy some stamps. Is it a post office near here? ....
     B: Yes, it's a post office in George Street.

     ....
3   It is a good idea to shop around before you buy a computer. ....
4   It used to be a second-hand bookshop in this street, but it's not here now. ....
5   Where's my mobile phone? Is it in the kitchen?

     ....
6   Did you know there is my birthday today? I'm 16.

     ....
7   I think we should go home now. There is nearly two in the morning. ....
8   Excuse me, how far is there to the airport from here? ....

4   Key word transformations

Complete the second sentence so that it has a similar meaning to the first sentence, using the word given. Do not change the word given. Use between two and five words, including the word given.

1   I can hear you perfectly so you don't need to shout. **no**
    I can hear you perfectly so .... to shout.
2   As Jack usually arrived on time I began to feel rathe worried. **unusual**
    As .... to be late, I began to feel rather worried.
3   How long was your flight from London to Bucharest? **take**
    How long .... fly from London to Bucharest?
4   Don't worry if you can't find Mexcafé, because most brands of coffee are similar. **matter**
    Most brands of coffee are similar, so
    .... if you can't find Mexcafé.
5   Why are the supermarket shelves empty? **nothing**
    Why .... the supermarket shelves?
6   Do you think this radio is faulty? **problem**
    Do you think .... this radio?
7   For the time being, planes can't land as it is too foggy at the airport. **fog**
    For the time being, planes can't land as
    .... at the airport.
8   I enjoyed seeing Angela again, didn't you? **lovely**
    Wasn't .... Angela again?
9   Will many people be waiting outside the cinema, do you think? **queue**
    Will .... outside the cinema, do you think?
10 It rained heavily last night and all the rivers have flooded. **storm**
    All the rivers have flooded because
    .... last night.

Reading Gapped text (Paper 1 Part 2)

1 Before you read

a Read the instructions for the reading task and the title of the article opposite.
What does *shy away from* mean?
A avoid using   B feel happy about

b Think of some possible answers to the question in the title.
EXAMPLE:
It is expensive to buy a computer.
....
....
....

2 Skimming

Skim the text. What answers does the text give to the question in the title? Mark those parts of the text and compare with your own ideas in Exercise 1b.

3 Gapped text

a Read paragraph 1 and sentence H carefully. Mark the words in sentence H that link to the highlighted words in the text.

b Read the rest of the text carefully. Then re-read the paragraph before and after each gap and think about what information is missing. Choose which option A–H fits in terms of topic and language links.

c Read the whole text again with your answers, to check that it makes sense.

4 Vocabulary

Read the text again. Choose five useful expressions or collocations connected with shopping on the Internet to add to your vocabulary notebook.
EXAMPLES:

The Internet
e-commerce site (= a website where you can buy
goods or services)
purchase (something) online

You are going to read a magazine article about shopping on the Internet. Seven sentences have been removed from the article. Choose from the sentences A–H the ones which fits each gap (1–6). There is one extra sentence which you do not need to use. There is an example at the beginning (0).

A Indeed, like most shoppers, Lunt's interviewees found it hard to navigate e-commerce sites, saying goods were not laid out logically, and how dull the websites were - particularly compared to things like computer games.

B Indeed, about 58 per cent of online shoppers fall into this category and Lunt suggests that this reflects their interest in books and CDs rather than clothes – but even so, men still aren't buying much in total.

C The more interesting question, however, is what the response from sellers will be because they have to find new ways of appealing to customers and offering services that include a mix of online and offline outlets.

D But underlying these stated reasons, there's also a fundamental difference between conventional shopping and online services: both the pleasure of unplanned purchases and the ability to examine products are missing online, and for many, the experience of shopping, especially for clothes, is as important as the products themselves.

E The location of the computer was another factor in this domestic mindset, with many people having theirs either in the sitting room as part of an entertainment set-up, or else in the study for work.

F The issues for such people are the broader social issues of privacy and the possible effects on the way we live – although surprisingly they are happy to use the Internet for other reasons.

G Given that these fans of internet shopping seem to represent such a small minority, is there something that will get the rest of the population shopping online?

H Amongst all these people, only 14 per cent had tried shopping online and a mere 5 per cent were regular users; most of their purchases were confined to those three commonest product types.

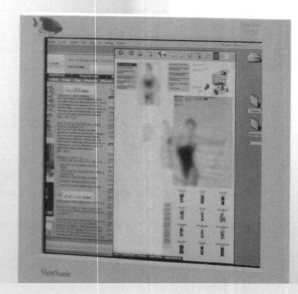

Why do shoppers shy away from the Net?

Shopping on the Internet should be easy and stress-free: no queues, no rude assistants. Yet, according to a recent study, people are still reluctant to buy from e-commerce sites. Dr
5 Peter Lunt, a London university psychologist, spent two years analysing Internet shopping and found that books, CDs and travel tickets are the goods most often purchased online. He surveyed almost 900 people, surfing the Net
10 with groups and talking to individuals in their own homes. **1** **H**

According to Lunt, the main explanations given for this reluctance to go e-shopping were the costs of computer equipment, fear of going
15 online and concerns about the delivery and possible need to return products. **2**

Acknowledging this difference, Lunt says 'People recognise the convenience of e-commerce in principle, especially for grocery shopping, but it
20 became clear that even the regular supermarket visit is a complex activity where personal and luxury items would be bought on impulse or with a specific occasion, person or meal in mind. It's hard to reproduce the pleasure of this
25 experience using an unfriendly list-based computer program.' **3**

Lunt believes there are three groups of people who do not shop online. The first has little knowledge of the Internet, but is potentially
30 interested. 'They're a prime target for limited e-services delivered by digital TV,' he adds. The second group tends to be older, less educated and, Lunt believes, may be left behind. Members of the third group are relatively wealthy and
35 computer literate, but have other reasons for not shopping on the web. **4**

And even amongst those who do shop online, most viewed it as an alternative. 'They are thinking more of the integration of e-commerce
40 services into their current household routine, rather than taking the opportunity to rethink how they organise their home lives,' says Lunt. **5**

Lunt sees this as a drawback because as he puts
45 it, 'PCs are not integrated into the places in the household where decisions about shopping are made.' Perhaps this is why single young men were most positive about e-commerce. **6**

50 The survey concludes that those who are most positive about e-commerce are focusing on the convenience and the price advantage in particular products and not on the shopping experience itself. **7** There seems to be
55 some doubt about this. More of us may be encouraged to shop online as manufacturers overcome bad web design and learn to safeguard our privacy, but will Internet shopping ever seriously replace the stress and thrill of the real
60 thing?

Vocabulary ▸ CB pages 136–137

1 **Topic: different kinds of holiday**

a **What type of holiday is each speaker describing? Match the holidays to the speakers below. Mark the words which help you decide.**
package holiday   adventure holiday   safari
city break   skiing holiday   camping holiday

1 'I love this kind of holiday. You do so many exciting things. Last year, for example, our group went to a remote part of Spain. We had a fantastic time – white-water rafting, rock climbing, canoeing and even hang gliding.'
....

2 'I go with my friends every year. We rent a chalet in the village and spend every day on the slopes. In the evenings, the only thing you want to do is warm yourself in front of the fire.'..........................

3 'I know that it's not as exciting as travelling on your own, but it's not as stressful. Basically, everything is organised for you – flights, accommodation, meals – everything. The tour company may even organise excursions to different places of interest, but it's up to you whether you go or not.'..........................

4 'It can get a bit tiring sometimes, especially if you spend a long time going somewhere by jeep. It's incredible, though, when you see lions or elephants in the wild for the first time.' ....

5 'Every year I go with my parents to the same place. We even put up our tent under the same tree each time. There are lots of facilities on the site – there's a cyber-café now for teenagers like me!'..........................

6 'I don't have much time for holidays. Occasionally, I take a couple of days off work and go to somewhere like Vienna or Prague. I stay in a luxury hotel and do as much sightseeing as I can. When I go back to work I feel like a different person.'
....

b **In your notebook, write a short paragraph about your favourite kind of holiday.**

2 **Things you need on holiday**
Match the items in the list below to the appropriate type of holiday and write them in your notebook. Some items may go in more than one category. Can you add any more words?

**Skiing holiday   Camping holiday   Beach holiday
Trekking holiday   Safari**

- a wide-brimmed hat
- sunglasses
- a sleeping bag
- a family tent
- a video camera
- a thermos flask
- a rucksack
- an airbed
- a walking stick
- antiseptic cream
- a pair of strong walking boots
- a warm anorak and bobble hat
- suntan lotion
- a one-man tent
- skis and ski-boots
- insect repellent
- a camera with telephoto lens
- a mask and snorkel
- a swimming costume
- plasters

3 **Verb + noun collocations**
a **Complete the sentences with a word or phrase from the list. Use each word once only.**
passport   reservation   inoculations   currency
credit cards   insurance   work permit   flight

1 When you've decided where you want to go, you need to go to a travel agent and <u>book</u> a .... Of course, you could also do this over the Internet.

2 It may be advisable to make a hotel .... so that you have somewhere to stay when you arrive at your destination.

3 Don't forget to apply for a .... in good time, if you don't already have one. Without this, you won't be able to go anywhere!

4 For some tropical countries, it's important to have .... for diseases like cholera before you set off.

5 Make sure you take out suitable .... , especially if you are going to be away for a long time. This will cover you if you are ill or lose your belongings.

6 If you intend to work in a particular country, find out if you need to apply for a .... beforehand.

7 It is useful to have a certain amount of cash with you as .... are not always accepted. Go to a bank and change some money into the .... of the country you are going to.

b **Mark the verb which collocates with the noun you have written in each space. The first one has been done for you.**

4 Exam practice: multiple-choice cloze (Paper 3 Part 1)

Read the text below and decide which answer **A**, **B**, **C** or **D** best fits each space. There is an example at the beginning **(0)**.

0 **A** source **B** spring **C** reason **D** origin

A FAMOUS TRAVELLER

Wilfred Thesiger's desert journeys in the Middle East are a constant **(0)** _A_ of inspiration to all those who **(1)**............ his love for the region. If you are **(2)**............ in travelling in the Middle East, reading Thesiger is a must.

Wilfred was born and **(3)**............ up in East Africa, where his father worked as a British Government official. Although he left Africa to study in the UK, he returned in the 1930s to begin his own career as an administrator.

In the late 1940s, he travelled to the Arabian peninsula to **(4)**............ information for a locust control project. There he first **(5)**............ across the Bedu, the traditional nomadic **(6)**............ of the desert, who would accompany him **(7)**............ two historic crossings of the absolutely **(8)**............ 'Empty Quarter' and introduce him to their harsh way of life.

Travel and exploration gave meaning to Thesiger's life. **(9)**............ he was travelling, he lived as a nomad, visiting remote **(10)**............ of the world, often on **(11)**............ , living simply among the local peoples and writing about his experiences. His books, more than any others, have caught our imagination and led us to **(12)**............ the beauty and solitude of the great desert expanses.

1 A keep	**B** share	**C** fall	**D** hold
2 A keen	**B** enthusiastic	**C** fascinated	**D** interested
3 A brought	**B** raised	**C** fetched	**D** reared
4 A gather	**B** learn	**C** listen	**D** search
5 A met	**B** encountered	**C** came	**D** got
6 A citizens	**B** tenants	**C** members	**D** inhabitants
7 A in	**B** on	**C** at	**D** by
8 A vast	**B** big	**C** large	**D** extensive
9 A While	**B** Throughout	**C** During	**D** Alongside
10 A sides	**B** edges	**C** corners	**D** surfaces
11 A horse	**B** foot	**C** camel	**D** bicycle
12 A fascinate	**B** appreciate	**C** delight	**D** amuse

Language development 1

Passives ▶ CB pages 138–139, GR page 193

1 Active or passive?

Mark the correct form of the verb in each pair.

1 A lot of people *suffer / are suffered* from travel sickness.

2 An excellent guidebook to France *has just published / has just been published*.

3 The number of visitors to the UK *was decreased / decreased* last year.

4 A new holiday resort *is being built / is building* on the south coast.

5 The hotel *will finish / will be finished* next year.

6 Anyone wishing to visit China must *apply / be applied* for a visa.

2 Passive forms

Rewrite these sentences in the passive to make them appropriate for a leaflet giving information to airline passengers. Begin with the word given. Be careful with word order.

Important information for passengers:

1 We kindly request passengers to keep their seat belts fastened during take-off.
   Passengers ....

2 We have banned smoking on all flights, in accordance with recent regulations.
   Smoking ....

3 You must put hand luggage under your seat or in the compartment above the seat.
   Hand ....

4 You can obtain information about the flight from the personnel on board.
   Information ....

5 We have trained all our flight assistants to deal with emergency situations.
   All ....

6 We will make every effort to ensure that passengers have a pleasant trip.
   Every ....

3 Verbs with two objects

Rewrite these sentences, making the words in italics the subject. Omit the agent (*by* …) if it is not necessary.

EXAMPLE: The travel agency posted us *the tickets*.
The tickets were posted to us by the travel agency.

1 The bank lent *me* £2,000.

....

2 The hotel management offers every guest *a complimentary bowl of fruit*.

....

3 Airlines have promised *travellers* cheaper flights for years.

....

4 One of our guides will show *you* the city's main attractions.

....

5 The judges awarded Peter *the first prize in the competition*.

....

4 Passive report structures

a Rewrite these sentences beginning with the words given.

1 People say that Prague is one of the most beautiful cities in the world.
  a Prague is said to ....
  b It is said that ....

2 Newspapers report that airport workers are going on strike next week.
  a Airport workers are reported ....
  b It is reported ....

3 People expect the government will introduce measures to boost tourism.
  a The government ....
  b It is expected ....

4 People think the missing tourist has been abducted.
  a The missing tourist ....
  b It ....

b Read the news report. Put the verbs in brackets in the correct form.

NEWS FLASH!

Hollywood star Rod Osbourne is believed
(1)........................... (*be*) in hospital in a small village
in Switzerland. It (2)........................... (*not/know*)
exactly what happened, but it (3)...........................
(*think*) that the Oscar-award winning actor
(4)........................... (*involve*) in an accident while
skiing in the Alps last week. Sources at the hospital
confirm that Osbourne's injuries are not serious. He is
said (5)........................... (*make*) good progress since
the accident and is expected (6)...........................
(*leave*) the hospital in a few days. At the moment his
wife, top model Lucy Evans, is believed
(7)........................... (*stay*) in a hotel near the hospital.
She is reported (8)........................... (*fly*) to the village
as soon as she heard the news.

---

5 Key word transformations

Complete the second sentence so that it has a similar meaning to the first sentence, using the word given. Do not change the word given. You must use between two and five words, including the word given.

1 One of the local people gave us directions. **given**
  We .... one of the local people.

2 The price of the ticket included refreshments. **included**
  Refreshments ....
  the price of the ticket.

3 The guide made us take our shoes off before entering the museum. **made**
  We .... take our shoes off before entering the museum.

4 They are going to publish a new series of guidebooks soon. **published**
  A new series of guidebooks .... soon.

5 They say that the Puppet Theatre is worth visiting. **said**
  The Puppet Theatre .... worth visiting.

6 The shop has not developed our photographs yet. **have**
  Our photographs .... yet.

7 It is believed that they cancelled their trip at the last moment. **believed**
  They .... their trip at the last moment.

8 The flight attendant offers the passengers sweets before take-off. **given**
  Sweets .... before take-off.

9 They don't let you use electronic equipment during take-off and landing. **allowed**
  You .... electronic equipment during take-off and landing.

10 The tour leader welcomed us when we arrived at the hotel. **welcomed**
  On arrival at the hotel, ...
  the tour leader.

Writing Report (Paper 2 Part 2)

▶ CB pages 140–141, WR page 204

Exam strategy

When writing a report, make sure you write for the reader specified in the task and choose the right style. Clear organisation is particularly important, so the reader can find the key information quickly. It is a good idea to group points under headings.

1 Understand the task

Read the task below and answer the questions.

1 What is your role?
2 Who are you writing the report for? What style will you use?
3 How many parts are there to the question? Mark the parts of the task that tell you what to include in your report.

> You work for the Student Travel Agency of your college. The principle of the college is interested in the experiences of students who have worked abroad during their summer holidays. She has asked you to find out this information and to write a report on the advantages and disadvantages of such work. In particular, she wants to know whether the college should recommend 'working holidays' to its students.

Write your **report** in **120–180** words in an appropriate style.

2 Check and improve a sample answer

a Read the report a student wrote. Does it include all the information required? Tick the parts of the task you marked.

b Complete the information at the top of the report and write a suitable heading for each section.

c The report is extremely short because not enough 'supporting details' are provided. Read the supporting details in the box below the report and decide which section you would add them to.

d The underlined expressions in the report are too informal. Rewrite them in a more appropriate way.

e Write out the improved report in your notebook.

> To: The Principal
> From: ....
> Date: ....
> Subject: ....
>
> (*Heading 1*) ....
> The reason I'm writing this report is to consider the advantages and disadvantages of working holidays abroad. (Supporting details: ....)
>
> (*Heading 2*) ....
> Lots of the students I spoke to said that they had enjoyed working abroad and had become more open-minded as a result. (Supporting details: ....)
>
> (*Heading 3*) ....
> I wasn't surprised when many students complained that they had worked too hard in certain countries. They believed that they had been exploited by their employers, who paid them very little money. (Supporting details: ....)
>
> (*Heading 4*) ....
> I'd say that the majority of students found the experience of working abroad very beneficial. Therefore, I believe that the college should recommend 'working holidays' to its students. (Supporting details: ....)

Supporting details

A Apparently, they felt they had learnt a lot about the local people and their way of life by working side by side with them.

B However, it should also warn them about the problems they could face and the precautions they need to take.

C Some students said that there had also been problems with documents such as work permits.

D To get this information, I interviewed more than 30 students who had worked in different countries.

Listening Sentence completion
(Paper 4 Part 2)

1 Before you listen
Read the instructions for the listening task opposite, and the notes. Think about the topic and try to predict the kind of information that is missing.

2 🎧 Sentence completion
a Listen to the recording and complete the notes using a word or short phrase.
b Listen again to check and complete your answers.

3 Structuring a talk

Exam strategy

In a good talk or presentation, the speaker explains what the talk will be about, and introduces each main point clearly before going into the details. Listen out for these signals, as they tell you when you have to listen for specific information.

In these extracts from the recording, the speaker introduces each main point of her talk. Number them in order.

☐ **a** 'The company regards the Reception desk as one of the most important places in the hotel. … So first and foremost, remember the three golden rules: …'

☐ **b** 'So the purpose of this meeting is just to quickly run through some of the training points that can get forgotten in busy periods.'

☐ **c** 'So that's check-in. Although there are busy periods for this, it's not as bad as checking out.'

☐ **d** 'Now, most guests have two main points of contact with the Reception desk. When they check in and when they leave. So I'll go through those two procedures in detail. When guests first arrive, …'

☐ **e** 'First of all I'd like to talk about the Reception desk.'

You will hear part of a staff training meeting in a hotel. For questions 1–10, complete the sentences.

CLIPSTONE HOTEL: STAFF TRAINING

The trainer refers the staff to a booklet entitled [_____ 1].

Receptionists should always use the guests' [_____ 2].

Receptionists should always [_____ 3] and apologise to waiting guests.

Receptionists mustn't forget to [_____ 4] at all times.

Rooms ready for guests checking in are marked by a [_____ 5] on the screen.

Staff should check whether a [_____ 6] room has been requested or not.

Staff should ask whether guests have a [_____ 7] with them.

Staff should check whether guests want a [_____ 8] in the morning.

When guests check out, a [_____ 9] on the screen means that extras need to paid for.

When checking out, guests may need information or a [_____ 10].

Vocabulary ▶ CB pages 142–143 ▶ Colloquial English page 124

1 Transport questionnaire

Do the questionnaire by choosing A, B or C for each of the situations below. When you have finished add up your score. For each situation, **A = 1 point, B = 2 points, C = 3 points.** Look in the box at the bottom of the page to find out what kind of traveller you are!

WHAT KIND OF
traveller
ARE YOU?

1 When you go to work / college in the morning, you:
- **A** use your car or get a lift in a friend's car
- **B** use public transport, even though you own a car
- **C** walk or cycle

2 When you want to go to the local supermarket, you:
- **A** get into your car and drive there
- **B** walk to the nearest bus stop and hop on a bus
- **C** walk or jump on your bike

3 If you have to catch a train and there is a delay of more half an hour, you:
- **A** lose your temper and start to shout at those around you
- **B** pace impatiently up and down the platform
- **C** sit on a bench, listen to your MP3 player and whistle to yourself

4 When a bus or underground train is very crowded, you:
- **A** squeeze on board but promise yourself that you will never travel by public transport again
- **B** get on and try to make yourself comfortable
- **C** wait for the next one to arrive

5 When the government talks about building a new metro line, you:
- **A** grumble about the amount of money it will cost
- **B** say that it'll probably never happen
- **C** congratulate politicians on their attempts to solve the traffic problems of the city

6 After a party, you don't want to drive so you:
- **A** take a taxi, though you know the fare will be outrageous
- **B** cadge a lift with someone going in the same direction
- **C** go to the nearest bus stop and wait an hour for the bus

7 When you go on holiday abroad, you usually:
- **A** book a flight through your travel agent or over the Internet
- **B** travel by car or train, even though this takes a long time
- **C** avoid flying at all costs because you worry about the damage jets cause to the environment

8 Your idea of luxury is:
- **A** jumping on a plane and staying in a five star Manhattan hotel for the weekend
- **B** sunbathing on the deck of a luxury cruise ship
- **C** going on a walking holiday and relaxing in a hot bath at the end of each day

9 While on holiday, you like to:
- **A** see the sights in style from a horse-drawn carriage
- **B** take a sight-seeing bus for tourists
- **C** stroll around with a guide book in your hand

10 Your idea of having a good time is:
- **A** traveling at high speed in a powerful sports car
- **B** feeling the wind in your hair on the back of a motorbike
- **C** peering at a map in the rain on the top of a mountain

What kind of traveller are you?

Score 10–16
You like to be comfortable when you travel. This is more important to you than how much you pay for the journey. You also think that it's important to arrive at your destination quickly, with a minimum of fuss. However, you like to spoil yourself when you're on holiday and will sometimes spend a lot of money in order to travel in style.

Score 17–23
You are a fan of fast, clean and efficient public transport and often grumble to your friends about the traffic and the pollution caused by too many cars. You like to arrive at your destination on time, but are not prepared to pay high taxi fares in order to do so. Finally, you are a bit of a romantic and would jump at the opportunity to travel on the Orient Express – but only if someone offered you some free tickets!

Score 24 –30
You would probably have been much happier living a hundred years ago, walking everywhere or riding a horse! You don't like the way cities have changed in recent years and often complain about traffic jams, car exhaust fumes and noise pollution. Finally, you like to keep fit and have a number of pastimes which keep your body in shape. Are you a vegetarian, by the way?

2 Word formation: negative prefixes and suffixes

a Make the adjectives and verbs in the list negative and write them in the correct column in the table.

careful   believable   understand   harmful
damaged   satisfied   approve   useful   honest
thoughtful   acceptable   behave   avoidable
hopeful   popular   like   attractive   suitable
agreeable   interpret   limited

un-	dis-	mis-	-less

b Use the word given in capitals to form a word that fits in the space in each sentence.

1 There is a lot of .... among local people about government plans to build a new airport nearby. **SATISFY**

2 Many people feel that they been .... and treated unfairly. **UNDERSTAND**

3 Not surprisingly, plans to build the airport near a conservation area are .... with environmentalists. **POPULAR**

4 People say that a planned hotel complex will be extremely .... and ruin the whole area. **ATTRACT**

5 Wildlife experts claim that the new airport will be .... noisy and destructive to the local ecosystem. **BELIEVE**

6 The local MP has voiced his .... of the plans in parliament. **APPROVE**

7 The .... of the government in the way they presented the scheme to the local community shocked a lot of people. **HONEST**

8 Government officials say their remarks have been .... by community leaders. **INTERPRET**

9 Government assurances about the levels of noise and pollution are considered to be .... inadequate. **HOPE**

10 'A certain amount of noise will be .... when planes land and take off,' said one spokesperson. **AVOID**

3 Key word transformations

Complete the second sentence so that it has a similar meaning to the first sentence, using the word given. Do not change the word given. You must use between two and five words, including the word given.

1 We enjoyed ourselves at the party last night. **time**
We had .... at the party last night.

2 Is there a party at John's house tonight? **having**
Is .... at his house tonight?

3 George read the newspaper quickly before going out. **look**
George had .... the newspaper before going out.

4 I've just thought of something really good! **had**
I've just .... idea!

5 Shall we go for a meal at that new restaurant? **eat**
Shall we have .... at that new restaurant?

6 I can't go out tonight because I am very busy. **work**
I can't go out tonight because I have a .... do.

Language development 2

Past tenses for hypothetical situations

▶ CB page 145, GR page 195

1 Wish + past, past perfect, *would* or *could*

a Mark the correct verb form in each sentence.

1 I wish there *are / were / would* be more cycle lanes in this town, but there aren't.

2 I wish I *can / am able to / could* ride a motorbike, but I can't.

3 They say the party yesterday was fantastic. I wish I *went / had gone / would go*, but I didn't.

4 What's the matter now? I wish you *stop / stopped / would stop* complaining.

5 There's a great film on TV tomorrow. I wish I *saw / could see / would see* it.

6 Mark is in a really bad mood. I wish he *would / will / had* cheer up, but he probably won't.

b Complete the sentences with the correct form of the verb in brackets.

1 I wish they .... (*tell*) us yesterday that taxi drivers were going on strike today.

2 I wish I .... (*can*) borrow my father's car, but he won't let me.

3 There's nowhere to park in this town! I wish they .... (*build*) an underground car park in the centre!

4 I wish I .... (*not/be*) so rude to Kate yesterday. I feel terrible.

5 You're always talking about your new girlfriend! I wish you .... (*talk*) about something else!

6 Tom said that the film on TV last night was fantastic. I wish I .... (*see*) it.

2 *I wish/If only*

What would you say in these situations? Complete the sentences, using the word(s) in brackets.

EXAMPLE: You are staying with a family in Milan but you don't know any Italian.
I wish ...... I could speak Italian .... (*speak*)

1 It's late at night and your neighbour is playing his stereo really loud.
I wish .... (*turn down*)

2 You feel terrible because you went to bed at three o'clock in the morning.
If only .... (*earlier*)

3 You failed an important exam because you didn't study very hard.
If only .... (*harder*)

4 You feel depressed because it's been raining all day.
If only .... (*stop*)

5 There is a rock concert on Saturday, but you can't go.
I wish .... (*go*)

6 Your sister lives a long way away from you.
I wish .... (*so far away*)

3 Other expressions for hypothetical situations
Mark the correct verb form in each pair.

1 I think it's time we *say / said* goodbye now. I'll see you in the morning.

2 I have a bad cold, so I'd rather you *wouldn't open / didn't open* the window.

3 Don't look at me as if I *were / had been* mad! I like walking in the rain!

4 What do you mean, you can't ride a bicycle? It's high time you *learned / have learned!*

5 Why did you tell my parents about last night? I'd rather you *didn't say / hadn't said* anything.

6 It's been over a week since your argument with Diana. Don't you think it's time you *phone / phoned* her?

4 Key word transformation
Complete the second sentence so that it has a similar meaning to the first sentence, using the word given. Do not change the word given. Use between two and five words, including the word given.

1 I think we ought to call a taxi to take us home. **time**
I think it .... a taxi to take us home.

2 I'd prefer you not to use my car. **rather**
I .... use my car.

3 I regret telling Julie about my plans for the future. **wish**
I .... Julie about my plans for the future.

4 It's a shame your friend can't go with you on holiday. **only**
If .... with you on holiday.

5 Mary, please stop humming to yourself while I'm driving! **wish**
Mary, I .... humming to yourself while I'm driving.

6 Don't you think we should set off for home now? **time**
Isn't it about .... for home?

7 I regret not being able to go on that luxury cruise of the Caribbean. **could**
I wish .... on that luxury cruise of the Caribbean.

8 I sometimes feel like a stranger in my own home. **if**
I sometimes feel .... a stranger in my own home.

9 Shouldn't you stop lying to her? **time**
Don't you think it .... her the truth?

10 You should have asked me before borrowing my car. **rather**
I .... me before borrowing my car.

5 Exam practice: open cloze (Paper 3 Part 2)

For questions **1–12**, read the text below and think of the word which best fits each gap. Use only one word in each gap. There is an example at the beginning **(0)**.

SCHOOL FOR DJS

I go out clubbing every Saturday night, and **(0)** ...my... favourite club is called Ocelot. They've got some really good DJs **(1)** .... play a good range of music including hip-hop, funk and boogie. But there is more to the club **(2)** .... just Saturday nights. During the week, they run DJ classes for people **(3)** .... me, who dream of becoming DJs themselves one day. I've already done the introductory course and learned the basics. So next week, I'm starting the Wednesday Masterclass, where one of the country's top DJs shows you **(4)** .... to put together a really great set of music. Apparently, they **(5)** .... you take along your own records if you want, but you don't **(6)** .... to because everything is supplied within the price. You get two hours' one-to-one tuition and then from nine o'clock **(7)** .... eleven, as people begin to arrive for a night out, you **(8)** .... the chance to perform as **(9)** .... you were a real DJ, under the supervision of your tutor. You never know, if people like **(10)** .... I do, someone might offer me a job. I **(11)** .... they would. Then I'd be able to give **(12)** .... the day job and go clubbing full-time!

Reading Multiple matching (Paper 1 Part 3)

1 Before you read
Look at the title of the article opposite and think about these questions.
1 What makes 'a good day out' for you?
2 What kind of things do you like to do?
3 What kind of places do you like to visit?

2 Skimming and scanning
Skim and scan the text. In which section are the following kinds of attraction mentioned? Write them on the line provided.

EXAMPLE: places of natural beauty ....

a homes of writers, artists, etc. .... *section A* ....
b theme parks ....
c museums ....
d amusement parks ....
e different kinds of buildings, e.g. religious buildings
....
f factories ....

3 Multiple matching
a Look at question 1.
  • Look at the key words marked in the question.
  • Scan the text to find the section(s) which may contain the answer.
  • Read this section carefully and mark the place where you find the answer.
  • Check that the text you have found exactly matches the question.

c Now continue with questions 2–15.

You are going to read an extract from a book about tourist attractions. For questions 1–15, choose from the sections (A–E). Each section may be chosen more than once.
Which section mentions

attractions where the design of the building itself is of great interest to visitors?	1
the possibility that visitors might spoil the places they visit?	2
the reasons determining where certain attractions are constructed?	3
attempts to make exhibits at some attractions seem more realistic?	4
the need for each attraction to have its own individual features?	5
attractions which do not have particularly impressive venues?	6
attractions that previously moved from one place to another?	7
attractions where visitors can watch a process in action?	8
a type of attraction that combines leisure with an educational purpose?	9
an attraction where consumer goods are on sale?	10
attractions associated with celebrated individuals?	11
the fact that attractions need to keep up-to-date with what visitors expect?	12
somebody explaining things to visitors at an attraction?	13
attractions that introduced the latest technology successfully?	14 15

El Greco's house in Toledo

Beamish, the North of England 'living museum'

A good day out

A

For some people, leisure means relaxing and getting away from it all, for example by visiting natural beauty spots in the country, or places for outdoor recreation. Of course, such natural attractions are
5 affected by the people who visit them, but the things that make them attractive tend not to alter greatly through time. Built attractions, however, are designed to appeal to people for whom relaxation means going somewhere and engaging in some kind
10 of specifically organised leisure activity. These attractions do, therefore, tend to change over time, in line with public taste and fashion. With each new attraction that is built, the competition to attract visitors increases, so great imagination and creativity
15 is required of designers and managers, in order to make their particular place stand out.

B

Over the past 30 years, there has been a marked trend in the leisure industry towards more exciting and sophisticated attractions of all kinds. Many
20 museums, for example, have seen quite dramatic changes, becoming more interesting and entertaining places to visit, while still maintaining their role of informing visitors about the past. Some have been converted into 'living museums' where
25 actors and actresses in costumes meet the public and play the roles of characters from the past, in attempts to make the exhibits come alive for visitors. In others, history is made vivid and exciting through the use of sounds, and even smells, to
30 conjure up a sense of the past. In a number of museums, audio-visual innovations have allowed very popular interactive displays to be developed.

C

Another trend which is emerging is for more places to be opened to the public as attractions, although
35 the original purpose for which they were built had nothing to do with leisure. Some of the earliest examples of this trend are religious buildings which attract tourists thanks to their great architectural value. These have come to serve a dual purpose, as
40 places of worship and as attractions for visitors. This trend, however, has now extended to various types of fascinating buildings, for a variety of reasons. Visitors often have an interest in exploring the homes of famous writers and artists from the past,
45 however humble the buildings themselves may be.

Not far from Madrid, in the town of Toledo, tourists flock to the tiny house of the famous painter El Greco, who lived there 400 years ago. Similarly, the parsonage which was the home of the Brontë
50 sisters, whose nineteenth-century novels include Jane Eyre and Wuthering Heights, brings many thousands of tourists each year to Haworth in northern England.

D

More recently, especially in the UK, there has been a
55 growing interest in the type of attraction where visitors can see a familiar object being manufactured. One example of this is the Edinburgh Crystal factory, which regularly opens its doors to the visiting public. Visitors are shown around the
60 factory by a guide and they see the famous Edinburgh Crystal glassware being manufactured in traditional red-hot ovens. After the tour, they have the opportunity to buy crystal decanters and goblets similar to those they have seen being made.
65 The visitors do not interfere with the glassmaking itself, so the factory serves a dual function of being both a real workplace and an attraction.

E

Amusement parks illustrate another trend. The concept of the amusement park grew out of the
70 travelling funfairs of a century ago. Over the years, these developed thrilling rides such as roller coasters alongside a range of things to do and see. As the equipment became more sophisticated, however, the larger funfairs tended to become fixed
75 in one place, creating wholly artificial worlds, completely devoted to the pursuit of fun and entertainment which enjoyed great popularity. Theme parks take this idea one step further, and the main difference is one of scale. Theme parks
80 stretch over vast areas of land, often the size of small towns. For this reason, most are situated in the countryside. Because theme parks are expensive attractions to construct, they are likely to be found in the more developed parts of the world. They are
85 also found in places which are within reach of large numbers of potential visitors, the customers of theme parks.

11A Happiness

Vocabulary ▶ CB pages 150–151

1 Topic: types of personality

a Write the character adjectives in the correct column in the table.
arrogant creative moody irritable ~~sensible~~ intellectual mean easy-going pessimistic sensitive witty ambitious vain punctual impulsive open-minded talkative generous suspicious sociable

Positive	Negative	It depends
sensible		

b Read the descriptions below. For each person, choose three adjectives from the list in Exercise 1a. Use each adjective once only. There are two adjectives you do not need.

1 Keith is very well-educated and likes discussing serious subjects with his friends. He's a junior lecturer in philosophy at the university, but he's determined to become a full professor by the time he's 35. Unfortunately, he thinks he's more intelligent and important than anyone else. ....
....

2 Joanna is very good at art. She has lots of original ideas and paints the most amazing pictures. She understands other people's problems and feelings very easily. When she talks, she says a lot of clever and amusing things, which make people laugh. ....

3 You have to be careful what you say to David, because he gets angry and annoyed very easily. He never believes that anything good is going to happen, so it usually doesn't! Although he's quite well-off, he hates spending money.
....

4 Sue loves being with people and has lots of friends. She talks a lot, which can sometimes be a little tiring. She tends to do things on the spur of the moment, without considering the possible dangers or problems. ....
....

5 Everyone loves Martin. He never seems to worry about anything or get upset or annoyed. He's ready to listen to other people's ideas and opinions, even if they are very different from his own. On top of that, he's always giving people money or presents. ....
....

6 Marilyn is an actress. She's very proud of her beauty. She can be a difficult person sometimes, and there are days when she is depressed or annoyed for no good reason. Marilyn finds it difficult to trust people, and seems to think that everyone is doing something bad behind her back.
....

c In your notebook, write a short character description of someone you know.

2 Verb/noun/adjective + preposition
Read this reference from a university tutor, and complete it with the correct prepositions.

I've been very satisfied **(1)**........................... Sebastian's performance over the past few years. I was a little concerned **(2)**........................... him when he first arrived at this college, but he has improved greatly since that time.

Sebastian is an extremely happy and cheerful student. He participates **(3)**........................... a large number of different activities and gets very enthusiastic **(4)**........................... everything he does. Sebastian belongs **(5)**........................... both the college football team and the basketball team, and is also involved **(6)**........................... the drama group and the environmental society. It is obvious that he has felt the benefit **(7)**........................... cooperating **(8)**........................... other students in these teams and groups. As regards his membership of the environmental society, I am glad that Sebastian has found something he believes **(9)**........................... and finds personally fulfilling.

While taking his final exams, Sebastian was both sensible and hard-working, finding a balance **(10)**........................... his studies and these other activities. This has resulted **(11)**........................... his obtaining an excellent degree from this university. I have every confidence **(12)**........................... his ability to do well in the future and recommend him to you without reservation.

3 🎧 Pronunciation

a **Look at the words below and listen to the recording. Mark the stressed syllable in each word.**

EXAMPLE: pessimistic

1 pessimistic enthusiastic artistic historic
2 cheer – cheerful delight – delightful
   wonder – wonderful beauty – beautiful
   disgrace – disgraceful
3 amaze – amazing confuse – confusing
   frustrate – frustrating satisfy – satisfying
   embarrass – embarrassing

b **Complete the pronunciation rule by ticking (✓) the correct answer A, B or C.**

1 When a word ends in -ic we stress:
   A the suffix **B** the second syllable
   C the syllable before the suffix
2 When we add the suffix -ful or -ing to a word we:
   A stress the suffix
   B stress the syllable before the suffix
   C do not change the stress of the word

4 Exam practice: word formation (Paper 3 Part 3)

Read the text below. Use the word given in capitals below the text to form a word that fits in the space in the text. There is an example at the beginning **(0)**.

CAN HYPNOSIS REDUCE STRESS?

When we think of hypnosis, we **(0)** usually think of those television shows where **(1)**............................ members of the audience are encouraged to do foolish things while they are **(2)**........................... . In such shows, the hypnotist is an **(3)**..........................., almost like a magician, whose main aim is to keep the audience happy. But hypnosis deserves to be taken more **(4)**........................... . If it is used properly, it can help people who suffer from **(5)**........................... related to stress.

We use the word *stress* to describe quite a large **(6)**........................... of different feelings, especially those connected with **(7)**........................... about our jobs. Hypnosis can help people to believe in their **(8)**........................... to do their jobs well. It also helps them to feel more relaxed about their work, which gives them greater **(9)**........................... to deal **(10)**........................... with any problems they may be facing in their daily lives.

(0) USUAL	**(4) SERIOUS**	**(8) ABLE**
(1) FORTUNE	**(5) ILL**	**(9) CONFIDENT**
(2) CONSCIOUS	**(6) VARY**	**(10) SUCCESS**
(3) ENTERTAIN	**(7) ANXIOUS**	

Language development 1 Clauses of

reason, purpose and contrast ▶ CB pages 152–153, GR page 186

1 Reason, purpose or contrast?

Read each sentence and decide if the clause is one of *reason, purpose* or *contrast*. Then mark the correct linking expression in each pair.

EXAMPLE: Recently I felt run-down *because / owing to* I was studying so hard for my exams. _____reason_____

1 *Even though / Despite* I took vitamin pills, I still seemed to have no energy. ....
2 I decided to take up jogging *in order that / in order to* do some exercise. ....
3 I went to a doctor one day *because of / as* I didn't feel very well. ....
4 The doctor said that my ill health was *due to / since* stress and overwork. ....
5 I decided to take up yoga *in order that / so as to* learn how to relax properly. ....
6 I now feel fitter and happier *despite / although* the fact that I am still very busy. ....
7 I even want to go to India *so that / in order to* I can learn more about yoga! ....

2 Which linking expression?

Read part of an interview with one of Britain's top runners, Paula Radcliffe. Complete the interview with an appropriate linking word or phrase from Exercise 1. There may be more than one possibility.

Interviewer: Paula, **(1)**........................... giving an amazing performance in the Sydney Olympics 10,000 metres, you didn't win a medal. How do you feel about that?

Paula: Well, it's true that three runners overtook me at the finish, **(2)**........................... I had led the way for 24 laps. It was obviously a disappointment **(3)**........................... I was sure I would win. But there's always another race to look forward to.

Interviewer: Has that always been your philosophy?

Paula: Yes. **(4)**........................... the fact that I was a top runner from the age of 12, I didn't win my first national championship until I was 17. There was no pressure on me. In fact, my coaches trained me carefully **(5)**........................... I wouldn't suffer from 'burnout' at an early age.

Interviewer: You often say that your greatest triumph was winning the Junior World Cross Country Championships in Boston in 1992.

Paula: Definitely. **(6)**........................... many great moments in my career since then, my victory in Boston remains a cherished memory.

Interviewer: Many people have commented on the red ribbon you wear when you run. Is it true that you wear it **(7)**........................... focus attention on the problem of drugs in athletics?

Paula: That's right. I wear a red ribbon **(8)**................... people can see my willingness to give a blood sample to the authorities. I'm very concerned about drug-taking among athletes.

3 Sentence combining

Read the statements below by Paula Radcliffe. Combine the sentences using an appropriate expression from the list. Use each expression only once. Make any other changes necessary. There may be more than one possibility.

in order to   due to   because   so that
even though   so as to   because of   since

1 A lot of male athletes at university wouldn't train with me. I was too fast for them.

   ....
   ....

2 I'm successful in athletics. I receive tremendous support from my husband and family.

   ....
   ....

3 I often discuss my diet with my dietician. I love eating out and trying new dishes.

   ....
   ....

4 Every year I go to a camp in Albuquerque, in the USA. I train there.

   ....
   ....

5 I want to spend some time in the USA. I will be able to run on the road circuit.

   ....
   ....

6 I love running on roads and mountain trails. I feel a sense of freedom.

   ....
   ....

7 I live a fulfilled life. I'm not concerned about my athletics career ending.

   ....
   ....

8 After athletics, I'd do something else. I could continue to channel my energy and ambitions.

   ....
   ....

4 Exam practice: open cloze (Paper 3 Part 2)

Read the text below and think of the word which best fits each space. Use only **one** word in each space. There is an example at the beginning **(0)**.

THRILL OF A LIFETIME

According **(0)**.........to.......... recent research, visiting a theme park in childhood can give people particularly happy memories. One thousand people aged between 18 and 22 took **(1)**........................... in a survey which was designed to find **(2)**........................... which happy childhood memories were most important to them. David Lewis is the child psychologist who led the research. He says that people remembered trips to theme parks much **(3)**........................... fondly than trips to the beach or to other leisure attractions **(4)**........................... as zoos. What is more, they remembered the most dangerous and exciting theme park rides best of **(5)**........................... .

Dr Lewis says that both adults and children go through various emotions **(6)**........................... a result of the 'white-knuckle' rides – the ones that provide the greatest thrills. These feelings include apprehension before the ride, fear during it, and relief **(7)**........................... it is all over. He has also noticed how often children want to repeat the experience immediately after getting off a ride **(8)**........................... that they can prolong the feeling **(9)**........................... achievement and satisfaction it gives them.

Dr Lewis also discovered that sharing the experience with close family members gave children strong family memories **(10)**........................... stayed with them as they **(11)**........................... older. His research helps us to understand why people love theme parks so **(12)**........................... . If you haven't been to one recently, perhaps it's time you did.

Writing Article (Paper 2 Part 2) ▶ WR page 202

Exam strategy

Start your article in an interesting and unusual way to catch the reader's attention. You can address your readers directly if you want. Make sure you finish your article with a strong, interesting sentence which summarises what you have said. Be humorous, if you think that it is appropriate in the kind of article you are writing. Finally, don't forget to give your article an interesting title!

1 Understand the task

Read the task below and answer the questions.

1 Where will the article appear? Who will read it?
2 What style should you use?
3 Would humour be appropriate in an article like this?

You see this competition in an international magazine for students of English.

WRITING COMPETITION

What was the happiest day of your life?

Write an article about the happiest day of your life, describing what happened and explaining why it was so special for you.

The best article will be published in our magazine next month!

Write your **article** in **120–180** words.

2 Check and improve a sample answer

a **Read the comments below and match them to the three introductions to an article (A–C) written by students.**

1 ☐ Inappropriate – more like the introduction of a discursive composition.
2 ☐ Inappropriate – more like the beginning of a formal letter than an article.
3 ☐ Appropriate – personal and slightly informal in style. It introduces the article in an interesting way and makes the reader want to read more.

A
> I am writing to you to describe the happiest day of my life. The happiest day of my life occurred when I celebrated my tenth birthday. I went with my parents to the London Aquarium.

B
> Imagine how happy and excited a little child from Africa feels when he or she sees snow for the first time. That's exactly how I felt when my parents took me to the London Aquarium on my tenth birthday.

C
> *Nowadays life has become so fast and complicated that people do not have time to feel happy. They are too busy making money or thinking about which car to buy next. In order to experience happiness, it is necessary to slow down and focus on the simple things in life.*

---

b **Read the continuation of the article below. Improve it by combining sentences.**

1 Combine sentences (a) and (b) using the phrase *as soon as*.
2 Combine sentences (c) and (d) by starting *As I was + -ing … .*

c **Now find and correct two mistakes with vocabulary.**

> **(a)** I woke up in the morning. **(b)** I realised that my parents had planned something special. They didn't say anything, though, until I had opened my presents. **(c)** I stared in delight at my new bicycle. **(d)** My father suddenly said, 'OK, let's go to London!'
>
> In the car, my father said me we were going to the London Aquarium. I remember that I had no idea what he meant. I only understood when I saw the photographs of fish outside. We spent hours there. I was so impressive by the sharks that I didn't want to leave!

d **Read the comments below and match them to the three sample conclusions.**

1 ☐ Inappropriate – too short and ineffective.
2 ☐ Inappropriate – more like the conclusion to a discursive composition.
3 ☐ Appropriate – it summarises the content of the article nicely and adds a touch of humour.

A
> I'll never forget that day. I really enjoyed my party later, but my visit to the London Aquarium made it a special day for me. You won't be surprised when I tell you that I'm now studying marine biology at university!

B
> In conclusion, it is obvious that happiness is the most important thing in life. It is easy to forget this simply because we are too busy at work. We should all make sure that we spend enough time with our families, doing things we enjoy.

C
> That is why my tenth birthday was the happiest day of my life. I will never forget what I did on that day.

e **Tick (✓) the title that you think is best for the article.**

A The happiest day of my life
B A day I'll always remember
C The London Aquarium

3 Do the task

Write your own answer to the task in your notebook.

Listening Extracts:
multiple choice (Paper 4 Part 1)

1 Before you listen
Look at the exam task opposite. Read the context sentence, the question and the three options. Think about the situation; who will be talking and what they will be talking about? Mark key words in each question.

2 🎧 Extracts
a Listen to the recording and do the task.

b Listen again to check your answers. Make sure the other options could not be correct.

You will hear people talking in eight different situations. For questions **1–8**, choose the best answer **A**, **B** or **C**.

1 You hear part of a radio programme about working conditions.
What is the speaker doing?
A suggesting how a problem should be approached
B recommending a particular course of study
C advising against conflicts with employers
[1]

2 You overhear somebody talking about a hotel.
At what point did she start to feel angry with the hotel?
A when her letter went unanswered
B when the service was not good during her stay
C when she phoned the hotel and spoke to somebody
[2]

3 You hear the beginning of a radio programme on the subject of human behaviour.
What question is the presenter going to ask the psychologist?
A why children are sometimes embarrassing
B how people learn to be tactful with others
C whether adults should try to be more honest
[3]

4 In a radio play, you hear two people talking.
Why doesn't the woman want to eat in the restaurant?
A Nobody else is eating there.
B A noisier place would be better.
C She doesn't like the music there.
[4]

5 On a visit to a college, you overhear part of a lecture.
What is the lecturer explaining?
A why laughter is important to us
B why laughter has been so widely studied
C why laughter is sometimes misunderstood
[5]

6 You hear a woman talking about a book she bought.
What is her opinion of the book?
A It fulfilled all her expectations.
B It surprised her how entertaining it was.
C It turned out to be more useful than she thought.
[6]

7 You hear a professional footballer talking about his retirement.
How does he feel?
A open to whatever new opportunities arise
B unsure whether he'll enjoy his new lifestyle
C determined to remain in touch with the sport
[7]

8 You hear a woman talking about her car.
Why did she decide to buy it?
A A friend suggested it.
B She liked the look of it.
C She needed to replace her old one
[8]

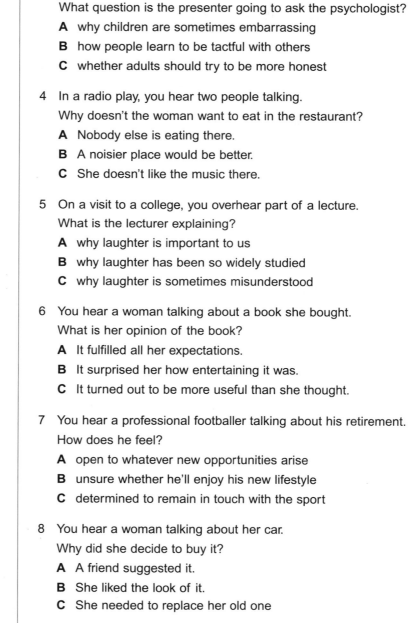

Vocabulary ▶ CB pages 156–157

Exam strategy

In Paper 2, you may have to describe different ways of keeping fit and healthy. You may also be asked to talk about this subject in Paper 5. Record useful vocabulary in your vocabulary notebook.

1 Commonly confused words

Read the texts below and mark the correct word in each pair.

The importance of diet

Nowadays, it is more and more common to hear that someone is a **(1)** *vegetation / vegetarian*. Many people have realised that eating vegetables, particularly lightly cooked or **(2)** *raw / crude* vegetables, is good for you. Frequent colds, headaches and other **(3)** *illnesses / diseases* are often symptoms of an unhealthy diet and a **(4)** *stressed / stressful* lifestyle. Eating more **(5)** *nutritious / edible* types of food and, if possible, living and working somewhere where the **(6)** *speed / pace* of life is slower, will result in a healthier body and mind.

Healthcare today

In the past 80 years, healthcare has changed a lot. You still often have to wait a long time for the doctor to see you in his **(7)** *office / surgery*, but many other things are different. Hospital **(8)** *wards / dormitories* are smaller and brighter, and doctors and nurses can **(9)** *treat / cure* you more effectively. If you are **(10)** *wounded / injured* in an accident, or have to **(11)** *make / have* an operation, you are much more likely to survive today than you were in the past. Then it was extremely common for wounds to become **(12)** *infected / polluted* and for complications to develop.

---

2 Collocations

a Write an appropriate verb from the list in each space below. It must collocate with all the words and phrases in the set. Use each verb once only.

take   have   make   break   catch   sprain   feel

1 .... a headache / earache / a sore throat / a high temperature / an accident / an operation / an injection

2 .... ill / dizzy / sick / depressed / fit and healthy

3 .... a quick recovery / an appointment with the doctor

4 .... a cold / flu / a virus from someone

5 .... your leg / your arm / your wrist / one of your ribs

6 .... your ankle / your wrist

7 .... your temperature / an X-ray / some medicine / an aspirin / a rest / some exercise / your blood pressure

8 .... you an injection / you a thorough examination

b Complete the sentences by putting a suitable verb + noun collocation from Exercise 2a in each gap. You may need to change the form of the verb.

EXAMPLE: What does the thermometer say? If I see that you <u>have a high temperature</u> , I'm going to call the doctor!

1 The doctor said that if I had appendicitis, I would need to go into hospital to ....

2 My sister was very ill last month, but she .... when the doctor prescribed antibiotics and was soon back at school.

3 Put your coat on when you go out! You'll .... if you don't wrap up!

4 The dentist asked me if I wanted to .... before he drilled my tooth.

5 Don't worry, you've only .... – you haven't broken any bones! You'll be able to walk again in a few days.

6 'I think you may have fractured your skull. We'll have to .... of the back of your head to check,' said Dr Benn.

3 Comparing photos

Look at the two photographs of people doing exercise and read how a student answered the question:

'Compare and contrast the two photographs, and say which form of exercise looks more fun.'

Complete the spaces with a word or phrase from the list below.

while   like   would choose
could be   kind of   however
show   personally   there are
on the other hand

Both photographs (1)_____ people taking exercise. In the first photograph, I can see a man cycling in the country, (2)_____ in the second photograph (3)_____ a lot of people in a room doing aerobics.

The man in this picture is on his own and he is cycling along a path. He is wearing a, er, a (4)_____ helmet on his head so it (5)_____ rather dangerous. The aerobics class, (6)_____ , is safe and organised, and there is a teacher – I think – who is leading them. The people are wearing – er – they're wearing those things people wear for doing keep fit – a bit (7)_____ stockings.

(8)_____ , I think both ways of exercising are fun. In an aerobics class you are with a lot of other people, doing exercises to music, and when you are cycling in the mountains you are surrounded by beautiful countryside.

(9)_____ , if I had to choose, I (10)_____ this one – cycling. It's hard work when you have to cycle up a hill but it's really enjoyable and healthy.

Language development 2

as/like, so/such, such as; too/very/enough ▶ CB page 159

1 so/such

a Make sentences by putting the words in the correct order.

1 such we have a view from beautiful our window
  We ....

2 such is a to day that I swimming nice want go it
  ....

3 such have never I delicious eaten food before
  ....

4 why it so to important exercise take is?
  ....

5 this so boring think documentary is that I will asleep I fall
  ....

6 he wants has so much can buy money that he anything he
  ....

7 weather we another such good on holiday had that stayed week we
  ....

8 many you not eat so hamburgers should
  ....

b Underline the correct phrase in the following sentences.

1 His diet contains *such a / a such* lot of cholesterol that I'm worried he'll develop heart disease in later life.

2 It was *such a / a so* good feeling when the doctor told me that I was suffering from a common food allergy.

3 There are *so few / so little* calories in lettuce that you can eat as much as you like.

4 Some processed food contains *so many / such many* preservatives that it might damage your health.

5 It was *such awful / such an awful* food that we agreed never to go again to that restaurant.

6 My boyfriend eats *such / so* quickly that he always has indigestion after a meal.

7 I had *so much / so many* to eat last night that I felt quite ill.

8 Rice is *so / so much* rich in carbohydrates that many parts of Asia have developed 'rice cultures'.

2 too, very or enough?
Complete the sentences with *too, very* or *enough*.

1 Those exercises are much .... difficult for me to do.
2 I don't think there is .... vitamin C in my diet.
3 Our gym instructor is rather serious but .... nice.
4 This tracksuit is not big .... for me, I'm afraid.
5 I think you put .... much sugar in your coffee.
6 My father thinks he is .... old to take up a sport.
7 Sheila doesn't spend .... time exercising every day.
8 Everyone knows that fresh fruit is .... good for you.

3 so, such, too, enough or very?
Complete the email with *so, such, too, enough* or *very*.

Hi Stephen

My exams are over at last! They were
(1)............... difficult that I didn't think
I'd pass. I did though, and now I'm a doctor! I
hope you're coming to my party on Saturday. It
should be **(2)**............... good. I can't
believe that **(3)**............... many of my
friends are coming. In fact, Tony thinks that
there'll be **(4)**............... many people
and that we won't have **(5)**...............
food and drink for everybody. I don't think that'll
happen. I've prepared **(6)**............... a
lot of food that I have **(7)**............... to
feed an army! I was thinking of having the
party in the garden, but Tony says it'll be much
(8)............... cold outside. I suppose
he's right. The weather changes
(9)............... quickly that it could even
rain, couldn't it? By the way, Stephen, could
you lend me some glasses? I don't have
(10)............... at home, I'm afraid.
Please give me a call as soon as you can.

Love, Anna

4 as, like or such as?
Complete the sentences with *as, like* or *such as*.

1 Dr Jones is regarded .... one of the greatest heart surgeons alive.
2 'I'm sorry I behaved .... a fool last night, Rod,' I said.

3 Many students work .... tourist guides during their summer holidays.
4 Famous people .... Bill Clinton and Madonna have visited this restaurant.
5 I'm 18 but my parents treat me .... a child.
6 I wish I could skate .... you! You're really good at it.
7 Vegetables .... red peppers, broccoli and brussels sprouts contain a lot of vitamin C.
8 Teachers described Luke .... a clever, hard-working student.
9 Cherie is really .... her sister, isn't she?
10 The new doctor seems .... a very nice person, doesn't he?

5 Key word transformations
Complete the second sentence so that it has a similar meaning to the first sentence, using the word given. Do not change the word given. Use between two and five words, including the word given.

1 You don't have the strength to lift those weights. **strong**
You .... to lift those weights.
2 Kate plays the piano so well even though she is only 16. **such**
Kate is .... even though she is only 16.
3 My father is a hospital doctor. **works**
My father .... a hospital.
4 The music at the party was too loud for us to be able to talk to each other. **so**
The music at the party .... couldn't talk to each other.
5 We had such a good time that we didn't want to leave. **enjoyed**
We .... we didn't want to leave.
6 You are not fit enough to take part in the competition. **unfit**
You .... take part in the competition
7 I left the party early because it was so crowded. **people**
There .... the party that I left early.
8 Dr Simmons treats his older patients like children. **if**
Dr Simmons treats his older patients .... children.
9 It looks like rain, doesn't it? **as**
It looks .... to rain, doesn't it?
10 Why can't you give up eating chocolate? **so**
Why is it .... give up eating chocolate?

Reading Multiple-choice questions
(Paper 1 Part 1)

1 Before you read
Read the instructions for the task, and the heading and subheading of the article opposite. Try to answer these questions.
1 What do you think a personal trainer does in his job?
2 What kind of people does Matt Roberts train?
3 Why do you think he took up this career?
4 What do you think Matt offers which makes him *more than just a fitness trainer*?

2 Skimming
Skim the text and check your ideas in Exercise 1. Write the numbers of the paragraphs in which you found the information and correct your answers if necessary.
Question 1: paragraph ....
Question 2: paragraph ....
Question 3: paragraph ....
Question 4: paragraph ....

3 Multiple-choice questions
Do the exam task below. Remember to do the following.
- First, read the questions and mark key words. Don't look at the options A–D yet.
- Find the place in the text where the information is contained.
- Find your own answer to the question and mark the relevant piece of text.
- Now read options A–D and choose the one closest to your answer.
- Read the piece of text carefully to check that your answer is right and that the other options are definitely wrong.

4 Vocabulary: expressions
Complete the second sentence so that it has a similar meaning to the first sentence, using the word given. Do not change the word given.
1 Matt's father played professional football and it looked as if Matt would do the same. **set**
Matt's father played professional football and Matt
.... do the same.
2 Being unable to exercise showed Matt what it's like to be out of condition. **taste**
Being unable to exercise ....
what it's like to be out of condition.
3 He arrived in the USA at a time when personal trainers were becoming fashionable. **with**
His arrival in the USA ....
the rise in the fashion for personal trainers.
4 It isn't surprising that news of Matt's skills spread by word of mouth. **comes**
It .... that news of Matt's
skills spread by word of mouth.

You are going to read a newspaper article about a personal trainer. For questions **1–8**, choose the answer **A**, **B**, **C** or **D** which you think fits best according to the text.

1 Why did Matt decide not to follow a career in football?
   A He realised it was a dangerous sport.
   B He was advised against it for medical reasons.
   C He discovered he was better suited to athletics.
   D He didn't want to do the same thing as his father.

2 The expression 'set his sights on' in line 22 refers to
   A a place Matt had seen.
   B a job Matt had tried.
   C something Matt had learnt to do.
   D something Matt hoped to achieve.

3 According to the article, when Matt went to the USA
   A he was able to take advantage of a new trend.
   B he was the first trainer to attract celebrity clients.
   C he was sure of finding work as a personal trainer.
   D he made good contacts amongst fashionable trainers.

4 In the writer's view, what did Matt's early clients appreciate most?
   A He wasn't well-known himself.
   B He respected their need for privacy.
   C He was recommended by their friends.
   D He provided a personal training package.

5 In London, Matt trained his clients in their homes at first because
   A that was what they preferred.
   B his gym was not in a fashionable area.
   C he couldn't afford to set up his own gym.
   D they were able to provide their own equipment.

6 What approach to training does Matt adopt?
   A He seeks to change people's attitudes.
   B He tries to teach people the best methods.
   C He works with people to achieve results.
   D He expects people to follow his example.

7 What is Matt's view of other personal trainers?
   A Cheaper ones may be just as good.
   B He prefers not to comment on them.
   C There may now be too many of them.
   D Few offer a service comparable to his.

8 In the last paragraph, the writer suggests that
   A Matt believes in the benefits of using his books.
   B Matt has plans to televise his books in the future.
   C Matt's books are amongst the best on the market.
   D Matt's books should be used together with a trainer.

FIT FOR FAME

He's the man who keeps the stars in good shape. But Matt Roberts is more than just a fitness trainer.

① At 33, Matt Roberts is Britain's leading personal trainer. His clients include the rich and the famous: people like supermodel Naomi Campbell and Mel C, the singer with the pop group Spice Girls. He has
5   already published two books about fitness and he is about to launch his own range of health and fitness products.

②   Unlike many of his clients, Matt has always been sporty. His father, John Roberts, played professional
10 football for top London club Arsenal in the early seventies, and Matt looked set to follow in his footsteps. Then, during an athletics match at school, his plans suddenly changed when he was knocked on the head by a stray discus. Doctors ruled out
15 team sports from then on, and for a few months he got no exercise at all. This gave Matt a brief taste of what it's like to be out of condition. After that, he decided to focus on another activity he had always excelled at: sprinting.

20 ③   Matt trained hard and once even represented England, but already by the age of 16, he had **set his sights on** becoming a fitness trainer with his own gym. He recalls: 'When my injury meant I wasn't getting any exercise, I just wasn't myself. It's the
25 same for people who are overweight or unfit, they aren't themselves.' For Matt remains convinced that fitness is the basis of a full and happy life.

④   After leaving school, Matt went to the USA. This was a lucky move because his arrival coincided with
30 the rise in the fashion for personal trainers amongst celebrities, and he became one of the pioneers in the field. His first big break came when a rock star who was preparing for a world tour employed him full-time. 'It was a great experience,' Matt recalls,
35 'coming up with the entire health package for somebody. But intense.' He's careful, however, even now, not to give away his employer's identity. And it is this acceptance of the confidential nature of their relationship that his clients value highly, perhaps
40 even more than the training itself. So it comes as no surprise that news of his skills spread through word-of-mouth recommendations.

⑤   After six months, Matt moved back to London, where he built up a base of clients whom he trained
45 in their homes, before spotting the premises he was looking for in the city's fashionable Mayfair district. As he was only 22, the banks wouldn't lend Matt the start-up money he needed and suppliers wouldn't lease equipment. But Matt worked hard to save the
50 capital and moved into what would be the first of his chain of gyms.

⑥   'It's great to see results in clients,' Matt says. 'I see myself more as a training partner. I don't think the pupil–teacher thing works with most
55 people.' He's probably right there, but it's clear to me that the best trainers are also psychologists of a kind, achieving the kind of mental transformation that changes a couch potato into a gymnast, helping us find the inner athlete just waiting to burst free.

60 ⑦   But then there are trainers and trainers. The £40-an-hour trainer down your local gym may not offer quite the same results as Matt, who charges between £80 and £110. What's more, he says he only knows of seven or eight really good trainers in the UK, adding
65 'although of course there might be a lot of good people I haven't come across'.

⑧   But if you can't afford a top trainer, you could, of course, try Matt's 90-Day Fitness Plan. As his editor insists: 'He's the real thing! As you read Matt's
70 books, you can almost hear him pushing you on.' Matt Roberts seems determined to broadcast the good news about health and fitness beyond his client base – which is a sincere, if also a profitable, objective. One can't help but think, however, that
75 even the best exercise book is bound to be less effective than one-to-one sessions with the man himself.

12A Bookworm

Vocabulary ▶ CB pages 164–165

▶ CB pages 164–165

Exam strategy

Crime is quite a common topic area in Paper 1, Reading, and Paper 3, Use of English. It also occasionally comes up in Paper 5, Speaking. Make sure you are familiar with the relevant vocabulary.

1 Topic: crime

a Label the picture using words from the list.

defendant   ~~defence lawyer~~   lawyer for the prosecution   judge
jury   witness   police officer   reporters

b Two journalists are discussing the trial. Match questions 1–8 to the appropriate answers a–h.

1 ☐ What crime did the defendant commit?
2 ☐ What did he do exactly?
3 ☐ How did the police manage to catch him?
4 ☐ Apart from the witness, is there any other evidence?
5 ☐ He'll need a good lawyer, won't he?
6 ☐ How do you think he will plead?
7 ☐ I wonder what verdict the jury will reach?
8 ☐ What kind of sentence is the judge likely to pass?

a Guilty, probably. I don't think it'll take them very long to decide.

b He certainly will. The lawyer for the prosecution is said to win almost all his cases.

c He's on trial for murder. He has a long record of burglary and other minor offences though.

d Oh yes. The police have found his fingerprints everywhere. They've also managed to get a DNA sample from some of his hair which they found at the scene of the crime.

e Apparently, he had broken into a house and was stealing some jewellery when the owner appeared. There was a fight and …

f Almost certainly the judge will sentence him to several years in prison. He may even give him life imprisonment.

g There was a witness who saw him leaving the house. She gave a description to the police and they arrested him the next day.

h I'm sure he'll plead innocent. He'll claim that he was attacked by the owner of the house and that he acted in self-defence.

c Read the sentences in Exercise 1b again, and find as many verb + noun collocations as you can. Add them to your vocabulary notebook. Then make a note of any other useful expressions related to crime.
EXAMPLE: commit a crime

2 Exam practice: multiple-choice cloze (Paper 3 Part 1)

Read the text below and decide which answer **A**, **B**, **C** or **D** best fits each space. There is an example at the beginning **(0)**.

0 A persuaded   **B** urged   **C** tempted   **D** provoked

AN OPPORTUNITY TOO GOOD TO MISS

It was something that might have **(0)** ...C... even the most honest teenager: the discovery of more than £3,000 in used bank notes in an unlocked night safe. That was what two British teenagers, aged 14 and 17, **(1)** .... across when they were hanging **(2)** .... outside a bank one Friday evening in January with **(3)** .... much to do.

As a joke, one of them decided to **(4)** .... the handle of the night safe a pull, and to his amazement it opened because it was unlocked. He couldn't believe his eyes when he saw the money inside. After a short discussion, he and his friend **(5)** .... the bank notes and ran away. Unfortunately for them, however, the **(6)** .... was being **(7)** .... by security cameras.

The money was reported missing on the following Monday morning and the teenagers were **(8)** .... for the crime within the week. Although neither of them would be **(9)** .... upon as a 'master criminal', they both nevertheless ended up with criminal **(10)** ....

At what's **(11)** .... a juvenile court they were each ordered to pay a £300 **(12)** .... In addition to this, they were ordered to write letters of apology to the bank they had stolen the money from. Lloyds Bank were later said to be reviewing their security systems.

	A	**B**	**C**	**D**
1	came	met	chanced	found
2	over	around	off	up
3	hardly	something	little	nothing
4	fetch	take	put	give
5	grabbed	swept	held	picked
6	burglary	fraud	theft	forgery
7	registered	recorded	recalled	received
8	charged	sentenced	arrested	convicted
9	looked	regarded	viewed	considered
10	notes	records	charts	documents
11	called	known	titled	named
12	fine	refund	fee	reward

Language development 1
Connecting ideas

▶ CB pages 166–167, GR page 186

Exam strategy

Remember to use a variety of connecting/linking expressions and structures to link ideas in your writing. But be careful: don't overuse the same structure. Also vary the length of your sentences: don't just use long sentences, use some **short** ones as well!

1 Which connecting expression?
Complete the sentences with an appropriate connecting word or expression from the list below. Use each word or expression once only. There are two that you do not need to use.
in order to   because   before   after   if who   which   while   and   but   such however

1 I read a lot of novels by Agatha Christie .... improve my English.
2 Agatha Christie is .... a good writer that I could read her novels all day.
3 Every night, I read a chapter of *Murder on the Orient Express* .... going to sleep.
4 .... I was reading last night, I heard a sound outside the window.
5 It was late .... obviously I felt a bit scared.
6 .... , I got up from my chair and walked to the window.
7 I couldn't see anything .... it was so dark outside.
8 I would have phoned the police .... I had a telephone.
9 .... thinking about it for a minute, I suddenly realised what the sound was.
10 There was a cat in the garden .... wanted to come inside!

2 Participle clauses

Rewrite or combine the sentences using the words given.

1 Simon spent all his time reading books because he was out of work.
Being .... , Simon
....

2 He heard the telephone ring. He put down his book. He got up to answer it.
Hearing .... , he
.... and ....

3 He felt annoyed at the interruption. He picked up the telephone. He shouted 'Yes!' as loud as he could.
Feeling .... , he picked
.... and ....

4 He put the receiver down again because he realised that the caller had hung up.
Realising .... , he
....

5 He got ready to go for a walk because he hadn't been out all day.
Not having .... , he got
....

6 He reached the door. He heard the telephone ring again.
On reaching .... , he
....

7 He ran to the phone. He picked up the receiver. He heard the voice of his girlfriend, who asked what the matter was.
Running .... , he picked
.... and ....

8 Despite the fact that he felt rather guilty, he couldn't help smiling.
Despite feeling .... , he couldn't
....

3 Combining sentences

Improve the following story by combining the groups of sentences using the words in brackets. Make any changes necessary. Write the story out in your notebook.

1 Peter arrived at his brother's house. He realised something was wrong. (as soon as)

2 It was a hot day. All the doors and windows were closed. (even though)

3 Peter was sure Tom was at home. He had phoned him an hour before. (as)

4 He opened the front door. He went inside. He looked in all the rooms. (opening, and)

5 Tom had gone out. He would have left a note. (if)

6 His brother was a sensible man. He always told others what his plans were. (who)

7 Peter was climbing the stairs. The doorbell rang. (as)

8 He rushed down the stairs very quickly. He almost fell. (so … that)

9 He saw his brother on the doorstep. He gave a cry of relief. (seeing)

10 Tom laughed. He told Peter that the police had arrested him in the afternoon. They had mistaken him for an escaped bank robber! (and, because)

4 Exam practice: open cloze
(Paper 3 Part 2)

Read the text below and think of the word which best fits each space. Use only **one** word in each space. There is an example at the beginning **(0)**.

AGATHA CHRISTIE, CRIME WRITER

Agatha Christie is probably the **(0)** ....most....... widely known writer of crime novels in the world. In **(1)** .... of the fact that her writing now seems rather old-fashioned, her novels continue to sell very well. What readers obviously like about them is the suspense and the atmosphere of mystery they create.

Agatha Christie was born in 1890. After **(2)** .... married to Colonel Archibald Christie in 1914, she worked as a volunteer nurse in World War 1, dispensing medicines. The knowledge of poisons **(3)** .... she gained during this time came in useful when she wrote her novels.

Her first novel, *The Mysterious Affair at Styles*, **(4)** .... published in 1920. The main character in the novel, Hercule Poirot, was **(5)** .... popular that she used him in another 40 books. In **(6)** .... to her novels, Agatha Christie wrote a number of plays. *The Mousetrap* was **(7)** .... a success that it ran in London for more than 50 years.

Agatha Christie's personal life was **(8)** .... exciting as the plots of her novels. She caused a sensation in 1926 **(9)** .... she disappeared for ten days, possibly suffering **(10)** .... amnesia. After **(11)** .... divorced her first husband, in 1928, she later married the famous archaeologist, Max Mallowan. They travelled widely in the Near East, and Agatha Christie carefully recorded her experiences in **(12)** .... to use them in later novels. *Death on the Nile* is one of these masterpieces.

Writing Report (Paper 2 Part 2)

▶ WR page 204

1 Understand the task
Read the task below and answer the questions.
1 What do you think your job or role might be?
2 Who are you writing the report for? What style will you use?
3 How many parts are there to the question? Mark the parts of the task that tell you what to include in the report.
4 Who would you need to talk to in order to obtain the information for the report?

The Mayor of your town is concerned about rising crime among teenagers. He has asked you to write a report for the town council, describing the crimes which teenagers commonly commit where you live and saying what you think could be done to solve the problem.

Write your **report** in **120–180** words in an appropriate style.

2 Compare two sample answers
a Look at the table, which lists the features of a good report. Then read Reports 1 and 2 and tick (✓) the features that you find in each report, to complete the table. Which report is better?

A good report:	Report 1	Report 2
has a clear title.	✓	✓
is divided into sections with useful headings.		
has an introduction stating the report's aims.		
says how the information was obtained.		
is written in an impersonal style.		
uses passive voice where appropriate.		
may use numbers to list points.		
ends with a conclusion or recommendation if requested.		

b Correct the errors which the teacher has identified in each report. (See page 9 for the key to correction symbols.)

Report 1

Report on teenage crime in this town

In order to write this report, I talked to lots of young people and local residents as well. Everyone agreed that there was a big problem in this town.

The main problems, according to most people, were (1) vandalism and (2) bad behaviour. There were lots of (3) burglaries, as well. Young people comitted [Sp] a lot of burglaries in this town. I spoke to one man who was so angry he could hardly answer my questions. They had broken into his house five times!

I don't really know what to recomend [Sp] I think that many teenagers my age don't have anything to do in the evenings. They feel bored and so they do things that are wrong. Obviously, the town council could build a sports centre. Teenagers would have somewhere to go then.

I strongly suggest building a sports centre. If this was done, crime would obviously decrease.

Report 2

Report on the problem of crime among local teenagers

Introduction
The aim of this report is to describe the types of crimes which are most common among teenagers in this town and to suggest possible solutions. The information for the report was obtained from local residents and teenagers.

The most common crimes
It seems that the three most common teenage crimes are vandalism, threatening behaviour and burglary. Most people beleived [Sp] that the third type of crime was the most serious. In recent years, there has been a huge increese [Sp] in the number of burglaries commited [Sp] by young people.

Possible solutions
Everyone who were [Gr] interviewed made at least one of the following suggestions.
1 More facilities for young people. For example, a sports centre could be built.
2 More police on the streets. There are parts of town where the police never goes. [Gr] Not surprisingly, crime was high in these areas.
3 Better street lighting.

Conclusion
It was widely felt that the town council was not doing enough to combatt [Sp] crime. For this reason, I strongly recommend that all the measures above should be taken. If this is done, teenage crime will certainly decrease.

3 Do the task
Write your own answer to the task in your notebook.

Listening Sentence completion (Paper 4 Part 2)

1 Before you listen
Read the instructions for the listening task opposite, and sentences 1–10. Try and predict what kind of information is missing. Remember to look at the words before and after the gap.

1 Which answer do you think will contain a number?

....

2 Which answers do you think will be adjectives?

....

2 🎧 Sentence completion

a Listen to the recording and complete the sentences.

b Listen again to check and complete your answers.

You will hear an interview with a novelist. For questions **1–10**, complete the sentences.

Laura explains that she studied [_____ **1**] at university.

Laura followed a career as a [_____ **2**] for many years.

Laura says she found her job both satisfying and [_____ **3**].

The first type of book which Laura attempted to write was a [_____ **4**] novel.

Laura noticed that novels dealing with the [_____ **5**] were doing well.

Laura's novel is about a man who believed he'd discovered a [_____ **6**].

Laura gives the example of [_____ **7**] as an historical detail she needed to research.

In Laura's novel, most of the [_____ **8**] are invented.

When planning a novel, Laura concentrates on the [_____ **9**] first.

When she's working on a book, Laura usually writes about [_____ **10**] per day.

12B The media

Vocabulary ▶ CB pages 170–171

1 Topic: the media

a Write these words and phrases in the correct column in the table. There may be more than one possibility for some words.

circulation   commercials   log on
documentary newscaster web page   download
gossip column reporter   editor   article   surf
server   tabloid   weather forecast   presenter
viewers   small ads

Television	Newspapers	The Internet

b Complete the sentences with words and phrases from Exercise 1a.

1 I worked on a local paper once. It was a weekly paper and had a .... of about 10,000.

2 I read a really interesting .... the other day about teenagers and crime.

3 Sometimes I .... the Internet for hours, looking for something interesting.

4 My father is a bit snobbish. He says that .... newspapers are no better than comics.

5 According to the .... on TV last night, today is going to be a lovely day!

6 If there are lots of photographs on the page, it can take ages to .... , so I usually go and make a cup of coffee.

7 The worst thing about TV is the number of .... They interrupt the programmes every 20 minutes on this channel.

8 Look in the .... of the local newspaper if you want to find some cheap second-hand furniture.

9 It's the .... of a newspaper who decides what news is reported every day.

10 I really like the .... on the *News Tonight* programme. She's quite humorous sometimes when she reads the news.

c Write the expressions in your vocabulary notebook. Add more expressions as you come across them in your reading.

2 Phrasal verbs

a Read the texts and mark the correct word in each pair.

Journalism has changed a lot in recent years. In the past, journalists were taken **(1)** *up / on* by a newspaper without any training at all. They had to pick **(2)** *up / on* their skills on the job. For example, the editor would tell them to go and hang **(3)** *by / around* the police so that they could find out what was going **(4)** *on / through*. Nowadays, a lot of journalists sit in front of their computers all day. They hardly get out **(5)** *of / from* their offices at all.

I'm going to study photography at university next year. My father is a sports photographer and he talked me **(6)** *up / into* becoming a photographer myself. It sounds like a really interesting job. A couple of years ago I wanted to go in **(7)** *for / at* law, but I think being a photojournalist or sports photographer will be more exciting.

What makes someone want to take **(8)** *on / up* a job in the media? I'm sure some people set **(9)** *out / off* to change the way people think and behave. But I think that most people who work in the media see it as an exciting job which puts them at the centre of events. I'd love to be a presenter on TV. To do that well you need to get **(10)** *on / across* well with people – and be able to express yourself clearly, of course.

b Replace the words in italics with phrasal verbs from Exercise 2a in the correct form. Make any other necessary changes.

1 I *acquired a knowledge of* Japanese while I was working there as a journalist. I didn't have any lessons. ....

2 Have you ever thought of *choosing* sports writing as a career? ....

3 My best friend *persuaded me to do* media studies at university. ....

4 I *have a good relationship* with my tutor at university. ....

5 A good reporter needs to know what is *happening* in the world. ....

6 That new newspaper is doing really well. It recently *employed* another 20 journalists. ....

7 If you *go everywhere with* Jim, you'll learn everything you need to know. ....

8 Tourists are being warned to *leave* town as quickly as possible – things are getting dangerous! ....

3 Exam practice: multiple-choice cloze (Paper 3 Part 1)

Read the text below and decide which answer **A**, **B**, **C** or **D** best fits each space. There is an example at the beginning (**0**).

0 **A** long   **B** far   **C** large   **D** deep

THE HISTORY OF JOURNALISM

Journalism has a very (**0**) ....A.... history. It dates back at least from ancient Rome, when written announcements of deaths, marriages and military appointments were (**1**)............. up regularly in public places. It wasn't until the fifteenth century, (**2**)............. , that the invention of the printing press made the rapid (**3**)............. of journalism possible.

Journalism as we know it today probably dates from the eighteenth century, with the (**4**)............. of daily newspapers that were written to spread the views of particular parties or social groups. There is a great variety of journalism on (**5**)............. in Britain, ranging from the scandals of the tabloid newspapers to the high-quality reporting of the more serious publications.

Changes in journalism in the twentieth century (**6**)............. place as a result of technological (**7**)............. : the teletypewriter, the radio, and then television. While the (**8**)............. of the newspaper journalist may have (**9**)............. in recent years, many radio and television journalists became (**10**)............. names as they reported events while they were (**11**)............. happening. News broadcaster Walter Cronkite, for example, will be remembered by millions of television (**12**)............. for his coverage of events such as the funeral of American president John F Kennedy and the landing of the first man on the moon.

1	**A** taken	**B** put	**C** given	**D** shown
2	**A** therefore	**B** however	**C** whereas	**D** indeed
3	**A** increase	**B** ascent	**C** extent	**D** growth
4	**A** appearance	**B** receipt	**C** release	**D** attendance
5	**A** choice	**B** market	**C** stock	**D** offer
6	**A** gave	**B** stood	**C** took	**D** held
7	**A** advances	**B** revisions	**C** amendments	**D** promotions
8	**A** mark	**B** influence	**C** command	**D** position
9	**A** reduced	**B** declined	**C** retired	**D** departed
10	**A** familiar	**B** known	**C** usual	**D** accustomed
11	**A** rightly	**B** truly	**C** actually	**D** certainly
12	**A** spectators	**B** passers-by	**C** observers	**D** viewers

Language development 2

need + -ing/to be (done); have/get something done ▶ CB page 174

1 *need + -ing* or *need to be (done)*?
a **Mark the correct verb form in each pair.**
1 We've run out of milk. We need *to buy / buying* some more today.
2 The battery in my camera needs *to replace / replacing*.
3 I've lost touch with Tania. I need *to write / writing* to her.
4 All my computer files are very old and need *to update / to be updated*.
5 My father is rather overweight. He needs *to go / going* on a diet.
6 This television is faulty. The shop needs *to give / giving* you a new one.
7 Yesterday my mother said that my hair needed *to cut / cutting*.
8 This letter is not very good. It needs *to rewrite / to be rewritten*.

b **Complete the sentences with the correct form of the verb in brackets. There may be more than one possibility.**
1 My car is due for a service – I need .... (*take*) it to the garage.
2 Your dog looks very hungry. Perhaps he needs .... (*feed*) more often.
3 I am going to the optician tomorrow. My eyes need .... (*test*).
4 The radio is not working very well. Do you think it'll need .... (*replace*)?
5 Did you need .... (*go*) to the doctor when you were ill?
6 That old pullover of yours really needed .... (*wash*). It was filthy!
7 When you fix the roof tomorrow, will someone need .... (*help*) you?
8 Our oven is really dirty. In fact, it's needed .... (*clean*) for ages.

2 *have/get something done*

a Complete the text. Use only one word in each space.

A couple of months ago, I bought an old house in the country, and I'm **(1)**.........................it done up. Most of the windows are broken, so I'll have **(2)**.........................replaced as soon as I can. A lot of the roof tiles are missing as well, and I **(3)**.........................probably need to **(4)**.........................the whole roof retiled.

Inside, I'm going to **(5)**.........................central heating put in, which will be another big job. Fortunately, the wiring of the house is fine, so I don't need to have **(6)**......................... rewired. That'll save some money. But the first thing I want to do is **(7)**.........................the wall between the dining room and living room knocked down to make one big room.

I'm going to redecorate the house myself rather than have it **(8)**.........................by professionals, because I love painting and I want to do it myself. The only problem is that I **(9)**.........................all my paints and brushes stolen a few days ago. I suppose it was fortunate my car **(10)**......................... not stolen as well!

b Complete the responses to the questions using the word(s) in brackets and the correct form of *have/get something (done)*.

EXAMPLE: Why is your hair such a strange colour?
Well, I ....had it dyed......... yesterday. (*dye*)

1 **A:** I've been having a lot of headaches recently. Why do you think that is?
   B: Maybe you should .... tomorrow. (*eyes/test*)

2 **A:** Why is your car always breaking down?
   B: I really don't know. I .... every six months. (*service*)

3 **A:** You look as if you're in pain. Do you have toothache?
   B: Yes. I haven't .... for ages. (*teeth/check*)

4 **A:** Why are there so many workmen in your garden?
   B: Well, we are going to .... there. (*swimming pool/build*)

5 **A:** Why is there so much smoke coming from your log fire?
   B: I don't know. We probably need to .... (*chimney/clean*)

3 Key word transformations

Complete the second sentence so that it has a similar meaning to the first sentence, using the word given. Do not change the word given. You must use between two and five words, including the word given.

1 Someone broke into Jane's house yesterday. **broken**
   Jane had .... yesterday.

2 Have they taken your photograph yet? **had**
   Have you .... taken yet?

3 I think we ought to get the house painted. **needs**
   I think the .... painted.

4 I can't email you because they are repairing my computer at the moment. **repaired**
   I can't email you because I am .... at the moment.

5 Peter wants them to put in central heating soon. **have**
   Peter wants to .... soon.

6 You need to get someone to knock down that garden wall. **knocking**
   That garden wall .... down.

7 I haven't been to the car wash for ages. **washed**
   I haven't had my .... for ages.

8 You should get some sleep now because it's late. **need**
   You .... to bed now because it's late.

9 Someone has just stolen my new watch! **had**
   I have .... stolen!

10 They are delivering Sue's new fridge today. **delivered**
   Sue is .... today.

4 Exam practice: open cloze (Paper 3 Part 2)

Read the text below and think of the word which best fits each space. Use only **one** word in each space. There is an example at the beginning **(0)**.

PRODUCT PLACEMENT

If you saw the latest James Bond film, you **(0)**....will.... have seen his new sports car in a number of key scenes. This is not, **(1)**................ , just because the car is important to the plot. It is the result of an agreement **(2)**................ the car's manufacturers and the film studio, aimed at promoting the luxury model on screen. And it works. **(3)**................ a result of the film, sales of the car in the USA have **(4)**................ up significantly.

This is an example of **(5)**................ is called 'product placement'. In other words, the products and logos that you see in films are **(6)**................ because of advertising deals. When Steven Spielberg made the film *Minority Report*, he got back around 25 per cent of his budget through such deals. He **(7)**................thought to have received £3 million simply for putting Tom Cruise in the driving seat of a particular car. For some products, **(8)**................ as mobile phones and fast food, companies may compete **(9)**................ each other to get on screen, pushing the price up even further.

But if you're there just to enjoy the movie, aren't the advertisements getting in the **(10)**................ of the story? Fortunately, advertisers do realise **(11)**................ advertisements which annoy film-goers will do more harm **(12)**................ good, so there is probably a limit to how many we will see.

Reading Gapped text (Paper 1 Part 2)

1 Before you read

Read the instructions for the task and the title of the text opposite and think about these questions.

1 What are the advantages and disadvantages of television?

2 Is the influence of television generally good or bad?

2 Skimming

Skim the text to answer these questions.

1 What main points does the writer make about television?

2 How does the writer answer Exercise 1, question 2?

3 Gapped text

Do the exam task below. Remember to do the following.

- Read the whole of the base text carefully.
- Read the text before and after each gap and think about the type of information that is missing.
- Look for the sentence that talks about this topic area.
- Choose the correct answer by checking the grammatical and lexical links between the base text and the key sentence. Look out for pronouns, synonyms, etc.
- Read the text again with your answers, to check that it makes sense.

4 Vocabulary: collocations

Read the sentences and decide which answer A, B, C or D best fits each space.

1 The writer .... a talk to a group of school-leavers.
   A made   **B** gave   **C** had   **D** led

2 Most of them wanted to .... into television.
   A work   **B** be   **C** go   **D** watch

3 In the UK, people .... up to four hours per day watching television.
   A pass   **B** take   **C** sit   **D** spend

4 Most of us rely .... TV as a source of information about the world.
   A at   **B** on   **C** in   **D** to

5 If a politician .... a fool of himself on TV, his career is over.
   A makes   **B** looks   **C** behaves   **D** does

6 TV has a very big influence .... our lives.
   A to   **B** with   **C** on   **D** through

7 That's why it's very important .... the programme makers show us.
   A that   **B** why   **C** if   **D** what

You are going to read a text about television. Seven sentences have been removed from the text. Choose from the sentences **A–H** the one that fits each gap (**1–6**). There is one extra sentence which you do not need to use.

A Despite this, the influence of television continues to grow.

B There is, however, a particular aspect of television which makes it unlike almost all other influences on our lives.

C It involves what happens to us during that time.

D But equally they can appeal to the worst sides of our nature, or turn everything into light entertainment.

E But most of the time, we turn it on to watch, and we give it our full attention.

F But the reality we get from television is not like that because we don't participate in it, we just watch it.

G We didn't use that rather nasty word then, of course: we had newspapers, radio and television.

H Similarly, if a book comes out based on one of these programmes, then bookshops stock up for the extra sales that will surely follow.

The influence of television

When I became a broadcaster in 1958, I didn't know, and neither did most other people, that I was entering what was going to become the greatest growth
5 industry of the next half century: the media. **1 [ ]** We've only started to talk about 'the media' relatively recently, but nowadays everybody seems to want to be part of it. When I gave a talk to a
10 group of school-leavers recently, I asked how many thought they might eventually look for a career in politics, medicine, the law. A few dozen of the 2,000 raised their hands for each. Then I asked who wanted
15 a career in the media. Half the hands in the hall went up, and most of them wanted to go into television.

Apart from sleeping, watching television is what people do most of in
20 the UK, each person spending, on average, just under four hours per day in front of the box. But the influence of television goes further, and cannot be measured just by the number of hours
25 people have their television sets on.
2 [ ]

Some people, certainly, treat it as background while they carry on having a meal, reading the paper or even listening
30 to a CD. **3 [ ]** As anybody with small children knows, we quickly become deeply involved in what's happening on the screen, and the language we use reflects this – we talk about being 'glued'
35 to the television.

What's more, most of us rely on television as the main source of information for what is happening out there in the world, and I'm not just
40 talking about the news or documentaries. We gain our impressions of what Australia or the USA are like from their soap operas. **4 [ ]** And even without the commercials, television can determine
45 what we buy, what we talk about and what children play with. As for the grown-ups, if a popular series is set in a specific area of the countryside, that is where the tourists will go. If a politician
50 makes a serious fool of himself on television, his career is over.

Television has become, for most of us, as much a part of our lives as the electricity that comes into our homes or
55 the air we breathe. It is now a central part of what makes us who we are.
5 [ ] It is not yet truly interactive. It speaks to us, but we do not speak back, except on a few phone-in programmes.
60 This is an interesting feature of something that has such a big influence on our lives.

When I was a child, a whole host of things and people influenced me, but the
65 one thing they all had in common was the fact that you got a reaction from them. That was how you learned what real life was all about, and how you fitted into it. **6 [ ]** In other words, we
70 don't have to do any thinking for ourselves. We just get reality given to us by those who make the programmes. That's why it matters so much what they decide to show us.
75 The television networks can present us with a picture of the world as it really is – complicated and interesting and full of variety – and they can make us think about it and about ourselves as a result.
80 **7 [ ]** If they do that, then that's how we will start to respond to the world too. My concern is that the trend is clearly in the wrong direction.

Colloquial English

Common idioms

Module 5A It's all in the MIND

In the sentences below, replace the words which are underlined with a phrase from the box. Put the verbs in the correct form.

make up (my) mind	cross (my) mind	frame of mind
rack (my) brains	be in two minds	have a brainwave
have second thoughts	it slipped (my) mind	

1 I've been <u>thinking really hard</u> all day about what to tell my wife. She'll never forgive me if I tell her the truth about what happened!

2 I hope you're not beginning to <u>have doubts</u> about taking part in the research project. You can't back out now.

3 It never <u>occurred to me</u> that you would be interested in going to Dr Aitken's lecture this evening.

4 Do you want to go to the party or not? You must <u>decide</u> fairly soon.

5 I <u>have just had a sudden clever idea</u>! Why don't we repeat the experiment using nitrogen?

6 My girlfriend <u>is unable to decide</u> about whether to accept the job offer.

7 I can't possibly solve this problem today. I'm not in the right <u>mood</u>.

8 I'm sorry about your birthday! <u>I completely forgot</u>!

Module 6A Making MUSIC

1 **Complete the sentences with a verb from the list. You may need to change the form of the verb.**

change   ring   face   play   make   blow   go   feel

1 What did you say her name was? Penny Tyler? The name .... *a bell*, but I just can't remember who she is.
2 Paul is always .... *his own trumpet*. Every day he tells us what a wonderful musician he is.
3 The flats in that area are .... *for a song*. We ought to buy one.
4 The boss wants to see you! It's time for you to .... *the music* for that mistake you made yesterday!
5 I didn't prepare for the interview at all – I just .... *it by ear*.
6 I know I was ill yesterday, but today I .... *as fit as a fiddle*!
7 Mick didn't want to play in the band at first, but he soon .... *his tune* when we told him how much money he would make.
8 There's no need to .... such *a song and dance* about a little scratch on your CD player!

At times Richard dreaded coming home, as he knew he'd have to face the music.

www.CartoonStock.com

2 Match the expressions in *italics* in Exercise 1 with the meanings a–h below. The first one
has been done for you.

You say this when:
a   you feel extremely healthy ...6...
b   someone boasts about what they've achieved   ....
c   you have to accept criticism / punishment for something you've done   ....
d   you behave according to the situation / improvise   ....
e   something is very cheap   ....
f   someone suddenly starts to express a different attitude   ....
g   you think you've heard a name before   ....
h   you complain too much about something unnecessarily   ....

Module 6B The COLOURS of the rainbow

1 Complete the idiomatic expressions in the sentences below with the correct colour. You
will need to use some colours twice.

1   I didn't know that Peter was the .... *sheep* of the family.
2   Gina telephoned me yesterday right *out of the* .... !
3   A famous artist lives next door to me, but I only see him *once in* a .... *moon.*
4   My boyfriend *saw* .... when I told him I wanted to go on holiday on my own.
5   You must have *painted the town* .... last night! You look terrible!
6   My brother was .... *with envy* when I told him I was going to Thailand.
7   I think you're seeing the situation *through* .... *-tinted spectacles*. Get real!
8   You look *as* .... *as a sheet.* Are you okay?

2 Match the responses a–h to the sentences in Exercise 1.

a   What do you mean? Just because I don't see anything bad in what's happening?
b   What a surprise! You haven't heard from her for ages.
c   I know – apparently, his father has never forgiven him for refusing to go to university.
d   Well, I can understand why he got angry. I would too.
e   Yes, I'm really tired. I can't remember all the clubs we went to!
f   No, I'm not. I really don't feel very well.
g   Why? Doesn't he ever leave his flat?
h   It's not surprising. Anyone would be jealous!

Module 7B My most attractive FEATURE is …

1 Complete the idioms with a part of the body. The first one has been done for you. You will
need to use one part of the body twice.

1   I can't *make* head *nor tail* of these instructions!
2   Zena and I don't *see* ...... *to eye* at all!
3   It doesn't matter if you don't go to the party. They'll *turn a blind* ......
    to it.
4   Ursula has such *a sweet* ......! Look at her eating that dessert!
5   Come out with me tonight. I know Milan *like the back of my* ....
6   Look at Mila's new coat. It must have *cost an* ...... *and a leg*!
7   Look at her! She's just ...... *and bones*!
8   Do you think Alberto said it *tongue-in-* ...... ?

"I'M AFRAID I HAVE BAD NEWS FOR YOU .
THAT SWEET TOOTH HAS GOT TO COME OUT."

www.CartoonStock.com

123

2 **Match the idioms in Exercise 1 (page 123) to the meanings a–h.**

a be very thin
b don't agree about anything
c like chocolate and cakes
d cost a lot of money
e be joking
f ignore
g know very well
h can't understand

Module 10B All the TIME in the world

1a Read the sentences below. Where might you hear people saying these things? Who do you think each person is talking to?

1 Phew! We've arrived *in the nick of time*! They're closing the check-in now!

2 I'm sure our flight to Berlin will leave *dead on time*.

3 *Nine times out of ten* the flight to Budapest is delayed.

4 I've told you *time and time again*, Albert, to take care of your passport!

5 It's okay, madam. *Take your time*.

6 It's amazing there was no traffic. We've arrived *with time to spare*!

7 The flight leaves in twenty minutes! *There's no time to lose*!

8 I want you to stay close to me *for the time being*. Okay?

www.CartoonStock.com

1b Match the expressions in *italics* with the meanings a–h.

a for a short period of time (from now)
b sooner than expected
c just before it's too late
d almost always
e don't hurry
f it's necessary to hurry
g at exactly the right time
h frequently

Practice exam

Paper 1 Part 1

You are going to read a newspaper article about Hollywood. For questions **1–8**, choose the answer (**A**, **B**, **C** or **D**) which you think fits best according to the text.

Mark your answers **on the separate answer sheet**.

I'm not a waitress – I'm an actress!

For every Kate Winslet or Catherine Zeta Jones, there are thousands of British 'wannabe' actresses who never make it in Hollywood. 'It is disheartening,' admits 28-year-old Rachael Nortance. 'I've been to so many auditions for film parts where I walk in and there's a room full of equally talented people, and I ask myself: "Why am I here?" But ironically, what Rachael finds hardest to accept is how nice people are to her at auditions. 'The organisers tell you they love your work, and for the first month or so I believed them, but eventually I realised it's totally fake because mostly you never hear from them again.'

During her four years in the USA, Rachael has been to more auditions than she can remember, has sent out thousands of photos of herself, and been to every celebrity party that she's been invited to. For all that, the closest she has come to
line 19   a camera is the one she takes snaps with to email home to her family in England. She has yet to land any film or TV work, and is currently working at a children's talent agency to make ends meet. 'Basically, I do my best to keep happy and focused on the industry,' she says. 'I was very realistic when I came to Hollywood – I presumed I would have to be a waitress, so I can't complain about a job that not only pays the bills, but which also gives me a lot of satisfaction.'

Rachael is just one of an estimated 1,000 hopefuls who arrive in Los Angeles every week, chasing dreams of stardom. Many are British, and almost all are unprepared for the intensity of the competition for acting jobs, and end up taking
line 34   menial jobs because they have to support themselves. 'British actresses think Los Angeles is the land of opportunity,' she explains. 'They see icons like Kate Winslet and think it's possible to be successful here. But for every one that makes it, there are thousands who end up doing dead-end jobs. Many get stuck here because they don't want to go home again, not so much because they can't afford it, but because that would be admitting defeat – they'd risk losing face.'

In spite of the constant rejection, Rachael keeps going. 'I'm passionate about acting and I think I've reached a standard where I can prove I'm a good actress,' she explains. 'But I do get down sometimes. That's when I cry on the phone to Mum, who talks me out of packing my bags and makes me realise I need to strive harder. There isn't a day that goes by when I don't wonder if I made the right decision to come here, but then a big audition comes up, or someone introduces me to a useful contact, and I realise how lucky I am.'

Rachael always wanted to act. She studied drama at Liverpool University before spending two years at the American Academy of Dramatic Arts, winning their best actress award. It was an instructor there who suggested she try her luck in movies. Four years later, even though she has yet to secure an acting role, she still feels she is doing the right thing. 'I know it takes time to make it here. At this stage it's all about contacts. A week ago, I had a meeting with a production company, and they've asked me to audition for a part in a possible film in two years' time. It's a long way off, but this could be where the ball starts rolling. It's like any goal you set yourself – you get so far and you can't give up.'

*There are photocopiable Answer Sheets in the Teacher's Resource Book.

1   What does Rachael find disheartening about auditions?

   A   Too many actors are invited.

   B   The wrong type of actors are invited.

   C   The organisers are insincere in their comments.

   D   The organisers refuse to give feedback on her performance.

2   The phrase 'the one' in line 19 refers to

   A   a social occasion Rachel attended.

   B   a picture Rachel has sent someone.

   C   an audition that Rachel remembers.

   D   a piece of equipment Rachel uses.

3   What does Rachael say about her job at the talent agency?

   A   She's not really suited to it.

   B   She finds it relatively rewarding.

   C   It's not as well-paid as waitressing.

   D   It's something she just does for the money.

4   What are 'menial jobs' (line 34)?

   A   jobs with low status

   B   jobs with good salaries

   C   jobs which provide useful contacts

   D   jobs for which there's lots of competition

5   According to Rachael, why do unsuccessful actresses stay in Los Angeles?

   A   They get used to the lifestyle.

   B   They are too proud to admit defeat.

   C   They lack the money to go back home.

   D   The have found alternative careers there.

6   On the phone, Rachael's mother often

   A   encourages her to keep on trying.

   B   tries to persuade her to return home.

   C   questions decisions that Rachael has made.

   D   makes useful suggestions about Rachael's career.

7   Why did Rachael initially come to Hollywood?

   A   as part of her university course

   B   on the advice of one of her teachers

   C   in order to receive an award she had won

   D   because she was being considered for a film role

8   How does Rachael feel about her latest audition?

   A   unsure whether it's worth attending

   B   encouraged by the timing of the project

   C   doubtful about the people she's already met

   D   optimistic about her chances of succeeding

Paper 1 Part 2

You are going to read a magazine article written by a wildlife cameraman. Seven sentences have been removed from the article. Choose from the sentences **A–H** the one which best fits each gap (**9–15**). There is one extra sentence which you do not need to use.

Mark your answers **on the separate answer sheet**.

The Chair Bear

When filming in Sri Lanka, wildlife cameraman Gordon Buchanan got the fright of his life.

When I was asked to spend a year in Sri Lanka, filming the local leopards, I jumped at the chance. The leopard is a shy animal which even the best trackers only see on rare occasions. There was, however, only one way to discover if it was possible to film them and that was to try. **9** [ ]

At first, I was put up in a four-star hotel. But what I gained in fresh towels and hot water, I lacked in leopards. Weeks passed with only glimpses of the animals. To have any chance of fulfilling my contract, I would have to locate signs of recent leopard activity in the jungle, and then sit it out overnight in a portable wooden hide. **10** [ ]

We set up the hide near the spot he'd indicated and I settled down to wait with my night-filming equipment, in the hope that the animal would come back to finish its meal. Soon after sunset, I was thrilled to see a mother leopard and cub silently appear on my infra-red monitor and begin to feed. **11** [ ]

I knew exactly what was making it, though this knowledge only alarmed me further. It was a sloth bear – a beast that is responsible for the most horrific attacks on humans. **12** [ ]

If you're wondering what makes these creatures so dangerous, it's said that they have the temper of a wasp and the jaws of a lion. I swung the infra-red camera around to get the animal in frame, but he was too close – something I only realised when a huge black nose appeared through a gap in the corner of the hide. **13** [ ]

I went back to my camera in time to see the bear sit down in front of the hissing mother leopard. I got ready to film the leopard as she fled. But just as the bear was about to grab the meat, she leapt at it, lashing out with her claws. **14** [ ] Within minutes the bear was back, this time with a friend. One fed as the other went around the back of the hide. Feeling exceptionally unsafe, I radioed for someone to come and get me.

Making our way back to the scene in daylight, I spotted something odd in the track. It was the folding seat I use when filming Looking down, I saw a set of bear tracks coming from the direction of the hide, while the teeth marks on the metal object confirmed that the bear had claimed it as its own. **15** [ ]

The front of that hide now had an oddly-shaped hole in it which looked as though it had been made by a bear leaving with a chair in its mouth – which must be exactly what had happened.

A But my pleasure turned almost instantly to barely controlled terror when, from behind the hide, there came an unearthly sound – a combined roar, growl, wail, scream and snarl, all at maximum volume.

B I grabbed my spotlight and flashed it in the animal's face, at which point it fortunately chose to move off.

C It was difficult to make out exactly how far away the animal was, but after a few minutes I heard the clatter of its claws on the rocks as it moved closer.

D I was sure I'd fastened the door shut, with all my gear inside, so cautiously we went to investigate – wary of what might be awaiting us.

E It wasn't long before KG, my right-hand man, found a deer which had recently been killed by a leopard – and so armed with this evidence, we headed into the forest.

F I was totally stunned – not only was this a completely unexpected reaction, but I had also captured the behaviour on film, including the cub continuing to feed with its mother until they both walked off.

G Nothing prepared me for what was to happen next, however, which was an experience I shall remember for the rest of my days.

H It was the idea of life in the jungle that really attracted me actually – sleeping under the stars and surviving on meals of wild fruits – but this wasn't quite how it turned out.

Paper 1 Part 3

You are going to read a magazine article about working in the music industry. For questions **16–30**, choose from the people **(A–D)**. The people may be chosen more than once.

Mark your answers **on the separate answer sheet**.

Which person ...

has only recently entered the music industry?	**16**
has fulfilled a childhood ambition to work in this industry?	**17**
chose to live in an area at the centre of the music industry?	**18**
wishes that his/her job was not so desk-bound?	**19**
has no regrets about turning down an alternative career opportunity?	**20**
mentions meeting some famous people?	**21**
once lost a job in the music industry?	**22**
took professional advice before finding a job?	**23**
has to stand in for colleagues in their absence?	**24**
has to balance work and family commitments?	**25**
mentions the excitement of working in the industry?	**26**
feels that qualifications are the key to getting a job in the industry?	**27**
mentions benefits received in addition to the salary?	**28**
says that circulating written documents is part of his/her job?	**29**
gained practical experience of working in the industry whilst still a student?	**30**

Jobs in the Music Industry

We talk to four people who work behind the scenes at a recording company.

A Dan Welney: Financial planning assistant

Dan worked for a merchant bank during university holidays to save up for a year out travelling. 'They offered me a permanent job,' he says. 'But I decided it wasn't for me. So I went to a firm of recruitment consultants who pointed me in the direction of the music industry and I started in January. I'm responsible for things like employees' expenses when they go on foreign trips so there's quite a bit of paperwork. But we're also the ones who say, 'You haven't got enough money to sign that band,' or 'You'll have to cut the video budget,' which is the interesting part. I don't get out of the office a great deal, which can be a drawback, but there are compensations – free concerts and CDs were certainly one attraction of the job. Although the celebrities tend to bypass my office, this certainly beats working for a bank, even if it's not as well paid.'

B Gemma Ortolano: Office manager

Although Gemma studied music at university, she chose courses that prepared her for the music business rather than the creative side. 'We learned about music law, tour management, all that side of it. Now I'm office manager in the marketing department here. It's a pretty varied job. I have to make sure everyone has what they need, I organise mailings to the press and I compile and send round reports so everyone in the organisation knows what's happening with the bands. I get to work across departments so it's an interesting job and I've mixed with my fair share of celebrities. I didn't know anyone in the industry when I started out, though obviously that can help. I chose to do a specialised degree instead and walked into a job afterwards. I would recommend it as a way of getting into the industry.'

C Sam Tysler: Music lawyer

Sam trained as a lawyer, but admits to being a frustrated musician. 'I played in a band as a kid at school and always dreamt of getting involved in entertainment sooner or later. I joined this company in 1994 and I'm now the senior lawyer in the department. It's not all desk-based and the day doesn't end at 6:30 p.m. because you've got to be out there in the public eye – although since I got married, I have had to cut back a bit on the partying. The artists and songwriters I represent are worth £70 million in record sales. One has sold 30 million records, others just have their 15 minutes of fame – that's the nature of the business. I find working in the industry is a thrill in itself because, although I just draw up the contracts, I still enjoy the buzz and the thrill of the deal.'

D Valerie Picot: Receptionist

As a French student doing International Business and English language, Valerie got to know the British music scene when she was over doing work experience as part of her course. 'After my degree, I returned and worked as an assistant at a recording studio,' she explains. 'Then last March I was made redundant and did temporary secretarial work before landing my present job. Music has always been a big part of my life so I came to where it all happens – London. I meet and greet visitors, and get to do cover across the departments if anyone is off sick. That means I've acted as PA to the Chairman, worked in international marketing – all good experience. I'm hoping it will lead to a more creative role.'

Writing

Paper 2 Part 1

You **must** answer this question. Write your answer in **120–150** words in an appropriate style.

1 An English friend, Chris, whom you met on holiday, has just sent you a letter with some photographs. Read Chris' letter and the notes you have made on it. Then write an email to Chris, using all your notes.

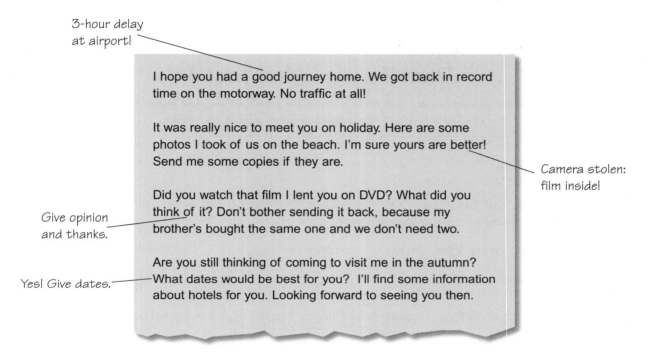

3-hour delay at airport!

I hope you had a good journey home. We got back in record time on the motorway. No traffic at all!

It was really nice to meet you on holiday. Here are some photos I took of us on the beach. I'm sure yours are better! Send me some copies if they are.

Camera stolen: film inside!

Did you watch that film I lent you on DVD? What did you think of it? Don't bother sending it back, because my brother's bought the same one and we don't need two.

Give opinion and thanks.

Are you still thinking of coming to visit me in the autumn? What dates would be best for you? I'll find some information about hotels for you. Looking forward to seeing you then.

Yes! Give dates.

Write your email. You must use grammatically correct sentences with accurate spelling and punctuation in a style appropriate for the situation.

Paper 2 Part 2

Write an answer to **one** of the questions **2–5** in this part. Write your answer in **120–180** words in an appropriate style.

2   Your teacher has asked you to write a story for your school's English language magazine. The story must begin with the following words.

As the bus climbed over the hill, we caught sight of the sea. Our holiday had begun.

Write your **story**.

3   You see the following notice in an international magazine.

> ### Describe your ideal friend
> *What qualities do you look for in a friend and which are the most important?*
> *The best article will be published in our magazine next month.*

Write your **article**.

4   Your class has had a discussion about advertising. Your teacher has asked you to write an essay, giving your opinions on the following statement.

Advertising has an important role to play in modern life.

Write your **essay**.

5   Answer one of the following questions based on your reading of one of the set books.

Either (a)   On a bookseller's website, customers can post reviews of the books which are for sale. Write a review of the book you have read for the website, including information about the characters and the plot, and say why you think other people might enjoy it.

Write your **review**.

Or   (b)   In the story which you have read, which character did you like most? Write an essay, describing this character's good and bad points with reference to the book or one of the short stories you have read.

Write your **essay**.

Use of English

Paper 3 Part 1

For questions **1–12**, read the text below and decide which answer **A**, **B**, **C** or **D** best fits each space. There is an example at the beginning **(0)**.

Mark your answers **on the separate answer sheet**.

Example:

0 **A** leads   **B** keeps   **C** passes   **D** follows

THE LIFE OF A COUNTRY VET

Don Strange, who works as a vet in northern England, **(0)**............. a busy life. As well as having to **(1)**............. pets which are unwell, he often visits farms where problems of various kinds await him. He has lost **(2)**............. of the number of times he has been called out at midnight to give **(3)**............. to a farmer with sick sheep or cows.

Recently, a television company chose Don as the **(4)**............. of a documentary programme it was making about the life of a country vet. The programme showed the difficult situations Don **(5)**............. every day, such as helping a cow to give birth, or winning the trust of an aggressive dog which needs an injection. Not all of Don's patients are domestic animals, **(6)**............. , and in the programme, people saw him helping an owl which had a damaged wing. It also showed Don **(7)**............. a meeting with villagers concerned about the damage a new road might do to their **(8)**............. environment.

(9)............. loved the documentary and, overnight, Don became a household **(10)**............. , known to millions of people. He continues to receive **(11)**............. numbers of letters which make a real **(12)**............. on him, especially those from teenagers who have made the important decision to become vets themselves as a result of seeing the programme.

1	**A** deal	**B** fix	**C** treat	**D** solve
2	**A** memory	**B** count	**C** score	**D** patienc
3	**A** suggestion	**B** warning	**C** advice	**D** recommendation
4	**A** feature	**B** subject	**C** case	**D** character
5	**A** faces	**B** greets	**C** copes	**D** stands
6	**A** although	**B** therefore	**C** yet	**D** however
7	**A** keeping	**B** holding	**C** carrying	**D** taking
8	**A** nearby	**B** area	**C** local	**D** close
9	**A** Onlookers	**B** Watchers	**C** Viewers	**D** Spectators
10	**A** word	**B** name	**C** fame	**D** star
11	**A** large	**B** wide	**C** great	**D** long
12	**A** effect	**B** impression	**C** emotion	**D** influence

Paper 3 Part 2

For questions **13–24**, read the text below and think of the word which best fits each space. Use only **one** word in each space. There is an example at the beginning **(0)**.

Write your answers **IN CAPITAL LETTERS on the separate answer sheet**.

Example: **0** **F** **O** **R**

NICER THAN CHOCOLATE

Sales of chocolate in Britain have fallen **(0)**............................ the first time in 50 years. According to researchers, this is largely **(13)**............................ children prefer to spend their pocket money on mobile phones. Schoolchildren who **(14)**............................ to visit their local shop to buy sweets are now buying top-up cards for their mobiles instead, **(15)**............................ that they can send their friends text messages. Sociologists see this move away **(16)**............................ sweets towards the use of mobile telephones as an example of **(17)**............................ teenage life is changing as a result **(18)**............................ new technology.

14-year-old Susannah Hedgely, **(19)**............................ has run up a bill of nearly £300 on her mobile phone in the past two months, **(20)**............................ majority of it on texting, is typical of the trend. Almost **(21)**............................ exception, the teenagers in her circle of around 50 friends own mobiles. Susannah was originally given one so she could **(22)**............................ her parents know when she was going to be late home from school, but she now sends up to 60 text messages per day. 'Rather **(23)**............................ go to the shop and get a chocolate bar to cheer **(24)**............................ up, I ring my friends and go out to meet them,' she says. 'I was once a big chocolate eater, but now I only have about one chocolate bar a week.'

Paper 3 Part 3

For questions **25–34**, read the text below. Use the word given in capitals at the end some of the lines to form a word that fits in the space in the same line. There is an example at the beginning **(0)**.

Write your answers **IN CAPITAL LETTERS on the separate answer sheet**.

Example: | 0 | P | O | P | U | L | A | R | I | T | Y | | | | | | | |

JOGGING IN THE PARK

Despite the increasing **(0)**.............................. of physical exercise in recent years, only 10 per cent of British people have taken out **(25)**............................. of a gym. One reason for this, **(26)**........................... suggest, is that gyms may have a negative psychological effect on people. In tests, **(27)**........................... environments were found to be far more **(28)**........................... than the artificial surroundings of a gym.

POPULAR

MEMBER

RESEARCH

NATURE

BENEFIT

Maybe this provides an **(29)**........................... for why there has been a steady **(30)**........................... in the number of people to be seen jogging in and around city parks in recent years. **(31)**........................... the gym, where people are limited to a certain range of machines, or **(32)**........................... classes, outdoor activity has no boundaries, and parks are **(33)**........................... becoming places of adult, as well as child, recreation, **(34)**........................... in the warmer weather.

EXPLAIN

GROW

LIKE

FIT

INCREASE

SPECIAL

Paper 3 Part 4

For questions **35–42**, complete the second sentence so that it has a similar meaning to the first sentence, using the word given. **Do not change the word given**. You must use between **two** and **five** words, including the word given. Here is an example **(0)**.

Example:

0 You must do exactly what the manager tells you.

CARRY

You must .... instructions exactly.

The gap can be filled by the words 'carry out the manager's', so you write:

0	C	A	R	R	Y		O	U	T		T	H	E		M	A	N	A	G	E	R	'	S	

Write **only** the missing words **on the separate answer sheet**.

35 I have never been as excited as I was during that football match.

HAVE

That football match was the .... ever seen.

36 After the race, Kerry asked a nurse to examine her swollen ankle.

HAVE

After the race, Kerry asked a nurse to .... her swollen ankle.

37 Steve had not expected to find archaeology so interesting.

IN

Steve was .... than he had expected.

38 People say that the pop star has given a lot of money to charity.

SAID

The pop star .... a lot of money to charity.

39 Simon decided to accept the salesperson's offer of a 20 per cent discount.

ADVANTAGE

Simon decided he would .... the salesperson's offer of a 20 per cent discount.

40 The heavy rainfall made it impossible for them to complete the walk.

PREVENTED

They .... the walk by the heavy rainfall.

41 A local garage always services my motorbike.

GET

I always .... at a local garage.

42 Tony regrets not being able to speak to his girlfriend last night.

COULD

Tony wishes that .... to his girlfriend last night.

Listening

Paper 4 Part 1

You will hear people talking in eight different situations. For questions **1–8**, choose the best answer **A**, **B** or **C**.

---

1 You hear somebody talking about a recent holiday.
   What disappointed her about the villa complex she stayed in?
   A the way it was laid out
   B the type of people it attracted
   C the facilities provided for guests
   `1`

2 You overhear a conversation about a missed appointment.
   How does the girl feel now?
   A embarrassed about the way she behaved
   B angry that she didn't see the dentist
   C satisfied that she made her point
   `2`

3 You overhear two colleagues talking about something which happened at work.
   What do they agree about?
   A Communications within the company are poor.
   B A mistake occurred as a result of human error.
   C It's important not to miss meetings.
   `3`

4 You hear an advertisement for sports clothes.
   What aspect of the clothes is being emphasised?
   A how practical they are
   B how durable they are
   C how attractive they are
   `4`

5 On the radio, you hear a man talking about children and computers.
   What is he doing when he speaks?
   A disagreeing with recent research
   B giving advice on how to approach something
   C explaining how a particular problem can be overcome
   `5`

6 You hear a programme in which a new book by a well-known novelist is being reviewed.
   What does the speaker think about this novel?
   A It is untypical of the writer's work.
   B It is not as well-written as she'd expected.
   C It seems to be lacking in originality.
   `6`

7 You hear part of a radio phone-in programme about problems at work.
   What is the caller having difficulty with?
   A attracting new members of staff to the company
   B convincing her staff that the pay and conditions are fair
   C encouraging members of staff to stay with the company
   `7`

8 You hear a conversation in a radio play.
   Where is the conversation taking place?
   A at a theatre box office
   B at a hotel reception desk
   C in a restaurant
   `8`

Paper 4 Part 2

You will hear part of a radio programme in which Peter Denison, a man who repairs clocks and watches, talks about his life and work. For questions **9–18**, complete the sentences.

Peter's [9] was the person who encouraged his early interest

in mechanical things.

Peter says that for him, old clocks represent a link with [10].

In Peter's first job, he worked as an improver in a jeweller's in [11].

The building where Peter works now used to be a [12].

As well as having good eyes, a watch repairer must be patient and have [13].

As a result of his work, Peter sometimes has health problems involving his [14].

The oldest clock Peter has repaired was made in the year [15].

Peter explains that people often have [16] feelings about old clocks.

Peter says that few people realise the need to [17] old clocks regularly.

In talking about his life and work, Peter describes himself as a [18].

Paper 4 Part 3

You will hear five women talking about living in blocks of flats. For questions **19–23**, choose from the list **A–F** the main reason each woman gives for choosing the flat where she lives now. Use the letters only once. There is one extra letter which you do not need to use.

A the size of the rooms

Speaker 1 ☐ **19**

B the proximity of local amenities

Speaker 2 ☐ **20**

C good transport links

Speaker 3 ☐ **21**

D the friendliness of the neighbours

Speaker 4 ☐ **22**

E a feeling of security

Speaker 5 ☐ **23**

F the level of maintenance

Paper 4 Part 4

You will hear an interview with a man who is about to go on a trip into outer space. For questions **24–30**, choose the best answer **(A, B or C)**.

24 What is Grant most looking forward to on his flight?

    A taking off from Earth

    B seeing the Earth from space   `24`

    C leaving the Earth's atmosphere

25 When asked if he is scared, Grant

    A denies this strongly.

    B insists that he's overcome his fear.   `25`

    C suggests that this is a normal thing to feel.

26 What will Grant be responsible for during the flight?

    A providing a commentary for the media

    B observing what the crew members do   `26`

    C operating some of the controls

27 What did Grant find most difficult about his training?

    A learning to deal with weightlessness

    B preparing for unexpected landings   `27`

    C improving his general level of fitness

28 Grant feels that the term 'space tourism'

    A gives people the wrong idea about what he's doing.

    B makes what he's doing sound attractive to people.   `28`

    C leads people to doubt whether he's really going.

29 Grant admits that many people wanting to do what he is doing

    A would find the training too challenging.

    B would get bored during the training.   `29`

    C would not have the necessary experience.

30 Grant thinks that in the future,

    A many people will be able to afford space flights.

    B more companies will be organising space trips.   `30`

    C most spaceflights will take paying passengers.

Speaking

Paper 5 Part 1 (3 minutes)

General questions

- What's your name?
- Where do you come from?
- Do you work or are you a full-time student? What do you do/study?

Now, answer one question from each section:

Home and family

- Do you have any brothers or sisters?
- Tell me about your favourite room at home.
- Do you like large family parties? Why (not)?

Daily life and special occasions

- Do you like getting up early in the morning. Why (not)?
- How do you travel to work/school/college?
- When is your birthday? How do you like to celebrate it?

Work/Education

- What's the most interesting thing you've ever studied?
- How important is English in your work/studies?
- What ambitions do you have for the future?

Health

- What sports did you enjoy when you were younger?
- What do you do to keep fit these days?
- Do you try to eat healthy foods? Why (not)?

Interests

- Did you have a particular hobby as a child?
- Have your interests changed as you've got older?
- Is there something you'd like to learn to do in the future?

Holidays

- Tell me about your last holiday.
- Do you like to travel on holiday or stay in one place? Why (not)?
- Where would you like to go on holiday in the future? Why?

Paper 5 Part 2 (4 minutes)

Interlocutor: Now I'd like each of you to talk on your own for about a minute.

I'm going to give each of you two different photographs and I'd like you to talk about them. (*Candidate A*), here are your two photographs. **They show people greeting each other**. Please let (*Candidate B*) have a look at them.

(*Candidate B*), I'll give you your photographs in a minute.

(*Candidate A*), I'd like you to compare and contrast these photographs, **and say why you think the people are greeting each other in this way**.

Candidate A: [*Approximately 1 minute*]

Interlocutor: (*Candidate B*), **how do you greet your friends**?

Candidate B: [*Approximately 20 seconds*]

Interlocutor: Thank you.

Interlocutor: Now (*Candidate B*), here are your two photographs. **They show people using computer keyboards**. I'd like you to compare and contrast these photographs, **and say how you think people feel about the equipment they are using**. Please let Candidate A have a look at them

Candidate B: *[Approximately 1 minute]*

Interlocutor: (*Candidate A*), **do you use a computer much?**

Candidate A: *[Approximately 20 seconds]*

Interlocutor: Thank you.

Paper 5 Part 3 (3 minutes)

Interlocutor: Now, I'd like you to talk about something together for about three minutes. I'm just going to listen.

An open-air music festival is being organised in the countryside. It will last a whole weekend. A large number of people are expected to attend the concert and the organisers need to provide adequate facilities for them. Here are some suggestions.

First, talk together about the facilities the organisers should provide. Then say which will be most important.

Paper 5 Part 4 (4 minutes)

- Have you ever been to a concert like this?

- What are the advantages of big events like this for music fans?

- What problems do you think the organisers might face during the weekend?

- Do you prefer to listen to live music or recorded music? Why?

- What type of music is it best to listen to in the open-air?

- Do you like being in a large crowd of people? Why (not)?

Key

Module 1A

Vocabulary p.6

1

1 b; 2 c; 3 a; 4 f; 5 g; 6 e; 7 d; 8 h

2

1 The phonemic transcription tells you how the word is pronounced and which syllable is stressed. In the word *inherit* /ɪnˈherət/ you stress the second syllable.

2 No. (The vowel in the middle of inherit is 'short *e*', as in *bed, men*, etc.)
   Note: Look at the Pronunciation Table at the beginning of the dictionary. Try and learn these symbols by heart.

3 Yes. (In the dictionary, the symbol [T] means that a verb is transitive – it takes a direct object. Verbs which are intransitive [I] do not take a direct object, e.g. *go*.)

4 The stress is on the first syllable (*house*hold).

5 Yes. (See meaning 2.)

6 Countable (so you could say, e.g. *several households*).

7 No. (The grammatical information in square brackets tells you that the adjective *household* must come **before** the noun. So you can say '*household items*' but not '*items which are household*'.)

8 Yes (meaning she is *well-known*).

Language development 1 p.7

1a

We put frequency adverbs such as *always, sometimes, often*:
after simple tenses of the verb *be*
before simple tenses of other verbs
after the auxiliary verb in complex tenses
before used to but **after** would.

1b

1 Adam always leaves for school at seven o'clock in the morning.

2 He goes to school by bus every day. / Every day he goes to school by bus.

3 In the past, he never used to wait very long for the bus.

4 The bus would sometimes be two or three minutes late.

5 Nowadays, the bus is often late.

6 As a result, Adam frequently arrives late for school.

7 Fortunately, his teacher doesn't usually complain.

8 Adam regularly does his homework on the bus.

9 He doesn't get home until after six o'clock on some days. / On some days, he doesn't get home until after six o'clock.

2

1 a has, b 'm/am having; 2 a see, b 's/is seeing;
3 a 'm/am feeling, b feels; 4 are (you) thinking, b do (you) think; 5 a appears, b 's/is appearing; 6 a are (you)
smelling, b smells; 7 a looks, b are (you) looking;
8 a expect, b 'm/am expecting

3

1 I remember how we would ~~have spent~~ *spend* hours waiting for a fish to bite.

2 Sometimes we didn't ~~used~~ *use* to come home until after dark.

3 ✓

4 My father used to ~~taking~~ *take* me with him on long walks in the mountains.

5 I used *to* love listening to him talk about nature.

6 Did I ever ~~used~~ *use* to get bored? Never! There were so many things to do.

4

1 used to; 2 was; 3 used to; 4 used to;
5 wouldn't/didn't use to; 6 used to; 7 brought;
8 would turn/turned; 9 would leave/left; 10 used to be

Listening p.8

2

1 B; 2 C; 3 C; 4 A; 5 A; 6 C

Audio script

W = *Woman;* **M** = *Man*

1

Cars in general have never been a real passion for me. However, my own car is another matter. I have three children under six, their toys, buggies and bikes to ferry round, plus an enormous supermarket shop to load into the boot every week. I may wave my husband off on month-long overseas business trips without a second thought, but when my car goes into the garage for an afternoon, I'm lost.

2

I've always loved music, but I wasn't sure what I wanted to do as a career, so I did a one-year course in music technology. At first, I still wasn't convinced it was for me, but once I realised I would eventually be able to put my own music together, I really started loving it. The course is a part-time one, so once I'd mastered the basics of how to use the microphones and mixing desk, I was able to get casual work in a recording studio. That was really useful and I haven't looked back. I love doing what I do and I wouldn't swap it for anything.

3

Some people say that shopping is a mindless kind of activity. Well, I love shopping, not for the things I buy, but just for the fun of it. So I was pleased to read that shopping is actually good for your brain. When scientists measured activity in the brains of shoppers, they found a lot of activity in the important back part of the brain in the two-and-a-half seconds that it took them to choose a product. In other words, it fires up the part of the brain used in making decisions. So it can't be mindless, can it?

4

W1: Do you wish you could learn a language or take up a new hobby, but it's too expensive or there isn't a class nearby? A new trend known as <u>'talent swapping'</u> could be the answer. On today's programme, two listeners reveal how it worked for them.

M: A neighbour told me she was having problems <u>filling in her tax forms, so I offered to help. In return she made me a lovely meal and now she's teaching me to cook.</u>

W2: <u>A friend was helping children at a local school with their reading and encouraged me to go too.</u> I love it because I get a real buzz from seeing them improving.

5

I went to university with quite <u>a few false ideas about how much living on my own and being a student in London would cost. Before I started, I gave myself a budget for food, rent, etc. and tried to stick to it, but it didn't work out, I'm afraid.</u> I realised that I'm quite fussy about things, like having the right kind of shampoo and eating well, and so <u>it was difficult to economise.</u> I ended up keeping a careful record of everything I spent, which made my friends laugh. You see, my mum's an accountant and I had always complained when she suggested doing that!

6

Travelling regularly in Europe and North America for my work means that I spend relatively little time at home. There's a lot of hard work involved, but one of the compensations of my job is staying in five-star hotels where the furnishings are cool and modern and the bathroom's out of this world. But you can get tired of all that. So when it came to my own place, I knew exactly what I wanted it to look like. <u>I decided to try and create the opposite of twenty-first century five-star hotel living.</u>

Writing p.9

1

1 a

2 b

3 accept the invitation; tell him/her about your brother/sister

2c Corrected email:

Hi Elizabeth,

Thank you for inviting me and my sister to stay with your family this summer. We would both love to come. Can we come for two weeks in August?

I know that you have never met my sister, Angela, but I am sure you'll like her very much. She is a very easy-going person. She is two years younger than me and is studying to be a doctor.

Like me, Angela likes walking and horse riding. She is also very good at tennis. There is only one thing that Angela is not very keen on. Swimming. It's rather strange because we used to go with our family to Lake Balaton every year when we were children. Our family even have a house there now.

I won't write any more, Elizabeth, because I'm taking exams at the moment and I am very busy. Thank you again for your invitation. I am looking forward to seeing you and your family this summer. I've told Angela all about you! Please let me know if we can come in August, won't you?

Best wishes/Lots of love

Suzanna

Module 1B

Vocabulary p.10

1

Photo A: olive leaves, medals, athletes, sports events
Photo B: university, degree, shake someone's hand, graduate
Note: in Paper 5 (Speaking) you get marks for using appropriate vocabulary

2a

1 show; 2 taken; 3 athletes; 4 medals; 5 degree; 6 Like; 7 and; 8 between; 9 event; 10 while / whereas; 11 graduate; 12 olive leaves

2b

Similarities: Both …. (and); Like the people in the first photo, she also ….;
Differences: The main difference between … is …; these athletes have … while / whereas the student …
Opinion: I think I'd prefer …
Paraphrase: some kind of …; a sort of …

Language development 2 p.11

1a

1 T; 2 F; 3 T; 4 F; 5 F; 6 T; 7 F

1b

1 a far larger … than; by far the most; nowhere near as many … as; a lot more … than; almost five times as many … as

2 slightly more … than; nearly as many … as

1c

1 The number of women who / that took part in the Atlanta Olympics was a lot smaller than in the Athens Olympics.
2 Athens organised slightly more events than Sydney.
3 Atlanta didn't organise nearly as many events as Athens.
4 Australian athletes were far more successful at the Sydney Olympics than at the Atlanta Olympics.
5 American athletes did far worse in the Athens Olympics than in the Atlanta Olympics.
6 Greek athletes won exactly as many gold medals in Sydney as in Atlanta.
7 The Olympic Stadium in Atlanta was nowhere near as big as the stadium in Sydney.
8 The Olympic Stadium in Athens was a lot smaller than the Olympic Stadium in Sydney.

2

1 The food I ate at that restaurant in Sydney was ~~the most spiciest~~ **the spiciest** I have ever eaten.
2 The first event we saw was ~~far better one~~ **far better** than the others.
3 The opening ceremony in Athens was much more exciting ~~that~~ **than** the ceremonies in Sydney or Atlanta.
4 ✓
5 He is a ~~more faster~~ **faster** sprinter than all the other athletes.
6 The people in the town were not nearly ~~as much friendly~~ **as friendly** as the villagers.
7 ✓
8 Unfortunately, we ~~didn't have~~ **had** nowhere near as much time to spend shopping in Athens as in Sydney.

Reading p.12

1
a

2a
1 two paragraphs;   2 two paragraphs

2b
1 Japan;   2 Australia

3
1 C;   2 A;   3 D;   4 B;   5 C;   6 A;   7 B;   8 D;   9 C;
10 B;   11 C

Module 2A

Vocabulary p.14

1
Note: in Paper 5 (Speaking) Part 3, you and your partner may have to choose three things from a number of things. It is important that you discuss the options with your partner and justify the choices you make. In this exercise, for example, did you say **why** the factors you chose were more important than other factors?

2a
1 scientist;   2 accountant;   3 lawyer;   4 musician;
5 architect;   6 journalist

2b
1 work on my own, creative;   2 really interesting;
3 salary is excellent, good career opportunities;
4 very creative, can take long holidays;
5 well paid, creative;   6 interesting, rewarding

3
1 A (you *pass/fail an exam* – you do not *succeed in an exam*)
2 B
3 B (you *go for* an interview)
4 C
5 B
6 A
7 A
8 B (you *strike* or *go on strike*)
9 C (your boss *gives you the sack* or *fires you* if he/she is not happy with your work)
10 A (you *graduate* from a college or university when you get your degree)

4
-t: passed, worked
-d: applied, earned, closed, offered
-id: wanted, attended, persuaded, promoted

Language development 1 p.15

1
1 took (last week);   2 haven't had (since then);
3 haven't learnt (still);   4 organised (in January);
5 has complained (up to now);   6 haven't found (yet);
7 answered (the other day);   8 enjoyed (the other day)

2a
1 just;   2 still;   3 yet;   4 already

2b
1 yet;   2 already;   3 still;   4 just

3a
1 lived;   2 been studying;   3 missed;   4 been working;
5 phoned;   6 been trying

3b
1 I've just written two letters of application. Can you post them?
2 George has been working on his CV all day, but he still hasn't finished it.
3 Joanna still hasn't arrived. Do you think she has got lost?
4 Although I have been learning English for over five years, I have never been to England.
5 Call the police! Someone has stolen the money from the safe.
6 I have been trying to phone Sue all afternoon, but I haven't been able to get through yet.

4
1 still haven't been to;   2 haven't seen Jenny for;
3 's/has never forgotten;   4 's/has been working;
5 has just phoned;   6 haven't met for

Listening p.16

1
1 five speakers;   2 they have all given up stressful jobs

2/3
1 D;   2 A;   3 B;   4 C;   5 E

Audio script

Speaker 1:
I worked as a City trader for 12 years and really enjoyed both the job and the lifestyle that went with it, but in the last two years I started to wonder whether it was what I wanted to do for the rest of my life. Because I commuted a long way across London by train, I saw my baby son for only a few minutes at the end of each day if I was lucky, and I'd spend all weekend sleeping. Fortunately, I'd always been a saver, and that made the decision to leave much easier. I had a keen interest in interior design and decided to use my savings to set up my own business.

Speaker 2:
Last summer, I resigned from my job as an insurance broker and started a year-long course to train as a wildlife artist. Learning a new skill was hugely satisfying. But I'll never forget the day I walked past a very expensive restaurant next to the college. I had dined there frequently with clients. Now I was a student in jeans and T-shirt, carrying a backpack. I felt odd. It wasn't that I missed it, but I did wonder if I would be able to afford to eat somewhere like that ever again. I'm excited, although obviously a little apprehensive, about the future. But I love being outdoors and travelling around the country, and everybody says I'm far more relaxed.

Speaker 3:
The first three years were very isolating. But as my wife and I got used to the life, we became very interested in the countryside and grew to love it. I know nothing about gardening and growing things, so taught myself by reading books. I no longer have to waste time on commuting or long business lunches, but my business only brings in about two-thirds of what I earned in my previous salary. But then we don't need so much money to live on. Our heaviest expenses are the two cars, because we are so remote. I grow all our own fruit and vegetables and we rear chickens to eat. We're about 90 per cent self-sufficient in summer.

Speaker 4:
The city had been my life. I worked for a public-relations company which specialised in art exhibitions and so my evenings were devoted to social events. Then without warning, I was made redundant. That made me stop and reconsider my priorities. I realised I was ready for a simpler, more enjoyable life and decided that with computers, faxes and email I could work from home, and didn't even need to be near London. Now I've got two children and so I can't work full time, but I'm doing some market research for a local hotel. I've no regrets; it's a happier, healthier and better quality of life for the whole family.

Speaker 5:
I'd start work at 6:30a.m. and often carry on until midnight if there was a big deal on. The pressure was incredible. There was no time for exercise or eating well and I found myself becoming a very tense and bad-tempered person. I was close to burning out in a totally unfulfilling lifestyle. By sheer chance I saw an article about how someone called a 'life coach' had changed someone's life. I got in touch and as a result of just one consultation, she helped me realise that I'd be much happier as a yoga teacher. I'm now running my own health club. It's quite demanding, but at least I know why I'm doing it.

Writing p.17

1
1   Peter Harlow, Phoenix Tour Group
2   to get the job
3   formal
4   details of previous work experience, why you think you're the right person for the job

2a
Relevant points: 1, 3, 5, 7, 9, 11

2b Suggested paragraph plan:
Paragraph 1: point 5
Paragraph 2: points 1, 3, 7
Paragraph 3: point 11
Paragraph 4: point 9

3a Suggested answers:
1   Dear Mr Harlow,
2   to apply for the position/post of
3   At present,
4   a good command of
5   I would be suitable
6   opportunity
7   consider my application
8   available to attend an interview/for interview
9   Yours sincerely

3c Suggested new paragraphs:
I would like …
I am 23 years old …
I feel …
I hope you will …

Module 2B

Vocabulary p.18

2
1 a teacher, b professor;   2 a check, b control;   3 a career, b course;   4 a lesson, b subject;   5 a train, b educate; 6 a grade, b degree

3
1 you think so;   2 What about;   3 you're right;
4 Don't you think;   5 suppose so;   6 couldn't agree;
7 up to a point;   8 quite true
Note: make sure you write down these words and expressions in your notebook. Use them in Paper 5 (Speaking) Parts 3 and 4.

Language development 2 p.19

1

1 the, Ø; 2 a, Ø, the; 3 a, a, Ø; 4 the, the; 5 Ø, the; 6 a, the; 7 a, the; 8 The, the; 9 Ø, the; 10 the, an

2

1 My flatmate, Mark, wanted to do *something* special last night.

2 ✓

3 He phoned <u>some</u> friends of his to ask them if they'd like to come as well.

4 ✓

5 ✓

6 ✓

7 Unfortunately, it was late and the owner said that he had hardly <u>any</u> pizzas left.

8 'Give us *anything* you have then. It doesn't matter what it is!' Mark told the owner in desperation.

9 The owner returned with two sad-looking pizzas and half a dozen sandwiches. Some of them looked distinctly stale.

10 'Next time we'll stay at home and make the food ourselves. *Anything's* better than this!' Mark groaned.

3

1 ✓; 2 hardly; 3 ✓; 4 the; 5 the; 6 the; 7 of; 8 ✓; 9 a

4

1 you got a computer at; 2 on the train to; 3 to be a bus driver; 4 he play the piano; 5 about Scotland on television; 6 we go to the cinema; 7 's/is telling the truth; 8 have a reputation

Note: in English there are a large number of prepositional phrases – e.g. *in prison, in hospital, by bus, at school,* etc. Keep a record of them in your vocabulary notebook.

Reading p.20

1a

1 a magazine 2 an older woman 3 semi-formal 4 coping with studying again, different kinds of courses, study skills

2

2 Photo B shows the writer.

3

1 D; 2 B; 3 A; 4 C; 5 B; 6 D; 7 A; 8 C

Module 3A

Vocabulary p.22

1a

a fairytale castle, b gloomy factories, c ugly Victorian buildings, d run-down slums, e restored 18th century warehouses, f prosperous mansions, g riverside offices and housing, h dilapidated building

1c 1 rewarding, 2 industrial, 3 present-day, 4 thriving, 5 live, 6 wonderful, 7 architectural, 8 popular

2 1 strength, 2 prosper, 3 prosperity, 4 optimism, 5 threaten, 6 threat, 7 economic, 8 achieve, 9 cultural, 10 architectural, 11 decline, 12 solution

3

1 residence; 2 impressive; 3 historical; 4 significance; 5 commercial; 6 exploration; 7 greatest; 8 famous; 9 romantic; 10 cultural

Language development 1 p.23

1

1 a well, b good; 2 a steady, b steadily; 3 lately, b late; 4 a hardly, b hard; 5 a wide, b widely; 6 a direct, b directly

2a

Gradable: decisive, lively, well-known, bleak, fragile, romantic, impressive, fast

Ungradable: tremendous, fantastic, furious, awful, unique

2b

1 absolutely; 2 very/extremely; 3 very/extremely; 4 very/extremely; 5 absolutely; 6 very/extremely; 7 absolutely; 8 very/extremely; 9 very/extremely; 10 absolutely

3

1 snowed hard; 2 have increased steadily; 3 quite a big; 4 a bit of an expensive; 5 hardly any; 6 was absolutely amazed by; 7 a direct flight; 8 got extremely angry

4

1 have; 2 them; 3 a; 4 Because/As; 5 by; 6 to; 7 been; 8 out; 9 what; 10 as; 11 that/which; 12 since

Writing p.25

1

1 a; 2 b; 3 You must include information about: a the organisation of the tour – was it well organised? b the museum – is it worth visiting? c the hotel – it was modern but … / what were the problems? d the lecture – there was a lecture / give some details

2a

There is no information about 1 the museum; 2 the hotel

2b, c, d Sample answer:

Hi Peter

Thanks for your email. I'm glad you are thinking of visiting Loxford. It's a really beautiful town.

The tour I went on last year was very well-organised. A coach took us to all the main sights. I particularly remember Loxford Museum. It was really interesting because it showed what life was like in Loxford Castle in the past.

The hotel where we stayed was quite nice. We ate all our meals there. Although it was modern, it wasn't very clean and my room didn't have a television.

After dinner, there was a lecture at the hotel by a local historian. His name was Dr Rawlings. It wasn't really a lecture at all, it was so relaxed and informal.

I think you should go on the tour, Peter. I enjoyed it and I'm sure you would as well. Tell me how you get on!

Lots of love

Maria

Listening p.26

2

Order of photographs:

1 D (immigrants arriving at Ellis Island by boat)
2 E (the Baggage Room)   3 C (the Registry Room)
4 B (Wall of Honor)   5 A (the Bunk Room)

3

1 1897 and 1924;   2 ferry (boat);   3 (B)baggage;
4 (an) interview(s);   5 (W)wall of (H)hono(u)r;
6 (B)bunk;   7 (H)hope and (F)fears;
8 11:10 (a.m.)/eleven ten (a.m.)/ten past/after eleven (a.m.);
9 Oral History Library;   10 ticket office

Audio script

Hello everyone. First of all, a big welcome to New York from all of us here at the hotel. My name's Bob and I'm here to make sure you enjoy your stay in the city. I've organised some great guided tours for you, and we start tomorrow with a trip to the Museum of Immigration on Ellis Island. Now I'm going to give you a few background details that will help you get the most out of your visit.

As you know, millions of people came to the USA from Europe in the late nineteenth and early twentieth centuries, especially during the period between <u>1897</u> and <u>1924</u> – that's the year when immigration controls were introduced – and Ellis Island was the place where they first landed. The buildings which immigrants had to pass through before they were allowed to come and live in the USA, were used right up till 1954. Then they stood empty until they were restored as a museum, which opened in September 1990. And that's where we'll be going tomorrow.

Your tour of the museum begins when you step off the <u>ferry</u> – at the very point where the immigrants stepped off the ships that had brought them on their long journey all the way from Europe.

The first place they passed through is called the <u>Baggage</u> Room. That's where they picked up their bags and other possessions, and you'll be able to see a display of typical baggage from the period there as you pass through.

You then go into what's called the Registry Room – just as the immigrants did. This is where they had medical check-ups and <u>interviews</u> and then, if all went well, they were allowed to enter the USA. Imagine how it must have felt to be so close to your new home, but still not be sure if you'd be accepted, or put on the next ship home again.

But most people were accepted, and it's incredible, but 100 million Americans can trace their family history in the USA to a man, woman or child who passed through this room. And 420,000 of them have their names written on what is known as the '<u>Wall of Honor</u>' which you can see at the museum.

If things were real busy, or if there was a problem, the newcomers might have to spend a few days on the island, and the next place you see on the guided tour is the sleeping area, known as the <u>Bunk</u> Room, and then after that what's called the Hearing Room – that's where people who'd been refused entry could have their case

heard by a judge.

The museum also has three theatres. Theatre 1 is a movie theatre and I've reserved tickets for you to see the 30-minute movie called <u>*Hope and Fears*</u>. In the movie, you'll see immigrants telling their own stories of how they pulled up their roots in Europe and came to live in the USA. Next door, in Theatre 2, there'll be the chance to see the play called *Ellis Island Stories*, which also lasts 30 minutes. This play features two immigrants and one immigration officer and it's based on real-life interviews recorded at Ellis Island. We haven't made reservations for the play, but it begins at <u>11:10 a.m.</u> and there'll be plenty of time to see it if you'd like to.

Or you might want to visit the <u>Oral History Library</u>. The Ellis Island Oral History Project has collected recordings of first-hand accounts of people's experiences at Ellis Island, and you can listen to some of these on a computer system with 20 individual listening stations.

And if there's still time after that, why not visit the exhibition called *The Peopling of America* which is located in the old <u>ticket office</u> which was across the water from the old railroad station. This exhibition places Ellis Island in the context of 400 years of North American immigration history.

So, all in all, it looks like being a great tour …

Module 3B

Vocabulary p.27

1a

Text 1 – B; Text 2 – A; Text 3 – E; Text 4 – D; Text 5 – C

1b

1 down; 2 catastrophe; 3 habitats; 4 species;
5 destroy; 6 extinct; 7 take; 8 greenhouse; 9 warming;
10 solar; 11 Poisonous; 12 dump; 13 Radioactive;
14 effect; 15 ban; 16 out; 17 recycle; 18 fertilisers;
19 modified; 20 grow

2

1 B
2 D (the writer was walking **down** the hill)
3 B (the only verb which makes sense here)
4 C (*hardly* = negative)
5 D
6 C
7 A
8 B (part of a fixed phrase)
9 A
10 A
11 C (if a single light bulb is *left on* all year = not switched off)
12 D

Language development 2 p.28

1

1 ✓; 2 enjoyed watching; 3 appeared to be; 4 ✓;
5 refused to give up; 6 managed to lift; 7 ✓;
8 having problems breathing; 9 ✓; 10 made millions of people feel

2
1 on; 2 in; 3 about; 4 in; 5 about; 6 to; 7 at; 8 for;
9 on; 10 for; 11 about; 12 for

3
1 a killing (*they no longer kill*); b to take (*we were driving there, so we stopped the car*)
2 a to bring (*I hope you didn't forget*); b putting (*it is a clear memory*)
3 a taking (*as an experiment*); b to persuade (*I attempted to do this*)
4 a to tell (*I'm sorry to tell you*); b paying (*I wish I hadn't done it*)
5 a to mention (*he didn't remember*); b seeing (*I still have the memory of it*)
6 a to take (*the government intends to take*); b changing (*it will require this*)

4
1 (really) can't stand travelling; 2 was my decision;
3 couldn't afford to go; 4 spent ages getting;
5 help smiling when I; 6 can hear people laughing;
7 threatened to go to; 8 looking forward to visiting;
9 was worth going to; 10 keen on the idea of

5
1 for 2 be 3 taking 4 to

Reading p.30

3
1 C; 2 E; 3 B; 4 F; 5 D; 6 A; 7 D/F; 8 F/D; 9 G;
10 C/F; 11 F/C; 12 E; 13 B; 14 A/B; 15 B/A

Module 4A

Vocabulary p.32

1
1 was born; 2 orphan; 3 childhood; 4 lonely; 5 was brought up; 6 well off; 7 late teens; 8 got on; 9 earn;
10 poverty; 11 put by; 12 luxury; 13 opportunity;
14 wealthy; 15 wedding; 16 achieve

2a
1 out; 2 on; 3 up; 4 into; 5 out; 6 without; 7 out;
8 with

2b
1 set out; 2 ran into; 3 do without; 4 put up with;
5 worn me out; 6 ran out of water; 7 giving up;
8 keep on

3
1 extremely; 2 challenging; 3 preparation; 4 fitness;
5 traditional; 6 inhospitable; 7 competitors; 8 heat;
9 endurance; 10 continental

Language development 1 p.33

1 Correct story order and verb forms:
a My girlfriend has a lovely black kitten called Max.
e She phoned me yesterday to say that she *had lost* him.
h She told me on the phone that she *had looked* everywhere.
b I *went* to her house, of course, to help her find Max.

d When she opened the door, I could see from her eyes that she *had been crying*.
j We *went* out into the garden to look for Max together.
i It was cold in the garden and it *was raining* heavily.
g 20 minutes later we still *hadn't found* Max, so we went back inside.
f We *were having* a hot chocolate when we heard a sound.
c There was Max! He *was lying* fast asleep in his basket!

2a
1 e; 2 d; 3 f; 4 a; 5 b; 6 c

2b
1 By the time we arrived at the party, everyone had gone home.
2 I was watching a horror film on television when the lights suddenly went out.
3 Once the air hostess had counted all the passengers, the plane took off.
4 I had never lived on my own before I went to university.
5 As soon as Peter heard the good news, he telephoned his wife.
6 We had been waiting for an hour and a half when the train eventually arrived.
7 The customs officer allowed us to go after he had searched all our luggage./After the customs officer had searched all our luggage, he allowed us to go.
8 While I was staying at my grandfather's house, I discovered an old photograph album.
9 Sarah didn't go back to work until she had recovered from the flu.
10 When my sister read her exam results, she burst out laughing.

3
1 had already started by; 2 when they heard;
3 had just taken; 4 had not expected them to;
5 as soon as I opened; 6 was midday when we set;
7 anything until he had read;
8 while I was; 9 she had never been to;
10 had been travelling for

Writing p.35

1a
1 students 2 Gillian; she

2a
(see paragraph breaks in improved story below)

2b
Paragraph 1: b
Paragraph 2: e
Paragraph 3: a
Paragraph 4: c
Paragraph 5: d

2c
1 past perfect 2 past simple

2d
1 walking; 2 cold; 3 fat; 4 smiling; 5 looked; 6 put;
7 started to cry; 8 got up; 9 liked

Improved story:

Gillian was cold and hungry and completely lost. She *gazed* around at the tall dark trees. Where was the village she had left that morning? She sighed and continued to follow the footpath through the woods.

It was Gillian's first visit to Wales. At first, she had *fallen in love with* the wild beauty of the place. It frightened her now, though, because she didn't know where she was.

After a while, she came to a shallow stream. She took off her boots and *dipped* her feet in the *freezing* water. Then she *burst into tears*. She had been walking for hours and felt too *exhausted* to take another step.

Suddenly, she heard a voice: 'Hello, can I help?' She looked up. A *plump*, cheerful woman was standing in front of her, *with a warm smile on her face*. She was holding a dog on a lead. Gillian *jumped up* and hugged the woman. She was safe!

When they got back to the village, Gillian realised how lucky she had been. She would never again go *exploring* alone in the mountains of Wales.

Listening p.36

1a

1 two speakers;   2 training for challenging physical activities

2

1 rower;   2 charity;   3 sailing;   4 100/one hundred kilo(gramme)s;   5 motivation;   6 challenge;   7 disappointed;   8 variety;   9 short(-)term;   10 lonely

Audio script

J = *Jennie*; **M** = *Malcolm*

J: In today's programme, we're talking about challenge and endurance. With me in the studio is someone who knows all about those qualities and how to find them in yourself, the champion rower Malcolm Price. Malcolm, welcome.

M: Hi.

J: So what's the secret if you're going to push yourself to the limit? It can't all just be physical strength and fitness.

M: Well, Jennie, many people these days do push themselves to the limit, physically and mentally to achieve their goals, and not only in competitive sports. You know, it could be a way of raising money for a charity, or just achieving something for personal satisfaction. But, whatever you choose to do, whether it's climbing a mountain, running across a desert or winning a sailing race, there's a lot of hard work involved to get yourself in top physical and mental shape, and success only comes through thorough training. That's the same whether you're

an Olympic champion, or just someone taking part in the local fun run.

J: But you've got to be fit to start with, haven't you?

M: Well, physical strength is part of it. I don't think I'd have gone into rowing if I didn't have the physical build for it. But when you're nearly two metres tall and weigh 100 kilos, there's not much chance of being a champion jockey or a sprinter. But I'm sure that I'd still have excelled at something, even if I'd been shorter and slimmer, because that's just in me as a person.

J: So, it's partly psychological then?

M: Well, I suppose it is, yes. If you're involved in sport as a kid, then the training becomes part of your life, and you learn a kind of strategy for success, whatever it is you're trying to do. But there's no reason why someone who starts doing physical activity as an adult shouldn't find the same level of motivation.

J: As long as you have a goal …

M: Exactly. You need to make sure you've got something to aim for, and it has to be something which you really can achieve, that's within your capabilities, but of course it's also got to be a challenge or else you'll have nothing to work towards.

J: And what about if you're trying really hard, but just not getting anywhere?

M: Well, it could be that you've set yourself the wrong goals, or it could just be impatience. The important thing is to aim to make progress in small stages; each week you should be getting closer to your target. But if you expect too much, too soon, you're almost bound to be disappointed.

J: So keep at it?

M: Yes, but vary your schedule. If you do the same things every day, you're tempted to make comparisons too soon. Apart from anything else, training becomes tedious if there's no variety in it. And you need time off from it too. At least one day a week, do something else, something completely unrelated.

J: So, don't worry too much about how it's going?

M: There's no point in doing that. You need to review your goals regularly, so that you know whether you're getting fitter or faster or stronger or whatever. But you should also be able to relax and enjoy yourself, otherwise what's the point? That's why short-term goals are useful. You know, for example, I'm going to be running five miles a day in two months' time, although my ultimate goal might be running a marathon next year.

J: But you've got to have one clear goal – like that marathon.

M: That's right, and friends can be useful too. Training with a friend means that you've got someone to share the ups and downs with, and it's also much harder to give up if there's someone else involved. To be honest, training can be a lonely business, and there will be setbacks, and so you need to enlist the support of those around you.

J: Malcolm, thank you. But don't go away because after the news, we'll be talking about how to prepare for the big day…

Module 4B

Vocabulary p.37

1a
Risk (extreme) sport: hang gliding (I), climbing (I), parachute jumping (I)
Track and field event: running (I), high jump (I)
Water sport: windsurfing (I), water skiing (I), scuba diving (I)
Winter sport: snowboarding (I), ice hockey (T)
Martial art: karate (I)
Ball games: tennis (I, T), basketball (T), rugby (T), golf (I)

1b
1 hang gliding; 2 water skiing; 3 karate; 4 tennis; 5 climbing; 6 scuba diving; 7 snowboarding; 8 ice hockey

2
1 B; 2 A; 3 C; 4 B; 5 A; 6 A; 7 B; 8 A

3
1 B; 2 C; 3 C; 4 B; 5 B; 6 A; 7 D; 8 A; 9 D; 10 A

Language development 2 p.38

1
1a a b ∅; 2a a b ∅; 3a some b a; 4a a b any; 5a a b ∅

2a
1 much; 2 ✓; 3 many; 4 ✓; 5 much; 6 ✓; 7 number; 8 much

2b
1 little; 2 a few; 3 a little; 4 little; 5 a few; 6 few (*few/a few* with countable nouns, *little/a little* with uncountable nouns)

3
1 a great deal of; 2 by very few; 3 much interest in; 4 lots of money; 5 no sports facilities at; 6 a small amount of

4
1 the; 2 few; 3 up; 4 up; 5 that; 6 well; 7 lot; 8 or; 9 because/as; 10 nothing; 11 but; 12 of

Reading p.40

2
1 The future of sponsorship – not mentioned
2 The advantages of sponsorship – paragraphs 2, 3
3 How commercial sponsorship of sports started – paragraphs 1, 2
4 The disadvantages of sponsorship – paragraphs 4, 5, 6

3a
2 the sports equipment manufacturer, Slazenger
3 of free publicity

3c
1 H; 2 E; 3 C; 4 F; 5 D; 6 A; 7 G

Module 5A

Vocabulary p.42

1a
1 science; 2 scientist; 3 genetics; 4 genetic; 5 psychology; 6 psychological; 7 linguistics; 8 linguist;
9 archaeology; 10 archaeologist; 11 astronomer; 12 astronomical

1b
The suffix *-ist* or *-er* is often used for a **person**.
The suffix *-ics* or *-y* is often used for a **subject**.
The suffix *-ic*, or *-ical* is often used for an **adjective**.

1c
1 psychological; 2 genetics; 3 astronomers; 4 linguistic; 5 archaeological; 6 scientific

2
science, scientist, scientific
genetics, geneticist, genetic
psychology, psychologist, psychological
linguistics, linguist, linguistic,
archaeology, archaeologist, archaeological
astronomy, astronomer, astronomical
Note: it is very important that you stress words correctly in English. If you stress the wrong syllable, people may not understand you. Check in a good dictionary (e.g. The *Longman Exams Dictionary*) if you are unsure which syllable is stressed.

3
1 the latest; 2 as a consequence of; 3 packed with; 4 hard to put down; 5 at the forefront of; 6 getting better and better; 7 in the widest sense; 8 to great effect

4a
1 e; 2 c; 3 g; 4 h; 5 f; 6 a; 7 b; 8 d

4b
1 present; 2 belief; 3 discovery; 4 design; 5 information; 6 theory; 7 breeze; 8 advertisements

5
1 A (*known as, referred to as, described as*)
2 B (= collocation)
3 D (= there was *little* information about DNA; *hardly anything* was known …)
4 A
5 B (*similar to, the same as*)
6 A (you accept something, but you *agree to* something)
7 D (you *do research* or you *carry out research* …)
8 A (*appeared* is usually followed by a *to-* infinitive)
9 C (you are *working on a problem* if you are trying to solve it)
10 B (you put *whereas* between two clauses in a sentence)
11 D (= *without saying anything*)
12 B (you *present someone with* a prize)

Language development 1 p.43

1
1 does the bank close; 2 I'll get; 3 I'm going to complain; 4 It's going to; 5 Are you doing; 6 He'll; 7 I'm meeting; 8 are you going to tell; 9 Will you; 10 will win

2
1 will discover; 2 'll/will be working; 3 'll/will have finished; 4 'll/will be painting; 5 'll/will have been; 6 'll/will go out; 7 'll/will be going; 8 'll/will have left

3

1 'll/will let you know, find out;   2 finish/have finished, shall we go;   3 Do you want, leave;   4 is, 'll/will start; 5 are, 's/is going to have;   6 stops, don't we go

4

1 A;   2 C;   3 C;   4 A;   5 A;   6 B;   7 C;   8 B

5

1 who; 2 to; 3 as; 4 than; 5 other; 6 if/whether; 7 (al)though/while/whilst; 8 in; 9 What; 10 which/that; 11 a; 12 must

Writing p.45

1

4 The points which should be included in the email: would a group of 20 students be a problem? / what is the best time to visit? / can the telescope be used? / is photography allowed?

3a

Paragraph 1: c, f, b
Paragraph 2: d, e, a
Paragraph 3: h, i
Paragraph 4: l, k, g
Paragraph 5: j

3b Ordered letter:

Dear Dr Good

I am secretary of the Science Club at Erasmus College. I saw your advertisement for the St Aubrey Open Day and would like to organise a group visit. However, there are some questions I would like to ask you beforehand.

Firstly, since all our members are interested in coming to the observatory, there will be about twenty of us. Would so many students be a problem? Could you also let me know the best time for us to visit?

I would also like to know if we will be allowed to look through the St Aubrey telescope? We have heard so much about it and would love to try it out!

Finally, several students are keen photographers. They want to know whether they can take photographs inside the observatory. I understand, of course, that photography may not be allowed.

I look forward to hearing from you.

Yours sincerely

Richard Zimler

Listening p.46

1b

1 a number: 3;   2 proper names: 1, 2;   3 parts of a face: 8; 4 adjectives 5, 6

2

1 China;   2 The Naked Face;   3 95/ninety-five;   4 mirror; 5 uncomfortable;   6 personal;   7 managers; 8 chin/lips (in either order)   9 make-up; 10 nodding/smiling (in either order)

Audio script

PR = *Presenter;* **L** = *Lillian*

PR: In today's programme, we're talking about faces and what they can tell us about a person's character. In the studio is Lillian Scott who's written a book about the skill of face-reading. Lillian, welcome.

L: Hi.

PR: So is this idea that you can tell a person's character from the shape of their face a new theory?

L: Oh no, it goes back centuries actually, but it's only now that people are studying it more seriously. The idea has reached us in Europe via Australia and New Zealand, but the skill was originally developed in China. I go into this in some detail in my book.

PR: And the book's called …?

L: Well, it took a long time to find a title. I wanted to call it Face to Face, but apparently there's already a book with that title, so that wasn't allowed. In the end, someone suggested The Naked Face, which sounded good because I wanted to focus on things which everyone can see, but which we tend not to notice. So we went for that.

PR: And the book begins by describing how the face works, doesn't it?

L: Yes, for example there are 14 bones in the face with around 95 muscles working around them. This means that we can do all sorts of things with our faces, revealing a great deal about ourselves in the process, because our faces are changing all the time as we speak, as we react towards the world around us.

PR: And can you observe this in your own face?

L: Well, yes, I mean when people look in a mirror, they tend to adopt a particular facial expression, the one they think looks best. They try to do the same thing when posing for photographs, but usually without success because you can't actually see what you look like till later. That's why people are always saying 'I look awful in that photo,' when to the rest of us they look perfectly normal. And of course, seeing yourself on video can be quite an uncomfortable experience, because then you see all your changes of expression and so on.

PR: And then some people think they have a best side, don't they, which they always turn towards the camera?

L: That's right. And, of course, each side is always different. It's a fact that's puzzled scientists for years, but it is true. Some face-reading experts say that people generally want to show the right side of their face to the world, because they feel the left is the personal side, you know, they want to keep it to themselves.

PR: Really? And what character traits can you see in people's faces? Give us some examples, things we could look out for.

L: Well, good managers generally have wide faces with the cheekbones wide apart, which is meant to indicate a strong desire to achieve things and meet targets.

PR: OK. Anything else?

L: Other good signs for success at work are a strong <u>chin</u>, which represents determination, and of course the shape of the <u>lips</u> has long been associated with that as well.

PR: Right. But what about if you don't look like that? Can you make the most of what you've got, in a job interview, for example?

L: Yes, you certainly can, and of course women especially try to do this. The first thing to remember is that you should look people straight in the eye when you speak, even if it means moving your chair. Some people use <u>make-up</u> or a new hair-do to emphasise or play down certain facial features, but it's best to get professional advice because too much, or badly applied make-up, for example, would be a mistake. It actually puts people off.

PR: Sure.

L: But basically it's more a question of how you behave at interviews. If you're tense, your face is likely to look tight and unrelaxed and people will think that's also your character. Whereas if you keep <u>nodding</u> and <u>smiling</u> to show that you're really interested in what they're saying, people tend to like you better.

PR: Thank you Lillian. And if you'd like to buy Lillian's book, it's …

Module 5B

Vocabulary p.47

1a
1 remote control;   2 DVD player;   3 keyboard;
4 optical mouse;   5 text message;   6 viewfinder;   7 lens;
8 earphones

1b
1 ring tone;   2 software;   3 channels;   4 focus;
5 website;   6 broadcast;   7 download;   8 images;
9 call;   10 zap

2
Correct order: 1 a;   2 d;   3 f;   4 b;   5 e;   6 c

Corrected discussion:

Peter: I think the computer is the most important thing ever invented. If you have a computer, you can do so many things that you couldn't do before. Computers and the Internet have changed the way people live.

Ingrid: Yes, that's *true*. But I don't think computers have changed our lives as much as cars. The car is a more important invention *in* my opinion. It's easy to live without a computer but you can't live without a car, can you?

Peter: No, I suppose *not*. Most people depend on them nowadays. Life would be *much* slower and more difficult without them. But I think other things are more important. What *about* fire, for example? I mean, that's something that changed the history of the whole human race.

Ingrid: Yes. You *are* right. I hadn't thought of that. I'm not sure if fire is a thing that we invented, though. It's a natural phenomenon. People discovered it. *Don't* you agree?

Peter: Yes, I suppose *so*. Well, writing then – writing was invented. That was a really important invention, I think.

Ingrid: I couldn't agree *more*. Without writing we wouldn't be able to live like we do today. The whole of our civilisation is based on things which are written down. Maybe it is the most important thing which has ever been invented.

3
1 a engine, b machine;   2 a electric, b electrical;
3 a appliance, b device;   4 a technician, b mechanic;
5 a discover, b invent;   6 a fix, b correct

4
1 impression;   2 entertainment;   3 products;
4 successful;   5 anxiety;   6 development;   7 immediately;
8 sale;   9 satisfied;   10 reception

Language development 2 p.48

1a
1 myself;   2 by;   3 ✓;   4 themselves;   5 yourself;   6 ✓;
7 each;   8 ✓

1b
1 blame yourself;   2 write it (yourself);
3 known each other;   4 relax;   5 looked at herself;
6 concentrate;   7 like each other

2a
1 b;   2 d;   3 a;   4 e;   5 f;   6 c

2b
1 how to use;   2 where I put;   3 what to do;
4 why he spoke

3
1 you enjoy yourself at;   2 you hurt yourself;
3 repaired my bicycle on my;   4 know how to use;
5 've/have forgotten what Mike;   6 sure who to ask;
7 went by myself;   8 know what to say;
9 been talking to each;   10 you draw this yourself

Reading p.50

1
1 negative meaning (*too clever for your own good* means you try to be very clever, but it doesn't work as well as a simpler solution)

2b
The main message of the text is A.

3a
2 it
3 something's not quite right

3d   1 H;   2 D;   3 G;   4 A;   5 B;   6 F;   7 E

Module 6A

Vocabulary p.52

1a
1 ambition;   2 replacement;   3 confidence;   4 popularity;   5 determination;   6 bravery;   7 creativity;   8 loneliness

1b
Note: This exercise will help you to see patterns in word formation. Some suffixes are used only for nouns, some

only for adjectives, etc. When you learn new words, pay particular attention to word stress – mark the syllable which is stressed. Check in a good dictionary if you are not sure. Look for pronunciation patterns as well as spelling patterns.

2a
1　am<u>bi</u>tion, determi<u>na</u>tion, satis<u>fac</u>tion, fasci<u>na</u>tion
2　crea<u>ti</u>vity, popu<u>la</u>rity, dependa<u>bi</u>lity, adapta<u>bi</u>lity

2b
c

3
1 in; 2 in; 3 out of; 4 by; 5 by; 6 on; 7 by; 8 in

4a
1 performance; 2 scholarship; 3 audition;
4 opportunity; 5 debut; 6 role; 7 offer; 8 impact;
9 album; 10 records

4b
Verb + noun collocation from the text are:
give + performance, win + scholarship, go for + audition, give + opportunity, make + debut, play + role, take up + offer, make + impact, release + album, break + record

5
1 has risen to; 2 gave an exceptional performance;
3 stands out as; 4 feel homesick; 5 by the popularity;
6 turned down; 7 lacks patience; 8 set off from; 9 been a very ambitious; 10 has no intention of leaving

Language development 1 p.53

1a, b
1　We're taking the plane that leaves Heathrow at six o'clock. (**D**)
2　Jennifer Lopez's perfume Glow, which was launched in 2001, quickly became the number one perfume in over nine countries. (**ND**)
3　Look! The pianist who played at the concert last night is sitting over there! (**D**)
4　Where are the tickets for *Cats* (that) I bought this morning? (**D**)
5　Jennifer Lopez, whose success as a singer has been phenomenal, has no plans yet to stop acting. (**ND**)
6　I'll arrange an interview with someone who can help you. (**D**)
7　The song which we enjoyed most at the Eurovision Song Contest was the Hungarian one. (**D**)

2　Complete article:

> Karaoke, **whose popularity has spread throughout the world in recent years**, originated in Japan. *Kara* is an abbreviation of the word **which/that means empty in Japanese (*karappo*)/** *karoppo*, **which means empty in Japanese**; and *oke* is short for *okesutura* or orchestra. Usually, a recorded song consists of both vocals and a musical accompaniment. However, recordings of songs **which/that consist only of the accompaniment** are called karaoke.
>
> For almost thirty years, Japanese people, **who have always enjoyed singing after work and at parties**, have been picking up microphones and 'singing karaoke'. Family karaoke sets, **which display the words and scenes of a song on a monitor**,

> are extremely popular in Japan. Apparently, they also help children **who/that have reading problems** to learn to read more quickly.
>
> In Japan, **where houses and flats are often built very close together**, noise can be a problem. So special places for people **who/that wanted to sing karaoke** started to appear in the towns and countryside. The first 'karaoke box' appeared in a rice field near Kansai as early as 1984.

3a
1　The musical *Moulin Rouge*, ~~which starred~~ Nicole Kidman and Ewan McGregor, was a huge success at the box office. **starring**
2　Many songs ~~which were written~~ more than 10 years ago seem very dated nowadays. **written**
3　One day I saw a busker ~~who was playing~~ four instruments at the same time. **playing**
4　Jennifer Lopez's second album, *J.Lo*, ~~which was released~~ in 2001, went straight to the top of the charts. **released**
5　All the money ~~which is earned~~ from ticket sales goes to charity. **earned**

3b　Read
A　The rock concert, ~~which was held~~ **held** last night in the main hall of the college, was a great success. I'm sure everyone who went last night will not forget it for a long time. During the performance, Jeff Stone, ~~who was constantly cheered and applauded~~ **constantly cheered and applauded** by his fans, amazed the audience by his skill as a musician. He played a number of old favourites, ~~which included~~ **including** Red Rose and Road to Heaven, and sang a number of songs from the band's latest album. At one point, the people ~~who were sitting~~ **sitting** in the front seats jumped up and started to dance in the aisles.

B　The classical concert on April 6th was disappointing. Beethoven's seventh symphony, ~~which was performed~~ **performed** by the University Orchestra, lacked passion throughout. In fact, the musicians ~~who were playing~~ **playing** in the strings section of the orchestra appeared to be positively bored. The conductor, James Oliver, who has led the orchestra for the past two years, surprised the audience by his unorthodox interpretation of the symphony.

4
1　Formal: That's the person to whom I spoke on the phone earlier.
　　Informal: That's the person (who / that) I spoke to on the phone earlier.

2　Formal: Bill is the sound technician for whom we work.
　　Informal: Bill is the sound technician (who / that) we work for.

3　Formal: They are redecorating the hall in which the concert will take place.
　　Informal: They are redecorating the hall (which / that) the concert will take place in.

4　Formal: Is this the tape on which you recorded the album?
　　Informal: Is this the tape (which / that) you recorded the album on?

5 Formal: Are these the tickets for which we paid so much money?
Informal: Are these the tickets (which / that) we paid so much money for?

5
1 which/that; 2 an; 3 well; 4 than; 5 what; 6 however; 7 to; 8 in; 9 with; 10 if/though; 11 when/once; 12 had

Writing p.55

1
1 in an English-language student magazine, for readers of this magazine;
2 to describe a concert you went to, in an interesting way for readers;
3 You must say a little about the musicians and the music they played; also whether you think the concert was successful (and why);
4 the review will be read by students, so the style should be fairly informal and include your personal opinions.

2

A good review:	Review 1	Review 2
has an eye-catching title.	✓	✗
has an interesting opening paragraph, which tells the reader *what* exactly is being reviewed.	✓	✗
is divided into paragraphs, each focusing on one aspect of the subject of the review	✓	✗
is written in an appropriate style and involves the reader by addressing him/her directly	✓	✓
describes clearly what the writer experienced, including important details	✓	✗
gives the reader a clear impression of the personal opinion (good or bad) of the writer	✓	✓
uses varied and interesting language	✓	✗
finishes with a strong sentence, which summarises what has been said	✓	✗

Review 1 is, of course, much better. In fact, Review 2 is **not a review** of a concert at all. The writer has simply written about his favourite band!

3a Corrected reviews:

Review 1

The *Flaming Lips* don't disappoint their British fans

It was obvious from the start that the *Flaming Lips* concert at the Brighton Centre was going to be different. When Wayne Coyle floated over the heads of the audience inside a huge plastic bubble, everyone knew this ~~is~~ **would be** a night to remember.

The *Flaming Lips* ~~are putting~~ **have been putting** on shows like this since the band was formed in 1983 in Oklahoma. They love to surprise their fans with special effects and surrealistic costumes. Wayne Coyle, the band's charismatic vocalist, loves to give people a good time.

In Brighton, the *Flaming Lips* played that old favourite Yoshimi Battles the Pink Robots, as well as The Yeah Yeah Yeah Song. The audience danced and sang along with the band, going wild with excitement when the *Flaming Lips* began to play Mr Ambulance Man.

The concert was a huge success. When I left, it seemed that the world had suddenly become more interesting – and more fun. If you love rock music, go and see them. They won't be in Britain for long!

[*180 words*]

Review 2

I like music and I love going to concerts. Last month I went to two concerts.

A band I really like is the *White Stripes*. ~~You have~~ heard **Have you heard** of them? They are an exciting band from Detroit in America. The *White Stripes* play back-to-basics blues. They have a ~~hugely~~ **huge** number of rock fans from all over the world. The band consists of Jack and Meg White, and they ~~are using~~ **use** just guitar and drums to accompany ~~the most~~ **most of** their songs. The *White Stripes* are from Detroit. They suddenly became famous in 2001. Before that, nobody knew anything about them. Meg and Jack always wear red, white and black clothes when they perform. Three really famous *White Stripes* songs are Aluminium, Blue Orchid and The Hardest Button to Button. Recently, these songs were rewritten for orchestra. I read ~~at~~ **in** a student magazine that the Royal Ballet is going to dance to these songs at the Royal Opera House in London. I ~~am wondering~~ **wonder** what the audience will think? They normally go and see Swan Lake!

I would like to go to that concert.

Listening p.56

2a
1 B; 2 B; 3 C; 4 C; 5 A; 6 B; 7 A

Audio script

PR = *Presenter*; P = *Peter*
PR: Last year, in a television series called *Faking it*, various people were given four weeks to learn the skills of a new profession. Peter Harris, a painter and decorator from Liverpool, was one of them and he joins me in the studio today. Peter, welcome.

P: Hi.

PR: So why were you selected to take part in the programme, Peter?

P: Well, one day, I got a phone call from someone asking me if I'd like to take part. They'd called lots of decorating companies all over the country looking for someone willing to spend four weeks learning to be an artist, you know instead of painting walls and doors, you'd learn how to do abstract art. And the cameras would be there to see how you got on. But they couldn't get anyone to volunteer. At first, I thought it must be one of my friends playing a joke on me, so I laughed and put the phone down.

PR: Really!

P: But fortunately, <u>they called back and gave me a number at the television company where I could call them and that's when I realised it was for real.</u>

PR: So what did your friends think?

P: They thought it was funny, because I know nothing about art but I think they admired me for giving it a try. Before the filming started, I went down to the local art gallery with them to have a look at some abstract art. <u>To be honest, I thought it was all a load of rubbish</u>, but I still wasn't convinced that I'd actually be able to do it.

PR: So what happened? How did you learn?

P: Well, at first, I actually found it exciting because I never knew what was happening from one day to the next. But basically, I had lessons. And of course I found it was harder than you'd think, especially with the cameras watching. <u>But the worst bit was having to film what's called a video diary every evening saying how the lessons had gone and how I was feeling.</u>

PR: But you enjoyed it?

P: I began to see that there really is something behind abstract art. People look at a painting and say 'What is it?' or 'It's just a load of paint thrown about,' but actually there's a lot more to it than that. I think people laugh at things they don't understand sometimes, but that doesn't mean it's no good. <u>The artist wants you to think, you know, which can be hard work!</u>

PR: Absolutely.

P: Then, one day, I was just painting freely, you know, experimenting, and suddenly I realised that what I'd painted looked like a wheelchair. I'd had a football accident as a child and I couldn't walk for a while. It was a frustrating and frightening time for me. Suddenly all those feelings came back to me. It was so unexpected, and I realised that a part of me was coming out in the painting. <u>It reduced me to tears.</u>

PR: Did other people see the wheelchair?

P: I don't think so, but funnily enough that was one of the pictures that went through to the final programme. The idea was that my paintings would be shown in a gallery alongside lots of real artists' work, and a panel of experts would try and say which ones were mine. It was all part of the idea of the television programme. Anyway, I was fairly

determined to prove that I could do it. <u>Lots of people were surprised when three out of four experts failed to spot which paintings were mine. But I was delighted.</u>

PR: So now you're an artist?

P: Sort of, yeah. Actually, since the show, I've sold about 15 paintings which has impressed my family more than anything. And I thought the other artists would really hate me, because they find it so hard to sell their work, but they were fine. <u>No, the only people I didn't like were some of the people who bought my work.</u> They only seemed to be interested in how much it would be worth in the future.

PR: Peter, thank you.

3

1 for real; 2 a load of rubbish; 3 bit; 4 hard work; 5 to tears; 6 to spot, delighted; 7 be worth

Module 6B

Vocabulary p.57

1

1 art exhibition; 2 street performance; 3 play; 4 TV show; 5 film

2

C	O	M	P	O	S	E	R
A	E	E	L	M	I	V	E
S	O	Q	C	W	S	N	V
T	S	I	H	N	T	B	I
V	C	L	A	P	A	H	E
O	R	M	P	U	G	P	W
D	I	E	T	C	E	L	X
U	P	B	E	P	R	O	S
P	T	E	R	F	O	T	T

1 cast; 2 script; 3 composer; 4 review; 5 plot; 6 clap; 7 chapter; 8 stage

3a

1 d; 2 h; 3 e; 4 g; 5 c; 6 b; 7 a; 8 f

3b

1 detective; 2 complicated; 3 popular; 4 abstract; 5 marble; 6 talented; 7 open-air; 8 oil

4

1 D

2 C (*bargain for/over, profit by*)

3 B (= occupy)

4 D

5 A

6 A (*fixed expression*)

7 D (*collocation*)

8 B

9 C (*show/teach something to someone, learn something from someone*)

10 A
11 B (= appears)
12 C

Language development 2 p.58

1

1 isn't/is not interested in;   2 's/is capable of becoming;
3 's/is no connection between;   4 's/is responsible for
choosing;   5 a quick solution to;   6 good at remembering;
7 's/is no comparison between;   8 a sudden increase in;
9 difficulty in understanding;   10 were disappointed to
miss/about missing/that you missed

2a

1 c; 2 f; 3 d; 4 b; 5 g; 6 e; 7 a

2b

1 Since David Blaine is now a celebrity, he is used to
   being approached by people on the street in America
2 He stopped appearing in public with his friend, Leo
   DiCaprio, because he couldn't ~~to~~ get used to the way
   people always called him 'Leo's friend'.
3 David Blaine is used to ~~be~~ spending a lot of time
   preparing for his difficult and often dangerous feats.
4 He recently tried to hold his breath underwater for
   longer than the world record of 8 minutes 58 seconds.
   In training for this, he had to get used to slowing down
   his heartbeat so that his body used less oxygen.
5 Although it was very unpleasant at first, David Blaine
   is now used to being attacked in the press by other
   illusionists and entertainers.

3

1 to;   2 for;   3 my;   4 few;   5 what;   6 the;
7 which/that;   8 all;   9 who;   10 when;   11 as;   12 of

Reading p.60

2

Paragraph 1: It's unusual because it's crowded with people
and has free events, puppet shows, samba bands, etc.
Paragraph 2: The museum is now trendy but didn't use
to be; the location used to be a well-off suburb, but is
now a poor district.
Paragraph 3: A new director was appointed to revive the
museum.
Paragraph 4: The free evening events are aimed at getting
people who wouldn't usually go to a museum to go.
Paragraph 5: Visitor numbers have gone up and people
who don't normally visit museums have started to do so.

3

1 B;   2 C;   3 C;   4 D;   5 A;   6 A;   7 D;   8 B

Module 7A

Vocabulary p.62

1

1 C (you *slice* meat, bread, etc. by cutting it into thin flat
   pieces; you *chop* into pieces with a sharp knife; you
   grate food such as cheese/vegetables with a *grater*; you
   shred food like cabbage by cutting or tearing it into
   long thin pieces)

2 B (you *roast* food – usually with a little oil – in the
   oven or over a fire; you *bake* cakes, bread, etc. in an
   oven; you *fry* food in hot oil)
3 A
4 A (coffee without sugar has a strong *bitter* taste;
   lemons have a *sour* taste; food which contains lots of
   spices is *spicy*)
5 D (your stomach *digests* the food you eat; you *sip* a
   liquid if you drink it slowly and in small amounts each
   time; you *gobble food up* if you eat it very quickly)
6 C (meat and poultry – chicken, duck, turkey, etc. – are
   rich in *proteins*; rice and pasta are rich in *carbohydrates*)
7 C
8 D (butter goes *rancid*; old food which is covered in a
   green/black substance – *mould* – has gone *mouldy*)
9 B
10 D
11 A (*starch* is a substance found in bread, rice, potatoes,
   etc.; *calcium* is a substance which helps bones and teeth
   to grow; *flour* is the basic ingredient of bread)
12 B

2a

1 d;   2 h;   3 f;   4 g;   5 a;   6 b;   7 e;   8 c

2b

1 got rid of;   2 runs;   3 turn to;   4 come up with;
5 came across;   6 put on;   7 find a way round;
8 cut down on

3

1 C (= collocation)
2 A
3 B (= when compared with the long time they have
   been eaten)
4 D (you *play a role*)
5 B
6 D (plants *belong to* a category/family/species)
7 A (*arrived in, appeared in, presented to*)
8 C
9 D
10 B (*joined to, added to, accompanied by*)
11 D (= used more generally)
12 A (= remark on something)

Language development 1 p.64

1a

1 You can take your own wine to that restaurant.
2 You shouldn't/ought not to eat junk food every day.
3 We can't sit here because the table is reserved.
4 Alice doesn't have to come with us if she doesn't
   want to.
5 I think you should/ought to leave your coat in the
   cloakroom.
6 Do we have to book a table at that restaurant?
7 You shouldn't/ought not to eat too much before going
   to bed.
8 You can't/mustn't park your car just outside the
   restaurant.
9 Can we sit at any table we want?

1b

1 had/ought;   2 can;   3 allowed/supposed;   4 should;
5 better;   6 should;   7 had;   8 have;   9 ought

2

1 didn't have to;   2 aren't/are not allowed to smoke;
3 'd/had better wear;   4 must not forget;
5 don't have to accept;   6 shouldn't have gone;
7 had to book;   8 mustn't go

3

1 by;   2 in;   3 with;   4 others;   5 Like;   6 or;   7 its;
8 on;   9 being;   10 the;   11 from;   12 have/need

Writing p.65

1a

1   The name of the hotel (Bristol)
2   How you get to the hotel from the station
3   What to do in Westbury in the morning (Castle)
4   Details about the restaurant meal in the evening

2b   Model email:

Dear Ms White

Thank you for your email. Here are the answers to
your questions.

I have booked you into the Bristol Hotel, which is a
pleasant hotel near the station. *When you come out
of the station, turn right and walk down the
High Street. Take the first turning on your left
and follow the road until you see the hotel on
the right.*

If you want to go sightseeing in the morning, why
don't you visit Westbury Castle? It's close to your
hotel and I am sure you will find it very interesting.

Finally, you asked me about the meal in the evening.
I have booked tables at a popular local Indian
restaurant, which serves both meat and vegetarian
dishes. I will pick you up at your hotel and we can
meet the students at the restaurant.

I look forward to seeing you in Westbury.

Yours sincerely

Julia Jacobs

2c

1 Why don't you …?;   2 You asked me about …;
Note: phrases which refer to questions are very common
in emails like this – make sure you use them in the emails
you write.

Listening p.66

2

1 C;   2 B;   3 C;   4 B;   5 A;   6 B;   7 A;   8 C

Audio script

P = *PR;* **W** = *Woman;* **I** = *Interviewer;* **G** = *Graham;*
M = *Man;* **NR** = *Newsreader;* **Dr B** = *Dr Blake*

1

PR: If nice, decent, ordinary food seems a bit boring and
tasteful, what about a light serving of cornflake
omelette washed down with tomato-and-banana
soup and a glass of delicious Pepsi and milk? After
dinner, you can enjoy coffee with a slice of cheese in
it. There are recipes for each of these culinary insults
– and several hundred more – on the aptly named
website, *Utterly Outrageous Recipes.* But the truly
amazing thing about these concoctions, which the
site's editor has collected from the thousands that
were sent in, is just how many of them contain
peanut butter – who'd have thought it was so versatile?

2

W: I don't eat much meat. I mean, you haven't got the
real taste we were brought up on, because the food is
so heavily processed nowadays. But I'm hardly a
vegetarian, either, although I do get through more
fruit than I used to. But you can't get by on that
alone, can you? I don't think that vegetarians are any
healthier than me actually. It's usually young people,
like my granddaughter, who go with it for a couple
of years to be like their friends, but it's not because
they're really against meat on principle or anything,
so they don't keep it up.

3

I: What do you think about the large-scale commercial
production of organic food?

W: Well, what I say is that when we buy food from
people whom we know and who are producing it
locally, we're making an investment in our culture,
whereas when we're buying it from a big
supermarket chain or food corporation, even though
it's in the organic section of the supermarket and
carries an organic label, it's not the same kind of
investment. But to be honest, it's certainly better
than buying from somebody who's not taking care of
the land at all, so it's a step in the right direction.

4

PR: So Graham, which of these series would you
recommend for this city?

G: Well, I suppose I'd go for *The Ultimate Guide* if I
had to choose one, although I'm rather disappointed
by it. I have no argument with the way the city is
described and the layout is clear. But apart from one
or two excellent diagrams, you couldn't call the book
well-illustrated. The other two have lovely
photography, but this one looks a little flat and grey.
No, it's the clear and precise information about
restaurants which really makes *The Ultimate Guide*
stand out, because if you're really going to use a
guidebook, that's what you need.

5

W: Which pizza do you want? There's Margherita, or
Four Seasons.

M: I always go for the plain one when I'm eating out,
because until they bring it, you don't know what the
topping's like.

W: Don't be daft, Four Seasons always has the same
things on it, it'll be like the ones I buy in the
supermarket.

M: Mmm. This advertisement doesn't tell you much.
The good thing about going to a pizzeria is that
there we'd be able to see what people at other tables
were having.

W: Look, <u>it's going to take them half an hour to deliver it, so if you want a pizza, we'd better get on the phone and order one.</u>

6

PR: <u>Do you feel that your current job doesn't allow you to fulfil your potential?</u> If so, you are not alone. According to a recent survey, nearly half of all full- and part-time workers feel the same way. Time for a change? A lot of people seem to think so. In the UK, more than one million people a month look for jobs through recruitment sites on the Internet. With such demand, it's not surprising that sites which aim to put job hunters together with job offers have sprung up in their thousands.

7

NR: Scientists at a week-long conference in Birmingham have been served smoked salmon flavoured ice cream with every meal <u>in an attempt to persuade them that savoury ice cream could be the food industry's next big marketing opportunity.</u> Dr Tony Blake, the scientist behind the experiment explains:

Dr B: Your brain is conditioned, when you see something that looks like ice cream, to expect the sweet and fruity taste that ice cream usually has. To change that, you have to educate people to try things several times. In my research, I've shown that after about eight helpings, your brain adjusts and you begin to get a taste for it. I'm hoping that commercial interest will now follow.

8

W: <u>I'm talking to the chefs all the time. I am a very important critic for the restaurant, but the staff have also got very good at it too. There's a constant atmosphere of inquiry and constructive criticism with regard to the food we serve.</u> It's not about consistency. It doesn't have to be the same from day to day. You know, one chef's bean soup is going to be very different from another's, because one of them is coming from an Italian viewpoint, the other from an Indian one, or whatever. <u>I feel all the time that I'm having this collaboration with some real perfectionists</u> – and you know, that's really stimulating.

Module 7B

Vocabulary p.67

1

A 1 A; 2 B (the *first impression* you get of someone is an expression); 3 C

B 1 A ; 2 A; 3B (the clothes a footballer wears is called his *kit*; soldiers wear *uniforms*; actors/actresses wear *costumes*)

C 1 C; 2 A; 3 A (*bright colours* is a common collocation); 4 C; 5 B (an old person's face is usually *wrinkled*; writing paper may be *lined*)

D 1 C; 2 C; 3 B (a room or house could be described as *messy* if it is dirty and untidy); 4 A (a *cloth* is a piece of material which is used for cleaning or drying something; a *substance* is a chemical or natural material which is either solid or liquid)

2

1 a size, b number, c figure; 2 a suit, b match, c fit;
3 a get dressed, b dress, c wear; 4 a put on, b try on,
c have on; 5 a take off, b loosen, c undo; 6 a costume,
b uniform, c suit

3

1 reaction; 2 unusual; 3 choice; 4 probably;
5 impression; 6 comfortable; 7 anxious; 8 foolish;
9 elegance; 10 outfit

Language development 2 p.68

1a

1 A; 2 C; 3 A; 4 C; 5 B; 6 A; 7 B

1b

1 can't belong; 2 may/might not like; 3 must be;
4 may/might have; 5 can't be; 6 must be having;
7 may/might be trying

2

1 Claudia must have been upset when she discovered … .;
2 The person who took it might not have realised it … .;
3 Anna can't have taken it because I … .;
4 Rachel is the same size as Claudia, so she might have taken it.
5 It was a fur coat, so it must have been worth … .;
6 Her father can't have been … .

3

1 ✓
2 Mr Dickens looks very smart these days. He must have found a new job.
3 ✓
4 Tina can't have paid £200 for that dress – it doesn't even fit her.
5 The neighbours are shouting at each other again. They must be having another argument!
6 ✓
7 Keith is late, isn't he? He may be doing overtime at the office, I suppose.
8 Emma looks very unhappy after her shopping trip. She may not have found a wedding dress she liked.

4 1 B; 2 C; 3 A; 4 D; 5 B; 6 C; 7 D; 8 A; 9 C;
10 A; 11 C; 12 B

Reading p.70

3 a self-assured = confidence; outward – inside;
respond positively – negative reaction
b 1 H; 2 B; 3 F; 4 A; 5 E; 6 C; 7 G

4

1 c; 2 d; 3 b; 4 e; 5 a;

Module 8A

Vocabulary p.72

1a

Eyes: stare at someone
Hands: clutch something, tap someone on the shoulder, push something into someone's hand
Feet: get to your feet, dash, give something a kick, slip (on a wet surface)
Head: give someone a nod

1b
Eyes: wink at someone, glance at someone
Hands: shake someone's hand, grab something, wave at someone
Feet: tap your feet, trip over something, jump up
Head: shake your head

1c
1 shook; 2 clutching; 3 tapped; 4 staring; 5 jumped;
6 grabbed; 7 glanced; 8 tap

Correct story order:
1 b; 2 d; 3 g; 4 h; 5 e; 6 c; 7 a; 8 f

2
1 get; 2 be; 3 fall; 4 celebrate; 5 have; 6 make; 7 go;
8 break

3a
1 relatives; 2 flatmate; 3 acquaintance; 4 fiancée;
5 colleagues; 6 best friend; 7 partner; 8 workmates

3b
1 we're not very close ✗;
2 we have a lot in common ✓;
3 she looks down on me ✗;
4 I've always adored her ✓;
5 we see eye to eye on most things ✓;
6 I really admired her ✓;
7 I can't stand him ✗;
8 I grew very fond of them ✓

4
1 B (if you *fancy someone* you feel attracted to them)
2 D
3 A (fixed expression = to have a chance)
4 B (phrasal verb *to chat someone up*)
5 D (*a tour* involves visiting several places, a *trip* involves going out or away)
6 C
7 D
8 C (phrasal verb = the result was)
9 B (*a part* = a role, *a play* = a piece of drama, *a show* = a piece of entertainment (singing/dancing, etc. at the theatre or on TV)
10 D (you *reach/arrive at* a destination, *achieve/manage to do* something)
11 C (fixed expression)
12 A

Language development 1 p.73

1
1 I asked her why ~~had she gone~~ *she had gone* there (WO).
2 She replied that she ~~wants~~ *had wanted* to improve her English. (T)
3 I asked her if she ~~will~~ *would* go to London with me in the summer. (T)
4 She said that she had spent some time there the ~~last~~ *previous* year. (WW)
5 I asked her why ~~didn't she want~~ *she didn't want* to go there again. (WO)
6 She ~~said~~ *told* me that it had rained all the time she was there (WW).
7 I said that we could ~~bring~~ *take* umbrellas with us. (WW)

2a
1 advised; 2 said; 3 refused; 4 admitted; 5 accused;
6 agreed; 7 threatened; 8 suggested

2b
2 g: Sue apologised (to me) for missing my birthday party.
3 i: Richard promised to be at the wedding/Richard promised that he would be … .
4 j: Maria warned me not to go out with Ken because he was dangerous.
5 c: Denise offered to help me write the invitations.
6 e: Keith threatened to tell my father if I went to the Oasis Club again.
7 d: Eve denied inviting my ex-boyfriend to her party/Eve denied that she had invited … .
8 b: Ruth suggested asking Dave out on a date/Ruth suggested that I (should) ask … .
9 f: Maureen advised me to break off my engagement/Maureen advised me that I should break … .
10 h: Rob accused me of telling him a lie.

3
1 promised not to tell anyone; 2 insisted on buying;
3 whether he could have; 4 why he hadn't arrived;
5 accused Simon of breaking his/having broken his;
6 warned Paul not to; 7 invited David to;
8 admitted that they hadn't/had not;
9 apologised for making/having made;
10 suggested going to (see)

4
1 for; 2 on; 3 other; 4 place; 5 what; 6 neither;
7 one; 8 than; 9 from; 10 were; 11 whether; 12 did

Writing p.75

1a
1 your teacher; 2 neutral, quite formal

2a
1 B; 2 A; 3 A; 4 C; 5 A; 6 B

2b
Paragraph 1: Introduction
situation now – many young people live with their parents
Paragraph 2: Advantages of living at home
Advantage(s): feel comfortable; cost of living is expensive
Example(s): don't need to cook, wash clothes, pay rent
Paragraph 3: Disadvantages of living at home
Disadvantage(s): don't become mature or independent living at home
Example(s): people who go away from home say they start to think for themselves, face problems
Paragraph 4: Conclusion
young people should stay at home if they want.

3
A good essay:
is divided into three or four paragraphs. ✓
has an introduction that makes a general statement about the topic. ✓
supports the main points with details. ✓
uses linking words to connect the ideas. ✓
states the writer's view in the conclusion. ✓
uses a neutral style consistently. ✓
is between 120 and 180 words. ✓

Listening p.76

2

1 C; 2 F; 3 D; 4 A; 5 E

Audio script

Speaker 1:

It used to be funny having a twin sister at school. People would mix us up, which was a laugh. Sometimes we wouldn't bother to correct them, but we never actually misled anyone intentionally. But we never thought the same way about things and we used to argue at least once a day. We even had fights, too. Sharon's bossier than me, but I'm physically stronger, so I'd normally win. We were both fiercely independent, but that didn't stop people either buying us identical birthday presents, which was dull, or one to share between us, which was a recipe for disaster! I didn't mind, but it used to infuriate her.

Speaker 2:

I used to enjoy sharing a bedroom with Katie because it was our own private space where we could go and be alone. We did argue now and again, and we had different ideas about music and clothes, but I'd definitely say we were closer than normal sisters would be. There was a real bond between us – even though she didn't always keep my secrets when I asked her to, so I could never trust her a hundred per cent. Even now, people tend to ask us to do things together, like being flower girls at a wedding recently. I always feel part of something when Katie's there, which is nice.

Speaker 3:

According to my mum, I was surprised when she told me that Emily and I were identical twins. I must have been about six at the time, and I hadn't really thought about it before, but I was happy enough. As kids, Emily and I were very much in tune with each other. It made me feel special. We'd have the same ideas about most things – clothes, music, boys – and although we always tried to be individuals, it never really worked because we were a team. Even now, Emily is the first person I'll turn to if I'm feeling down because I know I can rely on her.

Speaker 4:

I always found it hard being a twin because it meant I had to share everything – including a bedroom! I'm the oldest by ten minutes, but people just lumped us together. We both had our own tastes in clothes and we'd do our hair differently, but people still got us confused, which used to irritate me a lot. Although we spent most of our time together, Amy was never my best mate or anything. I'd talk to my other friends more than I chatted to her because they tended to listen to me more. Even now, compared to me, she's rather a quiet person, and I suppose that was why.

Speaker 5:

Compared to me, Lucy was really messy as a kid and it drove me mad. It would always be me who had to tidy up our bedroom because she'd left her clothes all over the floor. Luckily, we didn't have lessons together at school and we tried to keep out of each other's way.

Going shopping together was a real pain because we never wanted the same things. Even now, I'm happiest in T-shirts and casual trousers, whilst she prefers dressing up in skirts and dresses. We'd only really get on when we used to gang up on our older brother, Jamie, who we had frequent disagreements with.

3

A lumped, confused, irritate; C argue, fights;
D tune, ideas, team; E out of, way; F keep, secrets

Module 8B

Vocabulary p.77

1

1 weekly; 2 truth; 3 boring; 4 expectations;
5 unusual; 6 glamorous

2a

1 making models; 2 stamp collecting; 3 birdwatching;
4 gardening; 5 train spotting; 6 board games

3

1 lawn mower; 2 dice; 3 (tube of) glue; 4 anorak;
5 magnifying glass; 6 (pair of) binoculars

Note: in the interview, it is better to try to describe something using the words you know than to stop speaking. The words and phrases in this exercise will help you to do this.

4

1 spend
2 down (*wind down* = relax)
3 feet (*put your feet up* is an expression)
4 up (*take up* = start a new hobby)
5 passing
6 on
7 up (*springing up* = appearing)
8 give (*give someone a call* = telephone someone)

Language development 2 p. 78

1

1 have / 've been able to; 2 being able to; 3 was able to;
4 could; 5 couldn't / wasn't able to; 6 to be able to;
7 were able to; 8 will be able to; 9 haven't been able to;
10 can

2

1 managed to light; 2 succeeded in beating; 3 know how to speak; 4 'll/will manage to climb; 5 succeeded in winning; 6 managed to play; 7 didn't know how to use

3

1 I couldn't/could not go; 2 you be able to take;
3 isn't/is not capable of swimming; 4 know how to play;
5 could sing better; 6 be able to fix; 7 did you manage to make; 8 succeeded in passing; 9 wasn't/was not able to take; 10 managed to put up

4

1 than; 2 could; 3 few; 4 way; 5 able; 6 a; 7 as;
8 For; 9 who; 10 will; 11 why; 12 between

Reading p.80

3
1 C; 2 A; 3 B; 4 D; 5 A; 6 B; 7 C; 8 D; 9 C;
10 A; 11 B; 12 D; 13 C; 14 B; 15 A

Module 9A

Vocabulary p.82

1a
1 donation; 2 distribution; 3 suffer; 4 poverty;
5 volunteer; 6 inform; 7 support; 8 collection; 9 fund;
10 contribute

1b 1 d; 2 f; 3 b; 4 g; 5 h; 6 c; 7 e; 8 a

1c 1 volunteers; 2 raise; 3 relieve; 4 making; 5 set up;
6 poverty; 7 take; 8 donations; 9 collect; 10 distribute

2a
1 e (save up for); 2 d (keep up with something); 3 a (pay
back money); 4 f (set up a business); 5 b (take on staff);
6 c (take out money); 7 h (pay for something); 8 g (write
out a cheque)

3
1 account; 2 inherited, invest, donate; 3 market, shares;
4 worthless, auction; 5 turnover, bankrupt; 6 living, inflation

4
1 C; 2 B; 3 A; 4 D; 5 C; 6 B; 7 B; 8 D; 9 A;
10 C; 11 A; 12 D

Language development 1 p.83

1a
1 opens; 2 will close; 3 would put; 4 asks; 5 pays;
6 would be; 7 are; 8 makes; 9 were; 10 didn't give

1b
1 B; 2 B; 3 C; 4 A; 5 B; 6 C; 7 A; 8 B; 9 C; 10 C

2
1 if/provided that/as long as; 2 Even if; 3 if/provided
that/as long as; 4 unless; 5 if/provided that/as long as

3
1 'd/had invested, 'd/would have made;
2 'd/had supported, 'd/would not have closed down;
3 hadn't sold, 'd/would have lost;
4 wouldn't have set up, 'd/had listened;
5 hadn't left, would have given;
6 would have given, 'd/had asked;
7 wouldn't have been able, hadn't borrowed;
8 'd/would have bought, 'd/had known

4
1 If I **'d/had gone** into business with my best friend, I
might/would be rich and successful today.
2 If friends **hadn't supported** me when I lost my job and
home, I **would be** a beggar on the streets today.
3 If my brother **had taken** the advice of his teachers, he
wouldn't have apartments in New York and London
today.
4 If Julia **wasn't/weren't** a really good journalist, she
wouldn't have won the Journalist of the Year Award
recently.
5 Large numbers of people **wouldn't be** homeless today
if the government **had helped** the survivors of the
earthquake.

5
1 'd/would have sent her (some); 2 wouldn't be very/so
rich; 3 as long as you obey; 4 harder you'd/you would
get; 5 if you don't listen; 6 wouldn't speak German so;
7 provided that you don't; 8 earlier you wouldn't feel;
9 even if you work; 10 unless you get

Writing p.85

2c
1 Although; 2 also; 3 In fact; 4 Furthermore

2d
a   an immediate refund of £140 = my money back now
b   am writing to complain = (I) want to complain
d   received = got
e   so inaccurate = a load of lies
f   to my great surprise = I couldn't believe my eyes

2e Improved email:

Dear Sir/Madam

I am writing to complain about your advertisement for
the Handycam video camera.

I ordered the camera from your company last week.
Although you say that delivery takes less than 24 hours, I
received the camera three days later. To my great surprise,
I noticed that the leather case was dirty and scratched.

In your advertisement, you also mention that the
Handycam video camera is easy to use. In fact, it took me
two hours to read the instructions and I still could not use
the camera. When I telephoned for help, the girl I spoke
to was very rude.

If I had known your advertisement was so inaccurate, I
would never have ordered the camera. I expect an apology
and an immediate refund of £140. Furthermore, I feel that
you should change future advertisements so that they are
not so misleading.

I look forward to hearing from you.

Yours faithfully

Alex Vidal

Listening p.86

2a/b
1 C; 2 A; 3 A; 4 B; 5 C; 6 C; 7 B

Audio script

PR = *Presenter;* **M** = *Mandy*
PR: My guest today is Mandy Pagham, who five years
ago won a million pound prize after buying a single
lottery ticket. Mandy, it must have been an
incredible moment.

M: Well, at the time it was wonderfully exciting, of course. Although I'd bought the occasional ticket before, I'm not someone who usually gambles, so it wasn't as if I'd been building up my hopes or anything. I was just standing in a newsagent's shop with my friend Louise who used to buy a ticket every week, and she just said; 'Go on, buy one, you never know, you might be lucky.' So that's what I did.

PR: So how did you feel when your number was read out on the television?

M: Well, I wasn't even watching, I was helping my mum in the kitchen. I'd said to my dad, you know, 'Oh check this ticket for me, will you?' and he'd laughed and said something about 'wasting my money'. And then a few minutes later, he walked slowly into the kitchen, as white as a sheet. I mean some people would've been jumping up and down and shouting, but he was sort of speechless. So it was a few minutes before we realised what had happened.

PR: And when you did?

M: Well, we didn't know what to do at first, but you know, everyone at the TV station was very kind, and helped us to cope. Then, I went up to London to collect the cheque and so had my photo in the newspapers, although I never talked to any reporters. But that's when all the problems started. I mean, if I'd known, I'd have insisted on keeping my privacy, but I was just too thrilled to think straight, I'm afraid.

PR: So it was a problem, everybody knowing?

M: Oh yes. I mean, suddenly, we had phone calls from cousins we hadn't heard from in years, which was nice in a way, and all sorts of people I didn't know started coming up to me in the street for a chat and I thought: 'Gosh, this is what it must feel like to be rich and famous,' because you don't know whether people really like you or not. So that's when I started to have doubts about it all.

PR: I see. So did people ask you for money?

M: Not friends and family, no. I bought presents for all the people I felt close to, including the friend, Louise, who I'd been with when I bought the ticket – I bought her a really nice necklace, but I lost her as a friend. She was jealous, I suppose, because it could so easily have been her, anyway she was very nice about it, but we just drifted apart. I think she just didn't want to be with me anymore. But the worst bit was the begging letters.

PR: Did nobody warn you about that?

M: Oh yes, we'd been told to expect them, but it was still upsetting. People I'd never heard of started writing me letters, telling me all these terribly sad stories, and asking me for money. I mean the lottery people said: 'They're mostly untrue, throw them away – don't even open them,' I'm sure they were right, but I read them nonetheless. And there were so many that it really began to get me down. I mean I didn't regret winning the money, but I did begin to think that it wasn't fair that I should have it. And that's when I made my decision.

PR: To give it away?

M: Not all of it. I bought the things I wanted to buy – a house, a car, all the things people spend half their lives working for, so I'm certainly feeling the benefit of it now – and there's still a bit in the bank. But about half of it, I gave to charity. And I told everyone what I was doing, you know, gave newspaper interviews, let the whole world know that I wasn't enormously rich anymore, I was just myself – and fortunately, I have no regrets.

PR: Mandy, thank you for joining us today.

Module 9B
Vocabulary p.87
1a
1 D; 2 B; 3 C; 4 A; 5 B; 6 A; 7 D; 8 B; 9 C;
10 D; 11 A; 12 C

2
1 B (*out of stock* = not *in stock; on sale* = available to be bought in a shop; if something is *for sale*, it is simply available to be bought)
2 A (you follow a *recipe* when you are cooking something, the doctor gives you a *prescription* for some medicine; buy a *ticket* for the theatre)
3 D (you talk about a *reduction in price*; a shop sells something *at a discount* if it sells it cheaper than the normal price)
4 A (you pay e.g. a lawyer's or doctor's *fee*)
5 C (a bank or lawyer has *clients; shoppers* simply means people who shop)
6 C (a Mercedes is a *make* of car; you read the *label* on a jar of food or on an item of clothing for information about that product)
7 B
8 D (If you want information about a college or university, you read its *prospectus*; a *brochure* usually gives information about different holidays; a *directory* is normally a list of names, addresses or facts)
9 C
10 B

Language development 2 p.88
1a
1 is; 2 buy; 3 was; 4 is; 5 think; 6 has; 7 spend;
8 doesn't; 9 were (*premises* = the building that a shop, restaurant or company uses); 10 are; 11 have; 12 has

1b
Nouns + singular verb: euros, furniture, economics, everybody, politics, premises, the United States
Nouns + plural verb: people, the police, the majority of …, trousers, a number of …,

1c
1 have; 2 are; 3 was; 4 has/have; 5 are; 6 has;
7 have; 8 is/has been

2b
1 Both Britney Spears and Courtney Cox were born in the USA.
2 One of them was born in the 60s.
3 All of them have children.
4 One of them comes from the UK

5 Both Victoria Beckham and Courtney Cox are (apparently) happily married.

6 Both Victoria Beckham and Britney Spears have more than one child.

7 Neither Victoria Beckham nor Britney Spears has a daughter.

8 None of them is a film director.

9 One of them is a fashion designer.

10 Both Britney Spears and Courtney Cox are dancers.

3

1 ✓; 2 there, there's; 3 ✓; 4 There; 5 ✓; 6 it; 7 It; 8 it

4

1 there's/is no need/ there isn't any need; 2 it was unusual for Jack; 3 did it take (you) to; 4 it doesn't matter; 5 is there nothing on; 6 there's/is a problem with; 7 there's/is too much fog; 8 it lovely seeing/to see; 9 there be a (long/big) queue; 10 there was a storm

Reading p.90

1a A

3a/b/c

1 H; 2 D; 3 A; 4 F; 5 E; 6 B; 7 G

Module 10A

Vocabulary p.92

1a

1 adventure holiday; 2 skiing holiday; 3 package holiday; 4 safari; 5 camping holiday; 6 city break;

2 Suggested answers:

Skiing holiday: a warm anorak and bobble hat, skis and ski boots

Camping holiday: a sleeping bag, a family tent, insect repellent, a thermos flask, insect repellent, an airbed, antiseptic cream

Beach holiday: sunglasses, suntan lotion, a mask and snorkel, a swimming costume

Trekking holiday: a wide-brimmed hat, a pair of strong walking boots, a sleeping bag, a one-man tent, insect repellent, a rucksack, an airbed, plasters, a walking stick

Safari: a video camera, a camera with telephoto lens

3a

1 flight; 2 reservation; 3 passport; 4 inoculations; 5 insurance; 6 work permit; 7 credit cards, currency

3b

2 make a reservation; 3 apply for a passport; 4 have innoculations; 5 take out insurance; 6 apply for a work permit; 7 accept credit cards, change currency

4

1 B

2 D (*keen on* something, *enthusiastic about* something, *fascinated* by something)

3 A (phrasal verb meaning to be educated and cared for as a child until grown up)

4 A (you *gather* or *find out* information)

5 C (phrasal verb meaning to discover by chance)

6 D (the people living in a particular place are *inhabitants* of that place; you are a *citizen* of a country

and a *member* of a club or organisation)

7 B

8 A (*vast* is the only word which collocates with *absolutely*)

9 A

10 C (idiomatic expression)

11 B (you travel *on foot, on horseback, by camel* and *by bicycle*)

12 B

Language development 1 p.93

1

1 suffer; 2 has just been published; 3 decreased; 4 is being built; 5 will be finished; 6 apply

2

1 are kindly requested to keep …

2 has been banned on all flights in accordance …

3 luggage must be put under your seat or …

4 about the flight can be obtained from the personnel …

5 our flight assistants have been trained to deal with …

6 effort will be made by our staff to ensure that …

3

1 I was lent £2,000 (by the bank).

2 A complimentary bowl of fruit is offered to every guest.

3 Travellers have been promised cheaper flights for years.

4 You will be shown the city's main attractions (by one of our guides).

5 The first prize in the competition was awarded to Peter.

4a

1 a be one of the most beautiful cities in the world; b Prague is one of the most beautiful cities in the world;

2 a to be going on strike next week; b that airport workers are going on strike next week;

3 a is expected to introduce new measures to boost tourism; b that the government will introduce new measures to boost tourism;

4 a is thought to have been abducted; b is thought that the missing tourist has been abducted

4b

1 to be; 2 isn't/is not known; 3 is thought; 4 was involved; 5 to have made; 6 to leave; 7 to be staying; 8 to have flown

5

1 were given directions by; 2 were included in; 3 were made to; 4 is going to be published; 5 is said to be; 6 haven't/have not been developed; 7 are believed to have cancelled; 8 are given to the passengers; 9 aren't/are not allowed to use; 10 we were welcomed by

Writing p.95

1

1 You work for the Student Travel Agency of your college.

2 You are writing the report for the Principal of the college and you will use a formal, neutral style.

3 There are three parts – to write advantages, disadvantages and make a recommendation.

2b Suggested answers:

Heading 1: Introduction

Heading 2: The benefits/advantages (of working holidays)

Heading 3: The disadvantages (of working holidays)

Heading 4: Conclusions and recommendations

2c

1 D; 2 A; 3 C; 4 B

2d,e: Model report

Working holidays for students

Introduction

The purpose of this report is to consider the advantages and disadvantages of working holidays abroad. ***In order to obtain*** this information, I interviewed more than 30 students who had worked in different countries.

The benefits of working holidays

A large number of the students I spoke to said that they had enjoyed working abroad and had become more open-minded as a result. ***Apparently, they felt they had learnt a lot about the local people and their way of life by working side by side with them.***

The disadvantages of working holidays

Not surprisingly, many students complained that they had worked too hard in certain countries. They believed that they had been exploited by their employers, who paid them very little money. ***According to some students,*** there had also been problems with documents such as work permits.

Conclusions and Recommendations

It appears that ***the majority of students*** found the experience of working abroad very beneficial. Therefore, I believe that the college should recommend 'working holidays' to its students. ***However, it should also warn them about the problems they could face and the precautions they need to take.***

Listening p.96

2

1 *The Service Guide*; 2 name; 3 greet; 4 smile;
5 red flag; 6 (non) smoking; 7 car; 8 wake-up call;
9 blue arrow; 10 taxi

Audio script

OK, I don't want to spend too long on this, but we've got quite a few new members of staff with us this month, and some of you who've been here a while are going to be taking on new duties. So the purpose of this meeting is just to quickly run through some of the training points that can get forgotten in busy periods. They're all written in this booklet called *The Service Guide* which you all have a copy of, but I'll just remind you anyway.

First of all I'd like to talk about the Reception desk. Now whether you're actually staffing the desk or not, most of you will work in Reception at some time or another, and in busy times any of you may be asked to help out there, so it's imperative that you know, not just the basic procedures, but also our customer service policy.

The company regards the Reception desk as one of the most important places in the hotel. It's where people arrive, where they have direct contact with staff, and where they go if they want help, or if they want to complain.

So first and foremost, remember the three golden rules: Firstly, if you can, always address guests by name – this is quite often written on credit cards and booking documents, or type in the room number and it'll come up on the screen.

Secondly, it's important not to keep people waiting. If you have to, greet them and apologise for the delay, tell them how long you're going to be; anything rather than just ignoring them as they're waiting.

Thirdly, remember to smile, no matter how tired or harassed you're feeling or how horrid guests might be. We're there for them and we want them to feel welcome, whoever they are.

Now, most guests have two main points of contact with the Reception desk. When they check in and when they leave. So I'll go through those two procedures in detail. When guests first arrive, check whether or not they have a booking – most will have – and the list of guests expected will show up on the screen with their room allocation. Check this first. Room allocations change according to when departing guests check out and how this fits in with the cleaning rota. So make sure that there is a red flag against the room number on screen as this will indicate that cleaning is complete and the room is free. Most rooms are non-smoking, and any guests requiring a smoking room will usually need to have booked this in advance – check this with them and make sure the room allocated is correct.

Before handing over the key, there are a number of other questions to ask. Firstly, establish whether the guest has a car in the underground parking area and, if so, make a note of the registration number. Ask for the guest's credit card and take an imprint, explaining that this is a deposit against payment. And finally, check whether the guest requires a wake-up call in the morning and enter the details in the database. Then, if all is well, hand over the room key, and call a porter to show the guest to the room.

So that's check-in. Although there are busy periods for this, it's not as bad as checking out. Most people check out just after breakfast and this is when queues can occur. For normal checking out, the main thing is to make sure that there are no outstanding room service, bar or restaurant accounts. A blue arrow will appear on the screen if this is the case, or a green flag if there are no other payments to go on the bill.

Remember that guests who are leaving often ask for information about the hotel and may ask you to book a taxi for them. No matter how busy it gets, you must try to be as helpful as possible because how they were treated on departure often leaves a lasting impression on people.

Now I hope you're all familiar with the procedure for settling accounts ...

3

1 b; 2 e; 3 a; 4 d; 5 c

Module 10B

Vocabulary p.97

2a
un -: unbelievable, undamaged, unacceptable, unavoidable, unpopular, unattractive, unsuitable, unlimited
dis-: dissatisfied, disapprove, dishonest, dislike, disagreeable
mis-: misunderstand, misbehave, misinterpret
-less: careless, harmless, useless, thoughtless, hopeless

2b
1 dissatisfaction; 2 misunderstood; 3 unpopular;
4 unattractive; 5 unbelievably; 6 disapproval;
7 dishonesty; 8 misinterpreted; 9 hopelessly;
10 unavoidable

3
1 a good time; 2 John having a party; 3 a quick look at;
4 had a really good; 5 something to eat; 6 lot of work to

Language development 2 p.98

1a
1 were; 2 could; 3 had gone; 4 would stop;
5 could see; 6 would

1b
1 'd/had told; 2 could; 3 would build; 4 hadn't been;
5 would talk; 6 'd/had seen

2
1 I wish he would turn down his stereo/turn his stereo down.
2 If only I'd/I had gone to bed earlier.
3 If only I'd/I had studied harder.
4 If only it would stop raining.
5 I wish I could go to the (rock) concert (on Saturday).
6 I wish my sister didn't live so far away (from me).

3
1 said; 2 didn't open; 3 were; 4 learned; 5 hadn't said; 6 phoned

4
1 's/is time we called/to call; 2 'd rather you didn't;
3 wish I hadn't told; 4 only your friend could go;
5 wish you would stop; 6 time we set off;
7 I could have gone; 8 as if I'm/I am/I were;
9 's/is time you told; 10 'd rather you'd/you had asked

5
1 who; 2 than; 3 like; 4 how; 5 let; 6 have/need; 7 until/till;
8 have/get; 9 if/though; 10 what; 11 wish; 12 up

Reading p.100

2
a section C; b section E; c section B; d section E;
e section C; f section D

3
1 C; 2 A; 3 E; 4 B; 5 A; 6 C; 7 E; 8 D; 9 B; 10
D; 11 C; 12 A; 13 D; 14 B/E; 15 E/B

Module 11A

Vocabulary p.102

1a Suggested answers:
Positive: creative, sensible, intellectual, easy-going, sensitive, witty, punctual, open-minded, generous, sociable
Negative: arrogant, moody, irritable, mean, pessimistic, vain, suspicious
It depends: ambitious, impulsive, talkative

1b
1 intellectual, ambitious, arrogant; 2 creative, sensitive, witty; 3 irritable, pessimistic, mean; 4 sociable, talkative, impulsive; 5 easy-going, open-minded, generous; 6 vain, moody, suspicious

2
1 with; 2 about; 3 in; 4 about; 5 to; 6 in; 7 of;
8 with; 9 in; 10 between; 11 in; 12 in

3a
1 pessim<u>i</u>stic, enthusi<u>a</u>stic, art<u>i</u>stic, hist<u>o</u>ric
2 cheer, <u>cheer</u>ful; del<u>i</u>ght, del<u>igh</u>tful; <u>won</u>der, <u>won</u>derful; <u>beau</u>ty, <u>beau</u>tiful; dis<u>grace</u>, dis<u>grace</u>ful
3 <u>a</u>maze, a<u>maz</u>ing; con<u>fuse</u>, con<u>fus</u>ing; frustr<u>a</u>te, frustr<u>a</u>ting; <u>sat</u>isfy, <u>sat</u>isfying; em<u>bar</u>rass, em<u>bar</u>rassing

3b
1 C   2 C

4
1 unfortunate; 2 unconscious; 3 entertainer;
4 seriously; 5 illness(es); 6 variety; 7 anxiety;
8 ability; 9 confidence; 10 successfully

Language development 1 p.103

1
1 Even though (contrast); 2 in order to (purpose);
3 as (reason); 4 due to (reason); 5 so as to (purpose);
6 despite (contrast); 7 so that (purpose)

2
1 despite; 2 although/even though; 3 as/because/since;
4 Despite; 5 so that/in order that; 6 Despite;
7 in order to/so as to; 8 so that/in order that

3
1 A lot of male athletes at university wouldn't train with me **because/since** I was too fast for them.
2 I'm successful in athletics **due to** the tremendous support I receive from my husband and family.
3 **Even though** I love eating out and trying new dishes, I often discuss my diet with my dietician.
4 Every year I go to a camp in Albuquerque, in the USA, **in order to** train (there).
5 I want to spend some time in the USA **so as to** be able to/**so that I can** run on the road circuit.
6 I love running on roads and mountain trails **because of** the sense of freedom I feel.
7 **Since / Because** I live a fulfilled life, I'm not concerned about my athletics career ending.
8 After athletics, I'd do something else **so that** I could continue to channel my energy and ambitions.

4
1 part; 2 out; 3 more; 4 such; 5 all; 6 as;
7 that/when; 8 so; 9 of; 10 which; 11 got/grew;
12 much

Writing p.105

1
1 in an international magazine for students of English
2 the style should be fairly informal
3 humour would be appropriate

2a
1 C; 2 A; 3 B

2b
1 As soon as I woke up in the morning, I realised that my parents … ;
2 As I was staring in delight at my new bicycle, my father suddenly said …

2c
… my father ~~said~~ **told** me … ; … I was so ~~impressive~~ **impressed** by the sharks …

2d
1 C; 2 B; 3 A

2e
B (A day I'll always remember) is the best title. A (The happiest day of my life) is not really suitable because it simply repeats the wording in the exam task; C (The London Aquarium) does not summarise the content of the article effectively – it's also rather formal!

Complete sample answer:

A day I'll always remember

Imagine how happy and excited a little child from Africa feels when he or she sees snow for the first time. That's exactly how I felt when my parents took me to the London Aquarium on my tenth birthday.

As soon as I woke up in the morning, I realised that my parents had planned something special. They didn't say anything, though, until I had opened my presents. As I was staring in delight at my new bicycle my father suddenly said, 'Okay, let's go to London!'

In the car, my father told me we were going to the London Aquarium. I remember that I had no idea what he meant. I only understood when I saw the photographs of fish outside. We spent hours there. I was so impressed by the sharks that I didn't want to leave!

I'll never forget that day. I really enjoyed my party later, but my visit to the London Aquarium made it a special day for me. You won't be surprised when I tell you that I'm now studying marine biology at university!

Listening p.106

2a/b
1 A; 2 A; 3 C; 4 B; 5 C; 6 C; 7 A; 8 B

Audio script

W = *Woman;* **M** = *Man*

1
It's not unusual to feel angry or be at the receiving end of someone else's temper several times a day, especially at work. Understanding what triggers an angry response, whether in yourself or in others, helps you to avoid upsetting situations, however, and this means you're less likely to become a victim of your emotions. There are plenty of courses in conflict management which can help you; just try a quick search on the web to find one. But, if dealing with the general public is part of your job, do encourage your employer to take responsibility for this training. After all, it's as much for their benefit as yours.

2
I stayed in an expensive hotel last autumn and had a couple of minor complaints about the service. For once, there wasn't one of those irritating feedback forms to fill in, so I wrote a letter once I was home, pointing out my dissatisfaction and saying how things could be improved. While the original faults were not serious enough to make me mad, when the hotel failed to respond to my letter, I did get cross. So I called to see why the letter had been ignored, and the extraordinary response from the voice at the other end was: 'Was it clear that your letter needed a reply?' I was speechless.

3
The directness and honesty of children can be a source of deep embarrassment to their parents. Children lack the ability to be tactful, often hurting the feelings of ageing relatives by coming out with things like, 'I've already got three of those,' when they open a present. But wouldn't it be great to say what you really feel sometimes? I put it to psychologist Tamara Fenton that perhaps if only we could acquire a little of that childish directness and care a little less about what people thought of us, we'd be far better off.

4
M: Here we are, the restaurant's just through this doorway.
W: Oh dear. There's only a couple of people in there. I don't know if I fancy that. Look, there's something I want to talk to you about, but it's personal – I don't want anyone else to hear. They don't even have any music. Can't we go somewhere livelier?
M: All right. Is it something serious?
W: I'll tell you when we're sitting down. How about the pizzeria opposite the station? At least they've got piped music.
M: Yes, OK – if that's what you prefer.

5
Laughter occupies a special place in human social life and it's a fascinating feature of our biology. Scientists have studied all kinds of emotions and behaviour, but few have done research into laughter. Generally we associate laughter with pleasure, happiness and joy, but in some cultures it is also a sign of embarrassment or even fear. In fact, only 10–20 per cent of laughter is a response to humour. Most of the time it's a message we send to other people – it can be communicating a joyful mood, a willingness to be friends … but it can also be

unkind, and of course, you can always tell if it is.

6

It all started in a second-hand bookshop when I spotted a copy of Fiona Harrold's 'Be your own life coach'. It was less than a pound and I thought it would be a laugh to read a self-help book – something to chat to my friends about. The friendly orange cover promised to show me how to take control of my life and achieve my wildest dreams. <u>But, the truth is, with a few easy exercises and a few uplifting words, that book has helped me feel that I can take on the world.</u> I know people will smile at this, but I have nothing but praise for it.

7

Of course I love the club. It was part of my life for 20 years and I wish them nothing but success, but I'm moving on. I've got a place to study for a sports science degree and I start at the end of the month. It's a three-year course and I'm looking forward to it immensely because it sounds like fun. <u>Who knows if I'll go back into football at the end of it? I'm an optimist, so I make a point of never saying never, but that's why my horizons have no limit.</u>

8

I hadn't intended to buy another car. After all the trouble I'd had with the previous one, I said I'd settle for public transport in future, however inconvenient it was. <u>Then I saw Betsy.</u> She was parked outside a friend's house, with 'For Sale' written in the window. <u>25 years old, light blue and irresistible.</u> Other cars are faster, warmer, more economical and easier to drive, <u>but just walking past mine makes me smile,</u> and when I turn the key and hear the purr of her engine, well … I'm queen of the road.

Module 11B

Vocabulary p.107

1

1   vegetarian (*vegetation* = trees, bushes and plants in a particular place)
2   raw (vegetables which are *raw* are uncooked)
3   illnesses (an *illness* is a health problem that makes you feel ill; a *disease* is a specific illness that has a medical name)
4   stressful (a person feels *stressed*)
5   nutritious (food which is *edible* can be eaten – it is not poisonous)
6   pace (*pace of life* is an expression)
7   surgery (businesspeople work in an *office*)
8   wards (*dormitory* = a large room in a school or hostel where several people sleep)
9   treat (you can say you have been *cured*, if you are no longer ill after a course of treatment)
10 injured (soldiers are *wounded* in a battle)
11 have (you *have an operation*; the surgeon *operates* on you)
12 infected

2a

1 have; 2 feel; 3 make; 4 catch; 5 break; 6 sprain; 7 take; 8 give

2b

1 have an operation; 2 made a quick recovery; 3 catch a cold; 4 have an injection; 5 sprained your ankle; 6 take an X-ray

3

1 show; 2 while; 3 there are; 4 kind of; 5 could be; 6 on the other hand; 7 like; 8 Personally; 9 However; 10 would choose

Language development 2 p.108

1a

1   We have such a beautiful view from our window.
2   It is such a nice day that I want to go swimming.
3   I have never eaten such delicious food before.
4   Why is it so important to take exercise?
5   This documentary is so boring that I think I will fall asleep.
6   He has so much money that he can buy anything he wants.
7   We had such good weather on holiday that we stayed another week.
8   You should not eat so many hamburgers.

1b

1 such a; 2 such a; 3 so few; 4 so many; 5 such awful; 6 so; 7 so much; 8 so

2

1 too; 2 enough; 3 very; 4 enough; 5 too; 6 too; 7 enough; 8 very

3

1 so; 2 very; 3 so; 4 too; 5 enough; 6 such; 7 enough; 8 too; 9 so; 10 enough

4

1 as; 2 like; 3 as; 4 such as; 5 like; 6 like; 7 such as; 8 as; 9 like; 10 like

5

1 aren't/are not strong enough; 2 such a good pianist; 3 works as a doctor in; 4 was so loud (that) we; 5 enjoyed ourselves so much (that); 6 're/are too unfit to; 7 were so many people at; 8 as if they were; 9 as if it's/it is going 10 so difficult/hard for you to

Reading p.110

2

Question 1: paragraph 4 ('coming up with an entire health package for somebody')
Question 2: 1 (the rich and famous e.g. supermodels and pop singers)
Question 3: 2, 3 (always been sporty; 'convinced that fitness is the basis of a full and happy life')
Question 4: 6 (he's a partner 'I see myself more as a training partner')

3

1 B; 2 D; 3 A; 4 B; 5 C; 6 C; 7 D; 8 A

4

1 looked set to; 2 gave Matt a taste of; 3 coincided with; 4 comes as no surprise

Module 12A

Vocabulary p.112

1a

A reporters; B defendant; C police officer; D jury;

E defence lawyer; F witness; G lawyer for the prosecution;
H judge

1b

1 c; 2 e; 3 g; 4 d; 5 b; 6 h; 7 a; 8 f

1c

Verb + Object noun collocations:
commit + crime, pass + sentence, win + case(s), break
into + house, steal + jewellery, give + description, arrest +
criminal

Other useful crime expressions:
The defendant: is *on trial* for murder; *pleads guilty/
innocent* to the charge (of murder); has a *long record* of
minor offences, acted in *self-defence*
The police: have *found fingerprints*; have *got a DNA
sample* (from …); found evidence at the *scene of the crime*
The judge: will *sentence him to several years in prison/life
imprisonment*

2

1 A (phrasal verb meaning to discover by chance)
2 B (if you *hang around* somewhere, you are waiting
   there for no real purpose)
3 D
4 D
5 A
6 C (*theft* = stealing something; *burglary* = breaking into
   a house and then stealing things; *fraud* = obtaining
   money illegally in a deceitful way; *forgery* = copying a
   document/painting/money illegally)
7 B
8 C (you are: *arrested for a crime/charged with a crime* by
   the police. Later, in court, you are: *convicted of the
   crime* (if they find you guilty)/*sentenced to X years in
   prison*)
9 A (*regarded as/viewed as/considered to be*)
10 B (if someone has been convicted or found guilty of a
   crime/crimes, they have a *criminal record*)
11 A
12 A

Language development 1 p.113

1

1 in order to; 2 such; 3 before; 4 While; 5 and;
6 However; 7 because; 8 if; 9 After; 10 which

2

1 Being out of work, Simon spent all his time reading
   books.
2 Hearing the telephone ring, he put down his book and
   got up to answer it.
3 Feeling annoyed at the interruption, he picked up the
   telephone and shouted 'Yes!' as loud as he could.
4 Realising that the caller had hung up, he put the
   receiver down again.
5 Not having been out all day, he got ready to go for a
   walk.
6 On reaching the door, he heard the telephone ring
   again.
7 Running to the phone, he picked up the receiver and
   heard the voice of his girlfriend who asked what the
   matter was.
8 Despite feeling slightly guilty, he couldn't help smiling.

3

As soon as Peter arrived at his brother's house, he realised
something was wrong. *Even though* it was a hot day, all
the doors and windows were closed. Peter was sure Tom
was at home *as* he had phoned him an hour before.
Opening the front door, he went inside *and* looked in all
the rooms. *If* Tom had gone out, he would have left a note.
His brother was a sensible man, *who* always told others
what his plans were. *As* Peter was climbing the stairs, the
doorbell rang. He rushed down the stairs *so* quickly *that*
he almost fell. *Seeing* his brother on the doorstep, he gave
a cry of relief. Tom laughed *and* told Peter that the police
had arrested him in the afternoon *because* they had
mistaken him for an escaped bank robber!

4

1 spite; 2 getting; 3 which; 4 was; 5 so; 6 addition;
7 such; 8 as; 9 when; 10 from; 11 having; 12 order

Writing p.115

1

1 You are obviously someone the Mayor knows and
trusts; 2 the town council; the style will be fairly formal
in such a report; 3 There are two parts to the question –
you must describe the crimes and say what should be
done; note that the question does not ask you to analyse
the reasons why young people commit crimes.
4 teenagers, people who live locally

2a

A good report:	Report 1	Report 2
has a clear title.	✓	✓
is divided into sections with useful headings.		✓
has an introduction stating the report's aims.		✓
says how the information was obtained.	✓	✓
is written in an impersonal style.		✓
uses passive voice where appropriate.		✓
may use numbers to list points.	✓	✓
ends with a conclusion or recommendation.	✓	✓

Report 2 is obviously a much better report. Although
Report 1 contains some of the features of a report, it is
generally very informal and unhelpful. The introduction
gives no useful information to the reader at all and the
conclusion is weak and unsatisfactory.

2b

Report 1: committed; recommend
Report 2: believed; increase; committed; everyone who
was interviewed; where the police never go; combat

Listening p.116

1

1 Question 10; 2 Questions 3 and 4

2

1 modern languages; 2 teacher; 3 exhausting;
4 romantic; 5 history of science; 6 (new) planet;
7 clothes; 8 events; 9 plot; 10 500/five hundred words

Audio script

PR = *Presenter;* **L** = *Laura*

PR: My guest today is the novelist Laura Reddington, whose last novel, *The Lost Dream* was an international best-seller. Laura, did you always want to write?

L: I've always been interested in books, although not necessarily English Literature, because my degree was actually in modern languages. But I always thought it would be wonderful to be a writer. But I also knew it'd be very time-consuming and I didn't see that as a good career move when I was younger. I considered journalism, even publishing, but in the end I got a good job as a teacher, and that tended to come first. So this ambition to be a writer was, sort of, on hold whilst I did other things.

PR: But now you're so successful, don't you regret not starting earlier?

L: In a way, but maybe novelists shouldn't write until they've had a bit of experience of the world. Being out at work, you meet all sorts of people, see how they behave in different situations. I loved it and found it very satisfying, but also very exhausting. After twenty years, I'd had enough. That's when I decided to try my hand as a writer, because I was looking for a new challenge.

PR: So did you just sit down and start writing one day?

L: Well, my first thought was that I needed to make a living, so I tried romantic fiction – without success I might add. I thought it would be easy money because those novels sell in their millions. But, although I made up some great characters, the stories didn't work well. I just hadn't found the right thing, and so my work wasn't published. It took something a little deeper and darker, I suppose, to bring out my talent as a writer.

PR: A historical thriller. How did you get the idea for that?

L: I've always loved history and I could see from other novels that were doing well that the history of science interested people. I'm a fan of astronomy myself and I've always read widely on the subject. I was looking through my books one day when I came across the story of a man who thought he'd found a new planet. I realised this was going on at about the same time as a famous murder case in London. So I thought I could mix the two stories together to make a sort of detective novel.

PR: So lots of research?

L: Yes, I needed to get the historical details correct, you know, have people wearing the right clothes for the period, and things like that. But then, there are no records of what actually happened to people from day to day, and of course, the murder mystery was never actually solved in real life. So I made up most of the events I describe. In a novel, it all needs to seem real to the reader, but people aren't actually

checking the historical facts.

PR: And the actual writing. How do you go about it?

L: Well, that book took two years to write. I know some people can sit down and just write, you know, the inspiration just comes, and until they've finished they don't know how it will end. But for me, it's all about planning. Once I'd got all the plot clear in my mind, I was able to work the characters out in detail. Only then did I sit down and concentrate on the actual writing.

PR: Do you do a lot of rewriting?

L: No, once the ideas are in place, I just write – I know that some writers manage a thousand words a day, and I have done 750 on occasion, but usually around 500 words is the right amount for me. I keep reading through it, changing little things as I go, but most of it just flows from my brain to the page.

PR: And the new novel?

L: Well, that's a bit different …

Module 12B

Vocabulary p.117

1a

Television: commercials, documentary, newscaster, reporter, editor, weather forecast, presenter, viewers
Newspapers: circulation, gossip column, reporter, editor, article, tabloid, weather forecast, small ads
The Internet: log on, web page, download, editor, surf, server, weather forecast

1b

1 circulation; 2 article; 3 surf; 4 tabloid;
5 weather forecast; 6 download; 7 commercials;
8 small ads; 9 editor; 10 newscaster

2a

1 on; 2 up; 3 around; 4 on; 5 of; 6 into; 7 for;
8 up; 9 out; 10 on

2b

1 picked up; 2 going in for; 3 talked me into doing (media studies); 4 get on (well); 5 going on;
6 took on; 7 hang around with; 8 get out of

3

1 B (you *put up* a notice or announcement on a wall for people to read)
2 B
3 D (you talk about an *increase* in the number of … , the *ascent* of a mountain, the *extent* of an injury or problem)
4 A
5 D
6 C (fixed expression: *to take place*)
7 A (collocation)
8 B
9 B (*reduce* is a transitive verb – somebody *reduces* something; *decline* is intransitive and does not need an object; *retired* refers to a person not to *the influence* - it is important to read the whole sentence here.)
10 A
11 C

12 D (*spectators* = people who watch a game or event; *passers-by* = people in the street who see something happen by chance; *observers* = people who see or notice something)

Language development 2 p.118

1a
1 to buy;   2 replacing;   3 to write;   4 to be updated;
5 to go;   6 to give;   7 cutting;   8 to be rewritten

1b
1 to take;   2 feeding/to be fed;   3 testing/to be tested;
4 replacing/to be replaced;   5 to go;   6 washing/to be washed;   7 to help;   8 cleaning/to be cleaned

2a
1 having/getting;   2 them;   3 will;   4 have/get;   5 have/get;
6 it;   7 have/get;   8 done/redecorated;   9 had;   10 was

2b
1 have/get your eyes tested;   2 have/get it serviced;
3 had my teeth checked;   4 have/get a swimming pool built;
5 have/get the chimney cleaned

3
1 her house broken into;   2 had your photograph;
3 house needs to be;   4 having/getting my computer repaired;   5 have central heating put in;   6 needs knocking;   7 car washed;   8 need to go;   9 just had my new watch;   10 having her new fridge delivered

4
1 however;   2 between;   3 As;   4 gone;   5 what;   6 there;
7 is/was;   8 such;   9 with;   10 way;   11 that;   12 than

Reading p.120

2
1 main points: lots of young people want to work in television; most people in the UK spend a lot of time in front of the TV; we rely on TV for our knowledge of the world; TV can influence what we buy, read etc.; unlike other influences on us, TV isn't interactive; TV could have a better influence but at present doesn't.
2 generally bad

3
1 G;   2 C;   3 E;   4 H;   5 B;   6 F;   7 D

4
1 B;   2 C;   3 D;   4 B;   5 A;   6 C;   7 D

Colloquial English

5A It's all in the MIND p.122
1   racking my brains
2   have second thoughts
3   crossed my mind
4   make up your mind
5   have just had a brainwave
6   is in two minds
7   frame of mind
8   It (completely) slipped my mind!

6A Making MUSIC p.122
1   1 rings;   2 blowing;   3 going;   4 face;   5 played;
6 feel;   7 changed;   8 make

2   a 6;   b 2;   c 4;   d 5;   e 3;   f 7;   g 1;   h 8

6B The COLOURS of the rainbow p.123
1   1 black;   2 blue;   3 blue;   4 red;   5 red;   6 green;
7 rose;   8 white;
2   a 7;   b 2;   c 1;   d 4;   e 5;   f 8;   g 3;   h 6;

7B My most attractive FEATURE is ... p.123
1   1 head;   2 eye;   3 eye;   4 tooth;   5 hand;   6 arm;
7 skin;   8 cheek;
2   a 7;   b 2;   c 4;   d 6;   e 8;   f 3;   g 5;   h 1

10B All the TIME in the world p.124
1a   You might hear all these sentences in an airport.
Suggested answers:
1/2 Someone talking to his/her travelling companion as they arrive at the airport.
3   Someone complaining to a travelling companion or airport worker.
4   A woman talking to her son, or husband!
5   An airport official reassuring a passenger who is hurrying.
6   Someone talking to his/her travelling companion about their journey.
7   Someone talking to his/her travelling companion as they check in their luggage.
8   A parent talking to his/her child in a busy airport.

1b   1 c;   2 g;   3 d;   4 h;   5 e;   6 b;   7 f;   8 a

Practice exam

Reading

Paper 1 Part 1 p.125
1 C;   2 D;   3 B;   4 A;   5 B;   6 A;   7 B;   8 D

Paper 1 Part 2 p.127
9 H;   10 E;   11 A;   12 C;   13 B;   14 F;   15 D

Paper 1 Part 3 p.129
16 A;   17 C;   18 D;   19 A;   20 A;   21 B;   22 D;   23 A;
24 D;   25 C;   26 C;   27 B;   28 A;   29 B;   30 D

Use of English

Paper 3 Part 1 p.133
1 C;   2 B;   3 C;   4 B;   5 A;   6 D;   7 B;   8 C;   9 C;   10 B;
11 A;   12 B

Paper 3 Part 2 p.134
13 BECAUSE;   14 USED;   15 SO;   16 FROM;   17 HOW;
18 OF;   19 WHO;   20 THE;   21 WITHOUT;   22 LET;
23 THAN;   24 ME/MYSELF

Paper 3 Part 3 p.135
25 MEMBERSHIP;   26 RESEARCHERS;   27 NATURAL;
28 BENEFICIAL;   29 EXPLANATION;   30 GROWTH;
31 UNLIKE;   32 FITNESS;   33 INCREASINGLY;
34 ESPECIALLY/SPECIALLY

Paper 3 Part 4 p.136
35 MOST EXCITING (THAT) I'VE/I HAVE;   36 HAVE A LOOK AT;   37 MORE INTERESTED IN ARCHAEOLOGY;   38 IS SAID TO HAVE GIVEN;   39 TAKE ADVANTAGE OF;   40 WERE PREVENTED FROM COMPLETING;
41 GET MY MOTORBIKE SERVICED;   42 HE COULD HAVE SPOKEN

Listening

Paper 4 Part 1 p.137

1 B; 2 A; 3 B; 4 C; 5 B; 6 C; 7 C; 8 A

Audio script

Basically, I was looking for somewhere to get away from it all and relax, because the last few months have been so hectic at work, but I didn't want to feel cut off, because it's nice to meet people on holiday too. The complex sounded exactly what I was looking for – there were ten villas with a shared swimming pool and a restaurant, but each one had its own private sitting-out area. What I wasn't prepared for, however, was the fact that the place was popular with young families. So it was very noisy during the day, and extremely dull in the evening.

W = *Woman*; **M** = *Man*

2

M: How did you get on at the dentist's?

W: I'm afraid it's a bit of a long story. I got held up on the motorway, so I was 15 minutes late for the appointment. Anyway, the next patient had gone in, so I'd missed it, which is fair enough, but then the receptionist said I'd have to pay anyway. I'm afraid after rushing like mad trying to get there on time, I was a bit stressed out and I just lost my temper. I feel awful about it now because I really shouted at her in front of a waiting room full of people. It made me feel better at the time, though.

3

W: I feel sorry for Mandy really, I mean she spent hours preparing that report and no one thought to tell her that the policy had changed.

M: Well, you know, she's invited to all the meetings …

W: Come on, if we went to all the meetings we're invited to, none of us would ever get anything finished.

M: Well, even if you're not there, the minutes are circulated by email, you know, so I don't believe that she wasn't told. Either she wasn't listening, or she hadn't checked her in-box.

W: I guess so, but I still feel sorry for her.

4

Want to feel more confident in the gym? Swap your baggy T-shirt and track pants for racy sportswear that will make you look great. Our new autumn range of stretchy tops in bright colours is stylish and comfortable as well as allowing you to move freely. Our hard-wearing weatherproof jackets hold warmth in and keep the rain out, without making you look like a shapeless ball of plastic, and our must-have footwear, equally good for running or working out in the gym, wouldn't look out of place in the office. To view the full range, log onto our website now at *www. gymwear.com*.

PR = *Presenter*

5

PR: A listener, Mary, writes from Oxford to ask: what's the best age to introduce a child to computers? Well, Mary, recent research suggests that this can be a positive move for kids as young as three. It can enhance language and creative skills and give them a headstart in understanding technology. But that doesn't mean sticking the child in front of a screen and leaving them to it. Get a chair that's the right height, and keep each session to half-an-hour or less – more than enough time in one position for growing bones and a vulnerable spine. And sit with them, then you can answer any questions they might have.

6

There can't be many people around who haven't read at least one book by David Granham. His blend of subtle characterisation and superb plot lines makes his thrillers almost universally popular. But if you haven't sampled one yet, his latest offering *The Colne Verdict* is not the place to start. Although fans will find all the usual ingredients in place, and the writing is up to his usual standard, my impression is that the formula is beginning to wear a little thin, as if perhaps he's getting a little bored with it himself, and needs to try something a little different.

PR = *Presenter*; **S** = *Sally*

7

PR: And next we have a call from Sally, who works in a bank. Go ahead, Sally.

S: Hello, yes… I work in a big office and my department has hired and lost eight secretarial staff in as many months. I wouldn't say our salary structure was poor, and the hours and conditions are fairly standard, so what is driving new recruits away? As a section leader, I'm involved in recruitment discussions, but I'm at a loss to know how to reverse the situation.

PR: Right well, let's ask our expert, Tom Willis what he …

W = *Woman*; **M** = *Man*

8

M: I made a reservation for this evening. The names's Walters.

W: Mmm … Ah, yes here we are. The front row of the stalls and I think you've also booked dinner in the restaurant upstairs before the performance.

M: That's right – a table for two. What time is dinner served?

W: From six-thirty onwards, but we recommend that you take your seats in the auditorium by about seven twenty-five, because the curtain goes up at seven-thirty, so it's best not to leave it too late.

M: Oh, right. My wife's just gone to freshen up in our hotel room. It's only across the street, but I hope she's not long.

Paper 4 Part 2 p.138

9 uncle; 10 the past; 11 London; 12 stable; 13 sensitive hands; 14 back; 15 1650; 16 sentimental; 17 clean; 18 conservationist

Audio script

PR = *Presenter*; **P** = *Peter*

PR: Today, I'm visiting Peter Denison who makes his living repairing old clocks and watches. Peter, is this a family tradition?

P: Not really, my father was a farmer, but he preferred the animals to the machinery, and my grandfather had been a vet. But while I was growing up, I was always fixing bikes and taking things like radios to bits. And I remember going to see an <u>uncle</u> whose garage was full of tools and machines. I used to spend all day in there with him while my cousins were playing football. I guess he saw that I was interested and encouraged me.

PR: So why clocks in particular?

P: Well one day, when I was 14, I took my parents' clock to bits and discovered that clocks are actually beautifully made inside. It never worked again, but I'd made a thrilling discovery and that's when I decided to specialise in clocks. For me, clocks are something which connect us with <u>the past.</u> I like old things that haven't been altered or modernised, but still work perfectly.

PR: So what exactly did you study?

P: I did a course in what's known as horology at a college in Birmingham. I did well, and went on to get a job with a top firm of jewellers in <u>London</u> afterwards. I was employed as what's called an improver, doing all sorts of repair work for two years. It was excellent experience, but I didn't like city life, so eventually I decided to go home and set up my own workshop in the country.

PR: Was that easy?

P: Well, I began working in a corner of an old factory. Other craftsmen used the rest of the building, so it was relatively cheap. Actually I've spent my entire adult life working on my own in little rooms. I had a garden shed at one point, then a little office behind a shop, and my current workshop is in a converted <u>stable</u>. My workspace is made up of hundreds of little drawers and each piece of equipment has its place – so it's not as untidy as it might appear.

PR: And what qualities do you need for this kind of work?

P: Good eyesight, <u>sensitive hands</u> and a lot of patience are essential. Repairing a woman's watch the size of a small coin can be like doing micro-surgery and I work with my shoulders hunched forward, an eyeglass in my eye, just a few centimetres away from the watch or clock mechanism. Fortunately, my eyes are still sound, but like a lot of watchmakers, I do find I get <u>back</u> problems.

PR: And is it mostly old clocks you work with?

P: Yes, mostly from the period between 1850 and 1950, although occasionally I'll get one going back to 1750, and that's a real thrill for me. The oldest I've worked on was an Italian night clock dating from <u>1650.</u> A lamp shone behind the clock face so that the time was reflected onto the wall, a lovely piece of craftsmanship.

PR: And can most things be fixed?

P: Oh yes, if they were well-made originally. People are very <u>sentimental</u> about old clocks. They're often inherited, you know, handed down through the generations. But people generally don't bring them in to me until they break or stop working properly. In the old days people knew they needed to <u>clean</u> working things, but now it doesn't occur to them. It needs doing at least once every three years.

PR: And so what is it you get out of the job exactly?

P: I often think of myself as a <u>conservationist</u> because I'm devoted to repairing things and keeping old things going. Working with your hands doesn't seem to be as valued in modern society as it once was, which is a shame. The environment is very important to me and I try to grow my own vegetables and keep hens for eggs. So it's not just the clocks.

PR: Peter, thank you for talking to us today.

P: Thank you.

Paper 4 Part 3 p.139

19 B; 20 E; 21 A; 22 D; 23 F

Audio script

Speaker 1:
I've been here about five years. At first I wasn't sure that I'd made the right choice, because it was quite a while before I got to know the neighbours. <u>For me it was a question of position. I work from home, so it wasn't that I had to travel in to work or anything, but I wanted to be able to pop to the post office and get in a few basic provisions without wasting half my day.</u> All the bigger flats I looked at were a bus ride away from the shops. I don't have a car, and I didn't like the idea of being cut off, so I settled for less space.

Speaker 2:
I'm so close to the station you can hear the trains from my flat. I didn't realise that until I moved in, but I've got used to it now. I came here when I retired. I used to have a much larger place, but no longer needed the space. What attracted me was the fact that there's a man on the door downstairs <u>who checks who's coming in and what's going on – being on your own at my age, that's a comfort.</u> I thought he'd also do little maintenance jobs for me, but that's not part of his job apparently. Fortunately, I made friends with a nice couple downstairs who help me out when anything needs doing.

Speaker 3:
I was looking for somewhere close to my work because I didn't want to waste time travelling back and forth, so I wasn't really looking in this area at all. Then a colleague who lived in the block told me that this place was free. <u>As soon as I saw how much space you got for your money, I jumped at the chance.</u> I'd been looking at places with tiny rooms just because they were on good bus routes. It was only after I'd moved in that I realised how good the local shops are and what a nice part of town it is. You really feel safe walking round here – even late at night.

Speaker 4:
When I first saw this flat, I was put off by the fact that it's on a very busy road. It's the main commuter route into the city centre. But actually, I bought it from a friend, who <u>introduced me to the people upstairs. They were very welcoming and convinced me that it really wasn't a problem. I liked the idea of being close to such nice people so I decided that,</u> although I'd have liked bigger rooms, <u>it was probably a good buy.</u> It was only later that

I discovered how good the local shops are and that the block itself is well-maintained by the security guard who lives on the ground floor.

Speaker 5:
My last flat was very convenient, handy for the shops and well-connected for public transport. But the building itself was falling to pieces, and I got fed up trying to get the owner to do something about it. So, I moved out to this place instead because there's a caretaker who's paid to keep the place in order. I wasn't looking for much bigger rooms, but actually I've had no trouble using the space, and the other residents turned out to be really friendly. It gives you a nice feeling of security to know that if you have a problem, you can always pop next door for help.

Paper 4 Part 4 p.140
24 A; 25 C; 26 C; 27 B; 28 A; 29 A; 30 B

Audio script
PR = *Presenter;* **G** = *Grant*

PR: My guest today will soon be joining a very small and very special group of people. Ever since the idea of space tourism was first seriously considered in the late1990s, some people have had their name on the waiting list, as they saved up the fee. One of those people is Grant Sowerby, who is just about to leave on the trip of a lifetime. He'll be spending ten days on a space station as it orbits the Earth. Grant, welcome.

G: Hi.

PR: What are you most looking forward to about the flight?

G: There'll be so many experiences in those ten days that it's hard to know which will be the greatest moment. But I guess the launch is what I'm looking forward to most. There can't be many things as exhilarating as being in a rocket as it flies out of the atmosphere. The first experience of weightlessness and seeing the Earth from outside the atmosphere; those are going to be incredible too, but maybe not quite so thrilling.

PR: Don't you feel scared at all?

G: I wouldn't be human if I didn't. Because I'm not a military pilot or even a professional test pilot – this isn't something I do every day, you know. But I've done months of training alongside real astronauts, so I hope I'm up to the challenge.

PR: Will you have specific responsibilities on the flight?

G: Very much so. The spaceship is extremely small and so every seat has a set of controls in front of it. I'll be handling the systems that are controlled from the right-hand seat: for example, radio, TV, and some of the navigation systems. The flight commander sits in the centre and can take over from me on those functions if necessary, but hopefully I'll be a fully-functioning member of the crew.

PR: And was the training difficult?

G: Some of the survival training, you know, when we're prepared for an unexpected landing in the sea or in an extreme winter climate, has been physically very challenging. Much worse than the training for weightlessness, although that was pretty tough too.

PR: Some people are completely against the idea of tourists going into space. Do you see this trip as a holiday?

G: Actually, I see it very much as a life experience. People use the term 'space tourism' to describe what I'm going to do, but actually it's a bit misleading. I've been training flat-out for twelve months and I'll be working flat-out every day that I'm up there. So I'm going to need a real holiday when I come back.

PR: What sort of things will you be doing?

G: I'll be looking at different ways of measuring the energy an astronaut uses during a space flight, and how that affects the muscles. But the astronauts all tell me that the one thing they wished they'd had more of up there is free time. So I'm going to make sure that I have some, at least.

PR: And what advice do you have for other people who fancy a trip into space?

G: Well, the price is a bit steep at the moment which cuts a lot of people out, and then you've got to go through months of training. I mean, not everyone's up to that, physically, nor can they spare the time, and it can be frustrating for people. I mean, I was fortunate because if you don't make it through the training, basically they don't let you go.

PR: Right.

G: The best advice I can give is to say: 'Just keep patient'. I mean, space travel's going to become far more accessible, sooner or later, and I reckon it's going to be sooner than people think. I'm confident that with so many companies keen to organise trips, this market's going to open up considerably. I couldn't tell you what it might cost, but I'm confident that within ten years, I'll be able to buy a ticket and fly up there again without having to go through such a complicated training procedure.

PR: Grant, thank you … and best of luck with the flight.

G: Thanks.